Doing Theology in Plural Contexts

Doing Theology in Plural Contexts

Robyn Horner and Teresa Brown

t&tclark
LONDON • NEW YORK • OXFORD • NEW DELHI • SYDNEY

T&T CLARK
Bloomsbury Publishing Plc, 50 Bedford Square, London, WC1B 3DP, UK
Bloomsbury Publishing Inc, 1359 Broadway, New York, NY 10018, USA
Bloomsbury Publishing Ireland, 29 Earlsfort Terrace, Dublin 2, D02 AY28, Ireland

BLOOMSBURY, T&T CLARK and the T&T Clark logo are
trademarks of Bloomsbury Publishing Plc

First published in Great Britain 2026

Cover design: Elena Durey
Cover image © The Dance of the Trinity © Helen Bachmann

A catalogue record for this book is available from the British Library.

ISBN: HB: 978-0-567-72718-3
PB: 978-0-567-72717-6
ePDF: 978-0-567-72719-0
eBook: 978-0-567-72720-6

Typeset by Integra Software Services Pvt. Ltd.
Printed and bound in Great Britain

For product safety-related questions, contact productsafety@bloomsbury.com.

To find out more about our authors and books visit www.bloomsbury.com
and sign up for our newsletters.

The authors and publishers acknowledge and thank:

Fordham University Press for permission to reproduce pp. 120–4 of Phenomenologies of Scripture, *ed. Adam Y Wells (New York, 2017).*

For Saints Bosco and Gavin,
whose constant support
makes teaching and writing possible

CONTENTS

ACKNOWLEDGMENTS

Works such as these do not emerge solely in the silence of isolated withdrawal for research, but also from dialogue, prayer, and shared reflection. We wish to thank our colleagues in the Faculty of Theology and Philosophy at Australian Catholic University, who have supported our collaborative work and encouraged us to write about it, especially our colleagues in the Xavier Centre for Theological Formation (Maeve Louise Heaney, Jamie Calder, and Joel Hodge). Warmest thanks to Executive Deans present (Richard Colledge) and immediately past (Dermot Nestor) for allowing creativity and theological authenticity to flourish, in times that are always challenging. To our colleagues in the Teaching the Bible Community of Practice, thank you for sharing so generously and for graciously tolerating theologians who work with the Bible in different ways. Next, to our students, who have offered very insightful suggestions and reflections as we have tested some of our readings in class, and to our diocesan collaborators in Parramatta, Queensland, South Australia, and Victoria: we could not have written this book without your authentic and rich engagement in our classrooms. Thank you for realizing what is at stake and for being open to thinking about new ways of going forward. To our critical friends in this process, Gina Bernasconi and Christopher Reed, heartfelt thanks for your intuitive and careful readings, for your encouragement and for your honesty in feeding back your thoughts. And thanks most of all to our families, who perhaps sigh a little when we fly off to teach in other parts of Australia or the world, but who know that we are our best selves when we are doing theology together and who support us unconditionally.

Robyn and Teresa

PREFACE: WHO NEEDS TO READ THIS BOOK?

This book begins from the premise that Catholic theology is not theology unless it seeks to make sense of Christian faith in dialogue with the context in which faith is lived. In a letter to the Pontifical Academy of Theology in 2023, Pope Francis calls for theologians to engage in an "outgoing" theology that proceeds in a synodal way, that is, a theology that promotes the capacity to listen to the Holy Spirit and to each other, to dialogue with a multiplicity of voices and perspectives in a spirit of humility and friendship, and to discern and integrate new perspectives that shed light on faith and the issues at hand.[1] He calls for a "fundamentally contextual theology," which is "capable of reading and interpreting the Gospel in the conditions in which [human beings] live daily"—a truly incarnational theology that takes seriously God's revelation in Christ in human history.[2] Francis' exhortation emerges from an affirmation of the inextricable connection between the Church and the world, which is elucidated in the documents of the Second Vatican Council, and the recognition that God continues to reveal Godself in the realities of our times, in diverse contexts and human experiences.[3]

Since 2016, we (the authors) have been working together to support the theological formation of teachers and leaders in Catholic schools and systems throughout Australia (especially in South Australia, Victoria, New South Wales, and Queensland). We have worked to build the capacity of our participants to ask questions of faith, to think critically and reflectively about their own relationship with faith, and to bring their own experiences to bear in their reflection on how God speaks (reveals) through the word (scripture) and through the living tradition. Our approach is informed by the research undertaken by colleagues at Katholieke Universiteit Leuven (KU Leuven), which tells us empirically what we already perceive anecdotally—that the relationship with religion in modern Western contexts has changed and that this is having a dramatic effect on the development and articulation

[1]Pope Francis, "Ad theologiam promovendam," Apostolic letter issued Motu Proprio (November 1, 2023), n. 3, https://www.vatican.va/content/francesco/it/motu_proprio/documents/20231101-motu-proprio-ad-theologiam-promovendam.html.

[2]Pope Francis, "Ad theologiam promovendam," 4.

[3]See especially Vatican Council II, *Dei verbum: Dogmatic Constitution on Divine Revelation* (Libreria Editrice Vatican, 1965); Vatican Council II, *Gaudium et spes: Pastoral Constitution on the Church in the Modern World* (Libreria Editrice Vaticana, 1965).

of Catholic identity in Catholic schools.[4] We know from this research that if we are to support and enhance Catholic faith into the future, those working in Catholic schools and systems first need to be honest with themselves about where they stand in relation to faith. Then, they need to develop their capacity to engage with theological questions through authentic engagement with scripture and tradition, enter into dialogue with those who are similar to and different from themselves, and continue to ask questions about how God reveals Godself in the world today.

Our work with teachers and leaders in Catholic schools in support of these goals includes developing their ability to engage hermeneutically (i.e., interpretatively) with scripture and tradition and, in this way, to support their development toward a mature, discerning, and critically reflective faith.[5] In this hermeneutical engagement, we consider together how the text and the context speak to one another. We explore the way the context might interrupt assumptions we bring to the text and the meanings we associate with it, and how the text might, in turn, shed light on issues within the context and call us (the readers) to respond. In this process—the process of recontextualization—the text is placed into a new context and in the dialogue that ensues, new and deeper meanings emerge.

It is through this work that we came to develop the "four steps to recontextualization," which form the basis of this book. In each chapter, we bring a piece of scripture into dialogue with a particular experience and contemporary issue. In doing so, we seek not to provide ready answers to the big questions of our time, but instead to encourage deep and informed reflection on these questions through the lens of an authentic, incarnational, critically reflective, and relational Christian faith—or, for many, to invite an ever-deepening understanding and appreciation of faith.

This book is first and foremost a theological endeavor—it is our response to Pope Francis' call to "do" theology in ways that are informed by the Gospel and the realities of the human experience, attentive to the voices of people (both Christian and other-than-Christian) and enacted in the context of prayer or dialogical reflection.[6] To this end, it is a book that can be used by leaders and teachers in Catholic schools and systems (and those working in support of the same) for the development of their theological knowledge, skills, and

[4]We refer here to the Enhancing Catholic School Identity Research, the Victorian results of which were published in Didier Pollefeyt and Jan Bouwens, *Identity in Dialogue: Assessing and Enhancing Catholic School Identity. Research Methodology and Research Results in Catholic Schools in Victoria, Australia* (Lit Verlag, 2014). This research now contains well over 600,000 cases worldwide. For an extended discussion about this research and its implications for Catholic education, see Robyn Horner, Didier Pollefeyt, Jan Bouwens, Teresa Brown, Christiaan Jacobs-Vandegeer, Maeve Heaney, and Michael Buchanan, "Openness to Faith as a Disposition for Teachers in Catholic Schools," *International Journal of Practical Theology* 24, no. 2 (2020): 231–51; Robyn Horner, "Enhancing Catholic School Identity: A Response to Peter McGregor," *Irish Theological Quarterly* 88, no. 2 (2023): 112–36.

[5]Hermeneutics is often defined as "the art and science of interpretation."

[6]Pope Francis, "Ad theologiam promovendam," 4, 7.

dispositions—knowledge, skills, and dispositions that will support their work to enhance the identity of Catholic schools today. In short, this book is our humble contribution to the support of our colleagues and friends to "do" theology in ways that take seriously the realities of contemporary plural contexts.

Robyn Horner and Teresa Brown
Melbourne
January 2025

1

Introduction

The Context Is Always Evolving

The ancient philosopher Heraclitus is well known for saying something like "we do not step into the same river twice."[1] Seneca explains: "For the stream still keeps the same name, but the water has already flowed past. Of course, this is much more evident in rivers than in human beings. Still, we mortals are also carried past in no less speedy a course ...."[2] People often express a desire that things not change, or that they not change as quickly as they seem to, yet we know it to be the case that change is constant. This is part of what it means to live in time and history. Frequently, we must learn to translate or restate ideas anew so that they can be understood as the context changes. One aspect of this, for example, is that words evolve and the meanings we associate with words develop. As Karl Rahner states about the "development of dogma," "If we fail either to preserve or to change, we should betray the truth, either by falling into error or by failing to make the truth our own in a really existential way."[3]

In the Preface to the present work, we highlighted Pope Francis' call to do theology by being attentive to the context. He exhorts Catholic Christians to do "contextual" theology, and we have many fine examples of contextual theology in recent tradition from which we can learn: liberation theology, feminist theology, African theology, and so on. The present challenge, however, is to address multiple, changing contexts at once. Moreover, it is to address contexts where religious language—a language of transcendence—often has no meaning at all. This requires Christians to dialogue perhaps

---

[1]Heraclitus, *The Fragments of Heraclitus of Ephesus on Nature*, trans. George Thomas White Patrick (N. Murray, 1889; Digireads, 2013), Fragment LXXXI (otherwise numbered B12).
[2]Lucius Annaeus Seneca, *Epistles*. [62CE] *Volume I* (Harvard University Press, 1917), 58.
[3]Karl Rahner, "The Development of Dogma," in Karl Rahner, *Theological Investigations 1*, trans. Cornelius Ernst (Helicon, 1961), 45.

more thoughtfully with others than ever before. It requires a new sensitivity to questions of meaning as well as human dignity, and it requires a radical preparedness to let the Spirit go where it will (cf. Jn 3:8). For this process of cooperating with the Spirit to do its work in multiple new contexts, we have adopted the word "recontextualization." It seems that this is a very new word, for some, and we have heard rumors that it is sometimes understood pejoratively to mean a way of doing theology in complete ignorance of the tradition. Yet, as we will come to see, recontextualization describes a process that has been fundamental to Christian theology from the beginning.

Recontextualization

The first use of the English word "recontextualization" occurs in a book about symbols published by Philip Wheelwright in 1954: *The Burning Fountain*.[4] One of the ways in which the imagination works, he writes, is "by fusing or recontextualizing old ideas in such a way as to generate new ones." His point is that fusing old ideas with new—recontextualizing them—brings "liveliness and freshness" to expression.[5] Similarly in a later work, *Metaphor and Reality*, Wheelwright speaks of the frequent need to bring new life to traditional symbols. Writing in the field of literary studies, he observes: "Christian symbols, to be poetically effective, need to be discovered afresh in new contexts of imagery and of phrases." He cites as an excellent example "[T.S.] Eliot's recontextualization of the Christian symbol of the Dove by momentarily identifying it with a bombing plane" (*The dove descending breaks the air /With flame of incandescent terror*).[6] Such a violent overlay of images—the damaged bomber, screaming and aflame in uncontrolled descent into the city, and the dove, Christian symbol of the Holy Spirit bringing peace from the heavens—such incongruity wrenches open the symbol in Eliot's context of the Second World War London and reminds us that the flames of hell are real and present in war. Yet, the Holy Spirit is also symbolized by fire that cleanses in the book of Isaiah and inspires on the day of Pentecost. God is amidst the hell of the Blitz. Eliot revivifies the symbol by putting it to work in the experience of the lives of Londoners in the 1940s. Yet, the symbol can neither be fully conceptualized nor affectively exhausted by the thoughts and feelings it evokes in any single reader or context. We cannot be sure, in other words, that the resonances

[4]OED: "recontextualize, v." OED Online, December 2020, Oxford University Press, https://www.oed.com/dictionary/recontextualize_v?tab=factsheet#126632880.

[5]Philip Wheelwright, *The Burning Fountain: A Study in the Language of Symbolism*, 2nd ed. (Indiana University Press, 1968), 124.

[6]Philip Wheelwright, *Metaphor and Reality* (Indiana University Press, 1962), 97; T. S. Eliot, *Four Quartets* (Faber and Faber, 1944).

the symbol evokes for Eliot are those we have suggested here, but only that the symbol speaks anew because of his recontextualization.

If recontextualization is not included in the *Oxford English Dictionary* (OED) until 1954, it is not because the idea of putting something into a different context to express some new or perhaps deeper meaning has been lacking in English or in other languages. Recontextualization—perhaps by other names—is a common literary device, and we argue that it is also part of theological method throughout much of Christian history. At the same time, however, it is not usually a task undertaken with the particular kind of self-awareness that emerges in twentieth-century discussions by historians and philosophers. In these discussions, concepts such as "historical consciousness" and "hermeneutics" and their relationship to what Catholic Christians call "tradition" come to the fore. All three concepts are important for theology, and we will return to them in due course.

The impetus to think further and more formally about recontextualization in a theological context has come about for us because of the work of Lieven Boeve. In 2003, Boeve published *Interrupting Tradition: An Essay on Christian Faith in a Postmodern Context*, where he describes the process of recontextualization and its prominence in theological work after Vatican II. Specifically, he writes about the renewed attention of theologians to "the contextual character of tradition." "In principle," he says, every tradition "is inseparably *embedded in a specific historical context* that has made an essential contribution to the form thereof." This means that as the context changes, there is a need to recontextualize tradition. "Such *recontextualisation* of the tradition is simultaneously tied up with the actual life of faith, with concrete faith expression, on the one hand, and the transmitted tradition, on the other."[7] Importantly, Boeve argues that the purpose of recontextualization is not simply to continue or hand on the tradition as if nothing has changed, but instead to bring new contextual insights to bear on the tradition so that it can continue to speak in new and changing contexts. In this way, the context interrupts the tradition at the place where it no longer conveys meaning and the tradition undergoes a process of development so that the message of love revealed in the person of Christ can be understood in new and deeper ways.[8] In order to appreciate Boeve's insight, it is helpful to look

[7]Lieven Boeve, *Interrupting Tradition: An Essay on Christian Faith in a Postmodern Context*, trans. Brian Doyle (Peeters, 2003), 22.

[8]"Once a believing community has cast the dynamic relationship between tradition and context in a new form, it continues to narrate the Christian narrative which, paradoxically enough, is to be considered both the same as before and no longer the same … [T]he community remains faithful to its original inspiration and continues with the same narrative precisely by giving new expression to the same inspiration in a changed context." And many elements of the tradition—images, symbols, and so on—take up new forms of expression, even while some members of the community continue to hold onto the old forms. Boeve, *Interrupting Tradition*, 34.

at an example. While there are several such examples in the history of the Church, here, we look at a single theme of theological recontextualization to show its perennial, if largely unnamed, use.

Recontextualizations of Salvation

At different points in time, Christians have attempted to explain what it means to be "saved" by Christ. To begin with, let us note that the idea of being "saved" is often particularly difficult for twenty-first-century Westerners to understand, situated as we are in secular and highly pluralized and detraditionalized contexts. A friend who teaches theology describes the situation of teaching undergraduate university students pursuing studies in religious education. For the first half of the semester, this friend taught a group of students who were, by and large, uninterested in what she was saying. After several weeks on school placements, the students returned very animated and had begun to realize how their university seminars connected to their future work in schools. Yet, the whole class went silent when a young woman named Jess spoke up about her experience. She was teaching the year 8 religious education unit about Easter and she thought things were going really well, until she underscored for the students the Christian belief that Jesus had died on the cross to save them. At that moment, one shy, thirteen-year-old girl had put up her hand to ask a question: "But Miss," she said, "what do I need saving *from*?" Back at the university, Jess described the situation where she had very publicly realized she had absolutely no way of answering that question. She had blithely repeated a platitude that revealed she did not understand at all the faith about which she was teaching. A cradle Catholic, she had not even asked herself what Catholic faith meant.

From the perspective of Catholic faith, being "saved" is inexorably bound together with the concepts of sin, the sacrifice of Jesus and his work of salvation. Being "saved" from sin through the death of Jesus is a difficult concept to understand, even for those who profess to have Catholic faith. How much more difficult is it to understand for those who live without having been actively engaged in that tradition? In some of the earliest recorded theological reflections on the death of Jesus, embedded by Paul in 1 Cor. 15:3, we read that "Christ died for our sins in accordance with the scriptures." It is possible that the student teacher might have spoken about this early credal formulation (if she had known about it). To repeat the ancient creed, however, is clearly not enough in a contemporary context. For a start, what is sin? The Bible often speaks of *hhatah* (in Hebrew) or *hamartia* (in Greek), which means "missing the mark," using an image that comes from the context of archery (i.e., to sin means to miss the target). While the image of archery is still meaningful in a contemporary context (in the sense that many people would understand what archery is), it is not something that is commonly seen or experienced. Moreover, the concept of sin only has traction within a particular, religious view of the world. Sin is not the same as breaking the law, even if sometimes the same act can be both against the law and also sinful. Persons outside a religious framework have no need—and presumably no desire—to describe themselves using the language of sin, and in addition to the fact that it is poor form to presume to cast judgment, it makes no sense to call them "sinners" because the word has no meaning outside a relationship with God. Sin relates primarily to the ignorance of or resistance to (for original sin), or damaging of (for actual sin), a relationship with God, which subsequently gives a particular perspective to damaging a relationship with a human other, with the world or its creatures, or even with oneself (in the refusal to be honest with oneself, for example). Now, our description here of sin as damaging relationships is already cast from the perspective of persons who live in Western societies in the twenty-first century, where it is often personal relationships with individuals that orient our lives. Elsewhere and in other historical contexts, one might want to cast around for different imagery to augment this understanding of sin. This is already, then, a recontextualization in the appropriation of new meaning in relation to sin.

So much for sin. In terms of *how* salvation is effected by Christ, the Church has not defined dogmatically any single response (of many). Paul's reflection in Rom. 3:23-25 links the death of Jesus with sacrifice: "since all have sinned and fall short of the glory of God; they are now justified by his grace as a gift, through the redemption that is in Christ Jesus, whom God put forward as a sacrifice of atonement by his blood, effective through faith." While sacrifice is not the only theme explored by Paul in relation to Jesus' death, it is reasonable to expect that sacrifice is a concept that Paul's contemporaries understand, even if they have not previously thought about it in relation to human beings. Animal sacrifice is common practice in ancient Judaism and is practiced in Greek and Roman societies as well. Here, atonement (at-one-ment, making one, restoring relationship) is brought about by the blood sacrifice of an innocent victim. The ancient idea of martyrdom (or a "noble death") potentially develops the notion of human sacrifice in a more nuanced way—although Jesus' own death is not actually understood to be noble.[9] Some of the earliest theology about Jesus' action to save humanity from sin, then, is articulated in terms of the concept of sacrifice, and this bears some relation to the context of the times in which Christianity develops. Clearly, however, sacrifice is not a word that resonates in the twenty-first-century West. This is both because local temples in which animal sacrifices are conducted are hopefully few and far between—if they exist at all—and because the notion of sacrifice in a metaphorical (moral) sense has lost nearly all meaning in popular discourse. This makes it difficult

[9]Christopher J. Monaghan CP, "Paul's understanding of the death of Jesus," unpublished article, www.repository.divinity.edu.au, accessed February 4, 2021.

to understand; moreover, it tends to suggest to modern ears an image of a God who is vengeful and violent in demanding a blood sacrifice to atone for sin.

In the second century CE, Irenaeus of Lyons lived in what is now the south of France as a Greek-speaking bishop. While there are passages in his works that show his agreement with Paul in terms of Christ's sacrifice of atonement, another strong current in Irenaeus' thinking about how Christ saves humanity is the doctrine of "recapitulation." This theory has its basis in the solidarity between all humanity and the Adam of Genesis—in the fall away from God's likeness—and the subsequent solidarity between all humanity and Christ (the "new Adam") in the recovery of that likeness, the return (or recapitulation) to being like God.[10] Irenaeus' idea of recapitulation bears the optimistic style that comes to be distinctive of Greek (Eastern) in contrast to Latin (Western) Christian anthropology. The Eastern tradition has a less catastrophic view of original sin than that developed in the West by Augustine, since its vision of humanity is—to use modern terms—developmental and existential rather than ontologically determined.[11] For the Greek tradition, the fall takes place because human beings are children who have not yet grown up, whereas the Western tradition takes a stand on the thorough corruption of humanity. In the East, the doctrine of recapitulation allows that transformation takes place by growth in imitation, whereas the West casts its understanding in terms of a complete change in being—from good to bad. The Eastern view reflects a more positive notion of God than that implied in atonement by means of sacrifice and is perhaps easier for contemporary Christians to appropriate.

A third way of understanding salvation is reflected in the "ransom theory," which is developed most fully in the Patristic period. According to this theory, the Christ event occurs in the context of a great cosmic war. Adam has sold the souls of humanity to the devil (since human beings have sinned, the devil justly has ownership of them). Being God's Son, Christ is paid as a ransom for all those souls, that is, in return for God the Father's handing Christ over to the devil, and thus to death, humanity is released. However, since Christ is actually without sin, the devil cannot rightly keep hold of him by means of death. The "satan" (in Genesis, "the accuser" and not Satan) has nothing with which to accuse the Christ, and therefore Christ defeats death; the devil has effectively been tricked. Now, to critical Western

[10]Irenaeus, *Adversus Heresies*, [180], V.1.3., in Alexander Roberts, James Donaldson, and A. Cleveland Coxe, eds., trans. Alexander Roberts and William Rambaut, *Ante-Nicene Fathers*, Vol. 1 (Christian Literature Publishing, 2007).

[11]"Existential" means "having to do with existence or the meaning of existence," whereas "ontological" has to do with what one is, that in which one consists (in the history of philosophy, this is often termed a "substance"). The point is, the Eastern understanding relates to how human lives are oriented and can grow, whereas the Western understanding is more like how we are in ourselves—as though infected by a virus and thus forever changed for ill.

ears, this cosmic drama can sound like the makings of a Marvel movie. If contemporary persons struggle to believe in a transcendent God, they must also struggle to believe in a cosmic war and a supernatural agent of evil. The ransom theory is implausible fantasy to many, although it is often a part of charismatic theologies.

In medieval times, we see a similar kind of argument about how Christ saves humanity, this time developed using the terms of the feudal system. Anselm of Canterbury argues that because of the sin of humanity—which is a transgression against God's honour—human beings owe God (the feudal Lord) payment of a debt ("satisfaction"—hence, the "satisfaction theory"). Since humanity has no money with which to pay the debt, Christ steps in to pay with the highest price possible—his life. Anselm writes, "No man except this one ever gave to God what he was not obliged to lose, or paid a debt he did not owe. But he freely offered to the Father what there was no need of his ever losing, and paid for sinners what he owed not for himself."[12] Now, it is evident that if one were an impoverished serf living in a feudal system, this theory might make a lot of sense, but in the contemporary West, it has little experiential resonance. Along the same lines, but developed during the Reformation, the "penal substitution" theory maintains that the price of legal satisfaction—here, the price to appease God's righteous anger over human sin—is punishment of humanity by death. Christ substitutes for humanity in accepting the full force of God's wrath and dying on humanity's behalf. Given that this explanation of the process of salvation uses legal imagery, it potentially bears more relevance in the contemporary world. At the same time, however, the moral repugnance of many people with regard to the death penalty, as well as the doubts many bear about the kind of God who would exact such a penalty, once again distances the present generation from acceptance of this kind of understanding of the significance of Christ's life, death, and resurrection.

There are many other examples of theologians recontextualizing understandings of how salvation takes place; here, we note two that are more current in their focus. First, some writers think about salvation using psychoanalytic categories. Sebastian Moore OSB is pre-eminent amongst them in using the theory of Alice Miller to inform a thinking of original sin, the state whereby the true self of the person is constantly although unconsciously denied and seen to be unworthy of love. In this approach, the deepest desire of the self—the desire to be desired by one we desire—is endlessly frustrated because the *ego* mistakes the source as well as the goal of its desire. Salvation takes place first by means of the death of the *ego*, occurring where self-hatred is exposed in the face of Jesus' death on the cross (the disciples recognize both that they have killed Jesus and that they

[12]Anselm of Canterbury, *Cur Deus Homo* (*Why God Became Man*) [1094] Book Two, 18b. in Anselm, *Basic Writings*, ed. and trans. Thomas Williams (Hackett, 2007).

themselves are "dead" since they are separated from him). The path to authentic selfhood is then revealed in the resurrection, where it becomes possible to recognize through the non-judgmental and inclusive love of Jesus that one's true self is found in and with God, who is actually one's true desire and who desires us.[13]

Second, James Allison develops Moore's conceptualization of desire and comes to an understanding of original sin and salvation using the mimetic theory of French thinker, René Girard. According to mimetic theory, desire does not aim directly at an object (or another subject as such) but aims at *the desire belonging to another subject*. This is very visible in young children at play, where one child wants only the toy that another is holding and will sob and scream to obtain it. Once obtained, however, that toy often becomes meaningless and is cast aside once the child rival has a new interest. Girard maintains that societies are often based on such rivalry, which leads to violence and disorder. When the tension of fundamental rivalry reaches its peak and the community becomes completely disordered, former rivals turn to unite in their hatred of a single other in the group who is deemed to be responsible, and who is scapegoated—made responsible for the disorder and expelled from the group. In ancient societies, the scapegoat is often killed to restore order. In Girard's account, Jesus becomes the scapegoat of his society, but because he cannot actually be blamed for anything, he makes the scapegoating mechanism visible and overturns it, revealing the true nature of ordered desire. Alison uses Girard's account to show that Jesus is the "forgiving victim," and because of such, Jesus is able to reveal that God is not vengeful and violent but only loving.

> God raised up this man who had been killed in this way *for us*. The victim of human iniquity was raised up as forgiveness; in fact the resurrection was the raising up of the victim as forgiveness. This it was that permitted the recasting of God as love. It was not just that God loved his son and so raised him up, but that the giving of the son and his raising up revealed God as love for us.[14]

We have now touched on several theories about how Jesus saves humanity from sin. The point has been not to offer a developed understanding of these theories as such, but to demonstrate the fact that different generations in different contexts have refashioned their understandings of Christ's saving significance in terms that people of that generation and context can understand. This is one aspect of theological recontextualization. If

---

[13]Sebastian Moore, *The Crucified Is No Stranger* (Darton, Longman and Todd, 1977); Sebastian Moore, *The Fire and the Rose Are One* (Darton, Longman and Todd, 1980); Sebastian Moore, *Let This Mind Be in You: The Quest for Identity Through Oedipus to Christ* (Darton, Longman and Todd, 1985); Sebastian Moore, *Jesus the Liberator of Desire* (Crossroad, 1989).
[14]James Alison, *The Joy of Being Wrong* (Crossroad, 1998), 101.

the dogma (the formal teaching of the Church) in this case is "Christ died for our sins," then what it means (and what it does not or cannot mean) is forever the task for people of faith to explore. Moreover, if people of faith do not think about what they believe in the context of their own lives and the particular historical circumstances in which they live, this will sometimes give rise to some bizarre interpretations of Christian belief. For example, many priests and nuns (and undoubtedly lay people in their wake) who urged first communicants to swallow the host whole lest they chew the body of Jesus—in mistaken loyalty to a thirteenth-century understanding of the real presence of Christ—did not help those young people to respect the Eucharist but mainly to imagine some ghastly scene of cannibalism that was taking place in their own mouths.[15]

Historical Consciousness, Hermeneutics, and Tradition

In our discussion of the doctrine "Christ died for our sins," we can see that historical consciousness affects the ways it has been understood and interpreted at various times in history. Historical consciousness is normally contrasted with what is called "classical consciousness." Philosopher Martha Craven Nussbaum helps us to get at the meaning of classical consciousness when she sets out a classical view of ethical thinking as it compares with scientific thinking:

> The scientific version [of Platonism] thinks of ethical inquiry as similar to inquiry in the physical sciences ... In this picture, scientists studying nature inquire in a "pure" manner, undisturbed and uninfluenced by their cultural framework, their background beliefs, their wishes and interests. Their task is to walk up to the world of nature (as Plato's souls walk to the rim of heaven), to look at it, and to describe it as it is, discovering its real permanent structure ... The desires, beliefs, and ways of life of physical scientists—or, indeed, of human beings more generally—must not be permitted to influence their inquiry into its status or their choice of methods of investigation. The idea is that ethics, too, is scientific in just this way. Ethical inquiry consists of discovering permanent truths about values and norms, truths that are what they are independently of what we are, or want, or do. They are set in the fabric of things, and we simply have to find them.[16]

[15]A friend tells us her class was told the story of the sinful student who secreted a host home, cut it with a knife, and it bled!

[16]Martha C. Nussbaum, *The Therapy of Desire: Theory and Practice in Hellenistic Ethics*, Rev. ed. (Princeton University Press, 2009), 17.

A classical (or better, "classicist") consciousness proceeds on the assumption that what can be perceived is literal, universal, rational, essential, and unchanging.[17] Ideas and understandings "are set in the fabric of things, and we simply have to find them." It presumes that "the desires, beliefs, and ways of life of physical scientists—or, indeed, of human beings more generally—must not be permitted to influence [scientists'] inquiry into its status or their choice of methods of investigation." In contrast, historical consciousness recognizes that "desires, beliefs and ways of life" *do* in fact influence how human beings make meaning. It is not possible for the Gospel writers to speculate on Jesus' psychological state, for example, because there is no way of thinking that would correspond to such a question at that time in history.

At a first level, we can see the sample recontextualizations of salvation, above, as cumulative responses to Christ's role in salvation that expand and deepen our thinking of foundational revelation—the Christ event. This is how tradition functions and this is what is often meant by the phrase, the "development of dogma": reflective believers at different times in history have insights that enable them to explain dogmas in different ways or in ways that are innovative.[18] So, in *Dei verbum*, we read:

> This tradition which comes from the Apostles develop[s] in the Church with the help of the Holy Spirit. For there is a growth in the understanding of the realities and the words which have been handed down. This happens through the contemplation and study made by believers, who treasure these things in their hearts (see Luke, 2:19, 51) through a penetrating understanding of the spiritual realities which they experience, and through the preaching of those who have received through Episcopal succession the sure gift of truth. For as the centuries succeed one another, the Church constantly moves forward toward the fullness of divine truth until the words of God reach their complete fulfillment in her.[19]

---

[17]To use the language of theologian Bernard Lonergan: "classical culture appears as a somewhat arbitrary standardization of man. It distinguished the literal and the figurative meanings of words and phrases, and it conveyed more than a suggestion that literal meaning is somehow first, while figurative meaning is a dress or ornament that makes the literal meaning more striking, more vivid, more effective." Frederick E. Crowe, *Collection Papers of Bernard Lonergan*, 2nd revised and augmented ed., vol. IV, ed. Frederick E. Crowe (University of Toronto Press, 1988), 240; see also Bernard Lonergan, "The Transition from a Classicist World-View to Historical-Mindedness," in *A Second Collection: Papers by Bernard J. F. Lonergan, S. J.*, ed. William F. J. Ryan and Bernard J. Tyrrell (Darton, Longman and Todd, 1974).

[18]Cf. John Henry Newman, *An Essay on the Development of Christian Doctrine* [1845] (Cambridge University Press, 2010); Yves Congar, *Tradition and Traditions: An Historical and a Theological Essay*, trans. Michael Naseby and Thomas Rainborough (Burns & Oates, 1966).

[19]Vatican Council II, *Dei verbum*, 8.

At a second level, however, we have to be careful not to imply that we always and already have a clear conceptualization of that to which the dogmatic expression ("the words") refers "in itself" ("the realities"). Moreover, we have to be careful not to imagine we have somehow "captured" the full meaning of revelation in its original expression and just have to reinterpret it for each generation using images that are contemporary to that generation. To do so might be to imply that God can actually be "explained" using human language. Challenging the notion that we have a complete conceptualization of that to which the dogma refers is not to challenge the dogma as such, but to affirm that dogma always functions symbolically. In fact, creedal statements are sometimes called "symbols of faith." And, as Bernard Lonergan observes: "the human spirit expresses itself in symbols before it knows, if ever it knows, what its symbols literally mean."[20] Symbols themselves emerge from within particular points in history and within particular contexts, never presenting meaning as such but evoking it in ways that exceed our ability to exhaust it. So, there is always a complexity involved in recontextualization because it involves recognizing that symbols may speak anew in different historical contexts. We have to be attentive to shifts in hermeneutics; attentive to the historical rootedness of the symbol and its resonances in one context (and potentially other contexts), as well as the ways in which we engage with the symbol in the present, perceiving and understanding interpretatively—if we can quickly run together ideas from philosophers Martin Heidegger, Hans-Georg Gadamer, Paul Ricoeur, and Claude Romano.[21] Let us try to give an example.

When Jesus was crucified, crucifixion was a fate reserved for those who had committed a serious crime and who were not Roman citizens. It was brutal, and clearly intended to bring about a slow, painful death:

> Death, usually after 6 hours–4 days, was due to multifactorial pathology: after-effects of compulsory scourging and maiming, hemorrhage and dehydration causing hypovolaemic shock and pain, but the most important factor was progressive asphyxia caused by impairment of

---

[20]Bernard Lonergan, *Collection: Collected Works of Bernard* Lonergan, ed. Frederick E. Crowe and Robert M. Doran (University of Toronto Press, 1988), 241. See also Karl Rahner, *Theological Investigations Volume I: God, Christ, Mary, and Grace*, trans. Cornelius Ernst, XXIII vols. (Darton, Longman and Todd, 1961), 43: "[A]ll human statements, even those in which faith expresses God's saving truths, are finite. By this we mean that they never declare the whole of a reality." "[A]nyone who proposes to regard these propositions of faith, because they are wholly true, as in themselves adequate to the matter in question, i.e. exhaustive statements, would be falsely elevating human truth to God's simple and exhaustive knowledge of himself and of all that takes its origin from him."

[21]See especially Paul Ricoeur, *Hermeneutics and the Human Sciences: Essays on Language, Action and Interpretation*, ed. and trans. John B. Thompson (Cambridge University Press, 1981); Claude Romano, *At the Heart of Reason*, trans. Michael B. Smith (Northwestern University Press, 2015), chapter 22.

> respiratory movement. Resultant anoxaemia exaggerated hypovolaemic shock. Death was probably commonly precipitated by cardiac arrest, caused by vasovagal reflexes, initiated inter alia by severe anoxaemia, severe pain, body blows and breaking of the large bones. The attending Roman guards could only leave the site after the victim had died, and were known to precipitate death by means of deliberate fracturing of the tibia and/or fibula, spear stab wounds into the heart, sharp blows to the front of the chest, or a smoking fire built at the foot of the cross to asphyxiate the victim.[22]

We can imagine that the shock value of crucifixion was inspired to deter crime. If we were to search for a symbol that would now have a near-equivalent to that shock value, perhaps we might think of the electric chair (no pun intended).

In contrast, if we think about this description of crucifixion in terms of the hymn, "The Old Rugged Cross," we can be prompted to realize how far the symbol has shifted in its resonances over time. The real horror of crucifixion is gone, replaced by a focus on the individual sinner, and the music could now potentially be perceived as maudlin. In history, we note that the Cross (*crux*) was a symbol worn by the Crusaders (*crux-aders*)—killing took place in the name of Christ. Additionally, we see that the form of Christ on the Cross (the Catholic crucifix) was rejected by the Reformers in favor of the Cross alone, reflecting the theological tension between moments of crucifixion and resurrection. We observe with horror the ways in which the Cross has been used as a symbol for white supremacy, especially by the Ku Klux Klan.[23] In another remarkable shift, many people now wear crosses as no more than an item of jewelry and sometimes even as an artifact of kitsch. We should think about the ways in which crosses are ubiquitous in suburban, Western streets—very often, there are several crosses on the one street because there is a multiplicity of churches, and sometimes such crosses even double as mobile phone towers. And we could observe the ways in which old churches have often now been repurposed, complete with their cruciform symbols, to become cafes, restaurants, or private homes.

How does this example help us make sense of the problems arising in reflection on symbols in history? The Cross (whether as Cross or Crucifix) is the Christian symbol *par excellence*. In the early Church—and in spite of its link with unspeakable cruelty—the Cross comes to function as

[22]Francois P. Retief and Louise Cilliers, "The History and Pathology of Crucifixion," *South African Medical Journal* 93, no. 12 (2003): 938–41, 938.

[23]Joanne M. Pierce, "The History of the Cross and Its Many Meanings over the Centuries," *The Conversation* (September 11, 2020), https://theconversation.com/the-history-of-the-cross-and-its-many-meanings-over-the-centuries-123316.

a mark of discipleship (*take up your cross and follow me*) as well as a symbol of hope in the resurrection, or Christ's victory over death. Yet, if we consider how it has resonated at different times in history, we see how those resonances have changed in quality, not only because people in different times have different interpretations of symbols, but also because the symbol itself has repeatedly been embedded in new contexts in which it speaks completely differently. This is true of non-Christian contexts, as well as Christian and quasi-Christian ones (if we can sincerely claim such a distinction at all). Focusing on some of the different resonances of the symbol of the Cross—these would include the violence of the Church itself (crusades, inquisitions, condemnations, lynch-mobs, rampant sexual abuse of children and other vulnerable people, and cover-up of these crimes) as well as frequently domesticated good intentions (a preference for personal piety over involvement in politics, the promotion of prosperity theology). The Cross cannot help but be recontextualized, but in the very perception, understanding, or interpretation we have of it in our own context/s, we have to think about the ways in which it might speak with voices we might not (want to) recognize. These will include the victims of the Church itself. At the same time, in light of the theology of interruption as it is characterized by Boeve, such voices might actually offer an important opportunity for God to speak anew.[24] These voices might move the Church to become more self-critical and more compassionate, less judgmental and more humble.

Returning to the question of history with which we began, one of the most important insights of the twentieth century is the recognition that all our words are always and already embedded in contexts that invariably contribute to their meaning. To become aware of the importance of differences across time is not only to appreciate that people of different epochs think about things differently—which is one aspect of historical consciousness—but also to realize that what is framed by words in any context itself has no steady, easily recoverable referent (except in a dictionary) and that meaning has to be forged anew in every generation.[25] When it comes to the development of tradition, Christians are both inheritors and testators. They *participate* in the development of tradition by continually entering into a process of meaning-making in light of their contextual experiences.[26]

---

[24]"It is through the encounter with concrete others and otherness that the Christian narrative is challenged and interrupted. It is such interruption that has the potential to become the locus in which God is revealed to Christians today." Lieven Boeve, *God Interrupts History: Theology in a Time of Upheaval*, trans. Brian Doyle (Continuum, 2007), 48.

[25]See Merold Westphal, *Whose Community? Which Interpretation? Philosophical Hermeneutics for the Church* (Baker Academic, 2009).

[26]Boeve, *Interrupting Tradition*, 24.

Practical Implications

What has been said thus far clearly depends to a great degree on acquired theological and philosophical knowledge. In that sense, recontextualization would seem not to be a game for young players—and to an extent, that is true. At the same time, to insist on a kind of intellectual purity in the practice of recontextualization could be unhelpful, because it might simply repeat the mistake that has been made in many generations of the Church, which is to cut believers off from the expectation of growth, development, or maturity in their faith. It is time to move past the idea that some people do theology and other people do not, since the fact is that everyone who is part of a Christian community, in some way—Christian or otherwise—is actually doing theology all the time. The question is, are they doing it well or badly, and what criteria do we use to assess this? In a Catholic school, the teacher who sits up the back of the hall doing her marking during a whole of school Mass says as much about faith and her theological commitments as does the principal or religious education leader who works hard to articulate and bring to life the Catholic identity of their school amidst parent groups who are apathetic or who are focused only on high academic results. This exemplifies the hidden curriculum of Catholic schools. We say as much about faith when we work hard not to say anything about it as we do when we take to the pulpit.

In the oft-cited words of Anselm, theology is faith seeking understanding, and in order to recontextualize, it is first necessary to be open to and critically reflective about faith, whether that is Christian faith, another religious faith, atheism, or a different worldview altogether. In order to recontextualize in such a way as to enable others to "see" what Christian (or any other) faith is getting at, it is helpful to have a deep knowledge of and "feel for" the faith narrative and to recognize how different elements of contemporary culture can break open that narrative—in multiple ways.[27] It is also helpful to be able to name and have at least a preliminary understanding of those elements of contemporary culture that inevitably shape how any religious narrative is *heard in the current Western context*. One of the biggest mistakes that many of us involved in religious education in schools have made over the last thirty years is to have presumed that faith can continue to speak to culture in

[27]Boeve argues that the Christian narrative itself is an *open narrative*. By its very nature, he says, it has "an open sensitivity towards otherness," a recognition of the boundaries of particular discourses (that is, it reflects a particular understanding of the world in relation to God and does not seek to impose this understanding on other worldviews), and it involves a critical praxis that results in self- and world-criticism. Most importantly, he contends that when this open narrative closes in on itself and ceases to engage with the new, grace interrupts and breaks it open once again. See Boeve, *Interrupting Tradition*, 95–6; and Lieven Boeve, *Lyotard and Theology: Beyond the Christian Master Narrative of Love*, Philosophy and Theology Series (Bloomsbury T & T Clark, 2014), 73–4.

the same ways that it "always has" done in our own living memories. First, there simply is no "always has." Second, if we imagine there being any kind of continuity across time and cultures—at least in terms of a presumption of the existence of "God" or "the gods"—then we must recognize that such a presumption died long ago for many people. Chief amongst those elements of contemporary culture that inevitably shape how any religious narrative is *heard* in the West is what philosopher Charles Taylor calls "the immanent frame."[28] If one lives in the world as if what can be seen and touched is "all there is," then it can seem that talk of a God "up there" or a reality "beyond the world" is going to sound strangely like the faint echo of a dream one once had in childhood, perhaps something of which a grandparent spoke, a fantasy that has been left behind. To recontextualize in the contemporary context, one needs to be prepared to help open a space of genuine reflection in that immanence, without presuming that transcendence will be obvious to anyone.

At the same time, to recontextualize from the perspective of a religious tradition depends on a capacity to make that tradition meaningful, and this first involves a commitment to its meaningfulness. People who teach mathematics believe and frequently know that it is a system of meaning. The best teachers of English are those who have seen the beauty and truth of a poem or a piece of prose, for no matter how any of the students in the class judge the same work, such educators teach with a passion that can only come from a genuine knowledge and love of their subject. They do not need the affirmation of others before revealing this love. Instead, they bear witness to it constantly because they cannot do otherwise. The work has called to them unmistakably, and while students at first chuckle to think that their teacher can speak so passionately, they eventually come to know that there is something deeply consonant between the love and the work. Now, as it happens, some of the best teachers of English are also the best teachers of religious education, because they are often free to talk about what matters and what makes meaning. The technical word in religious (especially Christian) tradition that is used to refer to the capacity to speak this meaning has assumed a kind of awkwardness that is altogether misconstrued: the word is "witness," although it is also known as "testimony." From the perspective of a religious tradition—and especially Christianity—to witness is not, as might be imagined, to hold someone hostage and try to convince them to take on one's own commitment. Instead, it is to "[give] an account of the hope that is in you" (1 Pet. 3:15). St Francis of Assisi is often quoted (and apparently misquoted) as saying "Preach the Gospel at all times. Use words if necessary." To account for one's hope does not mean to give embarrassingly personal sermons, to "overshare" or to give

[28]Charles Taylor, *A Secular Age* (Harvard University Press, 2007), chapter 15.

"too much information," but to reveal—often silently—that the source of one's hope is a love that is experienced as genuine.

One of the purposes of the present book is to assist practitioners in thinking about how to recontextualize religious beliefs. Since we ourselves are situated in the Catholic Christian community, we reflect on how to recontextualize largely, although not exclusively, from a Catholic Christian point of view. We have noted, above, three points of emphasis: that everyone who is part of a Christian community in some way—Christian or not—is actually doing theology all the time; that to have faith in a transcendent God can be entirely outside the experience of many contemporary Westerners, so that there is nothing obvious or even natural about belonging to a faith tradition; and that to recontextualize from a Christian perspective demands a capacity to enter deeply into and speak from that tradition, while also engaging others who speak from a different position or worldview, and to be sensitive and open to the context. In light of our experience, we have developed what we call "Four Steps to Christian Theological Recontextualization" as one way of conceiving the task. We readily acknowledge that it is not the only way, and that some of the best recontextualizations are more like miracles which take place *despite* what we do instead of *because* of it. Sometimes, images and texts and stories seem to come to us rather than we to them. At other times, recontextualizing is just painstaking work. Either way, it can be an immensely creative and life-giving activity.

Four Steps to Christian Theological Recontextualization

Listening to the Text

While it is possible to imagine beginning a recontextualization with a statement from tradition (where tradition is conceived as the other-than-biblical tradition of the Church), there are many circumstances where beginning with something from the biblical tradition is more straightforward. For a start, it is more ecumenical. Moreover, since we advocate commencing with prayer, and since it is less customary to pray with dogmatic or doctrinal texts (although sometimes other sorts of traditional writings are amenable for use in prayer—for example, the spiritual texts of significant figures in the tradition), starting with a biblical text makes sense. It is also possible to begin with other symbols, that is, other-than-textual symbols, perhaps visual or other artistic renderings of a narrative. We begin with biblical texts partly because they represent a proximity to the life of Jesus that underscores their preeminent place in tradition, and partly because the narrative is frequently organized into relatively short stories that are often readily available to the mind's eye.

Now, to begin Christian recontextualization with prayer demands one also recognize that some members of a group undertaking the recontextualization might not feel able to come before the text in this way. Recontextualization requires an openness that begins in truly listening to the text: for Christians, this involves the belief that God might reveal Godself by means of the text, whether by the words, or by the affect that signifies through the words. The appropriate stance for Christian participants is one of humility before the text and the desire, or the desire to desire, that God will speak.[29] For others, however, a preparedness to enter into the exercise in an open way is to be encouraged. The most that one can ask is that there is respect between all participants, wherever they stand in relation to the authority of the text. This need not be framed as *negative* respect (listen respectfully even if you don't believe in God!) but can and should be framed much more positively (persons who are of different worldviews and beliefs have much to offer when reading a Christian text).

The first step in recontextualization is evidently the selection of a text (or other symbol) to recontextualize. Very often, it is good advice simply to choose a text from the lectionary readings for the day. While this can seem somewhat arbitrary, it is often surprising what comes of such a choice and it avoids over-reliance on or bias toward one's usual preferences. Evidently, sometimes one has reason to choose a particular reading, instead. We have no hard and fast advice to give on the best type of text to select, except to say that if one is leading a recontextualization activity, it is important to do some preliminary reflection on some of the possibilities onto which a text might open. A hermeneutically rich text—one that opens onto several possibilities—is more likely to yield a rich recontextualization than a text that is more limited in scope. One also has to bear in mind the conceptual breadth of those undertaking the task, as well as any potential tendencies to hear the text in a literal way.

Next, we have to allow sufficient opportunity for the text to speak. We suggest beginning with *lectio divina* (divine reading). *Lectio divina* is an ancient monastic tradition of taking a passage of Christian scripture and praying with it. This means that the one reading endeavors to be open to hearing the word of God addressed directly to them in the text. The text is read very slowly, more than once, and allowed to "wash over" the person in prayer. Different words are "savored." In some ways, this is more like eating than reading: "taste and see that the Lord is good" (Ps. 34:8). Over the course of the prayer, it sometimes happens that a particular word or phrase from the text strikes or deeply moves the person, and this becomes the focus of prayer in the context of the person's or the community's life: in other words, the one praying allows that word or phrase to resonate with

[29]See Jean-Yves Lacoste, *In Search of Speech: Talking, Reading and Praying in an Age of Words*, trans. Oliver O'Donovan (Bloomsbury, 2024), 128–31.

their present concerns. It is important for participants to record such words or phrases in writing.

A different opportunity for the text to speak can be brought about by imaginatively entering into the scene of the text. In this book, we have developed a number of hermeneutical-phenomenological readings of the biblical texts we are using. Entering into a text phenomenologically involves the suspension of both belief and disbelief in order to focus more fully on aspects of its lived experience.[30] A phenomenological reading of the narrative focuses on what in the text gives itself, which might be invisible, and *how* it is given (as memory, perception, imagination, and so on). Very often, these are things that are missed in an ordinary reading. The hermeneutic aspect of phenomenology relates to our attention to the interpretative dimensions of our response to its givenness.

Conceptually different from undertaking a phenomenological reading, another way of experiencing a Gospel text is to immerse ourselves in the scene and engage in an imaginative contemplation using the senses. The process may be self-led, where we ask ourselves what we can see, hear, smell, taste, touch, and feel as we experience the narrative unfolding around us. Alternatively, it may be guided, with a leader retelling the narrative, using highly descriptive language and prompting questions that enable us to imagine our responses. Sometimes the leader might pose questions that prompt imaginative dialogue with the characters. We might be invited to ask questions of the characters and to imagine what they might say. This approach borrows from the Spiritual Exercises of Ignatius Loyola, where it is a question of using the senses metaphorically in order to "[indicate] the ways in which we react to the world under the influence of God's grace."[31] Examples of sensory contemplation are given in Chapters 6 and 8, but there are other resources available to support this method of prayerful engagement in a text.[32]

Again borrowing from Ignatius Loyola, sometimes we enter the text by means of a "colloquy." A colloquy is a conversation. It is a way of entering the text by means of an imaginative conversation with God. Here, we write in direct address to the person who is the subject of the text. "[The] colloquy, Ignatius says, 'is properly made by speaking, as one friend speaks to another, or as a servant speaks to his master; now asking for some grace, now blaming oneself for some misdeed, now communicating one's affairs, and seeking counsel in them'. In the colloquy, the heart speaks—it communicates freely

[30]See Robyn Horner, "Towards a Hermeneutic-Phenomenological Methodology for Theology," *International Journal of Practical Theology* 22, no. 2 (2018): 153–73.

[31]Philip Endean, "The Ignatian Prayer of the Senses," *Heythrop Journal* 31, no. 4 (1990): 391–418.

[32]See "God Communicates in Many Ways," and "Pray with Your Imagination," in David L. Fleming, *What Is Ignatian Spirituality?* (Loyola, 2011); Timothy M. Gallagher, *Meditation and Contemplation: An Ignatian Guide to Prayer with Scripture* (Crossroad, 2008).

with God, according to the stirrings it feels."[33] An example of a colloquy is given in Chapter 5.

Still another way of entering the text more fully is to engage in *Bibliodrama*, which has been defined as "combining a close reading of biblical texts with searching, imaginative questions" in acting out the story.[34] In its fullness, the process of *Bibliodrama* can readily be linked with that of recontextualization:

> Religious narratives from existing and living traditions may evoke memories of, and reveal connections with, a person's own life experiences. These narratives can provide elements for the ongoing process of identity construction, i.e., elements that are incorporated in an individual's personal narrative—in a reworked form or not. In addition, such elements can further be integrated in the ongoing narrative of the respective tradition as well. The activity of remembering contributes to the rewriting of one's own biography, but also contributes to new insights in the tradition. A person's own story, which includes words, images and fragments of a particular tradition, becomes part of that tradition, while the story simultaneously reconstructs the worldview/life orientation of that person.[35]

One of the benefits of *Bibliodrama* is that it has evolved in multireligious contexts, and attention to the method can assist in the development of skills in dialogue between different traditions and worldviews.

A final suggestion we have for this stage is to ask participants in the recontextualization to find or create images of the narrative. An important part of this process is for participants to use the images to tell and retell the story until they have a clear memory of the characters and sequence of events. This can be undertaken in pairs or in larger groups where one of the tasks is to help each person remember the story. In a further development, participants can find or create images of how they *feel* about the story or any of the characters, as appropriate, and to share those feelings (and the reasons why they are evoked, if possible). However, the creation of images

---

[33]Gallagher, *Meditation and Contemplation*, 86.

[34]This quote comes from the founders of the method, Susan and Peter Pitzele on their website, *Bibliodrama*, http://www.bibliodrama.com/, accessed March 10, 2021. See also Peter Pitzele, *Scripture Windows: Toward a Practice of Bibliodrama* (Alef Design Group, 1997). For recent engagement with the method, see Jean Agten, "Bibliodrama: Introducing Stories from Narrative Traditions in the Development of Young People's Life Orientation," *Education Sciences* 9, no. 2 (2019): 107; Natascha Kienstra, Monique van Dijk-Groeneboer, and Olav Boelens, "Religious-Thinking-Through Using Bibliodrama: An Empirical Study of Student Learning in Classroom Teaching," *Religious Education* 113, no. 2 (2018): 203–15; Bas van den Berg and Fortuin-van der Spek, "The Appropriation of Symbolic Language in Worldview Education Through Bibliodrama," *Education Sciences* 9, no. 2 (2019): 88.

[35]Agten, "Bibliodrama: Introducing Stories," 2.

of aspects of the text can lead participants to assume a literal position in relation to the text. We suggest a process for opening up such literalism in the next section.

Entering into Dialogue

When each participant has had time to listen carefully to the text, it is time to enter into dialogue with others who have read that text in different ways. First, it is important to consult reputable biblical scholars to ensure that any unfamiliar or potentially misread terms are clarified. It is easy for the imagination or the intellect to be misled and to create anachronisms by reading contemporary concepts back into the text. For example, a common one for children—and for quite a few adults—is that Jesus was a Christian. It is also important to approach the text in its increasingly larger contexts: the context of its surrounding verses; a biblical chapter; a greater story, a biblical book—as it may have been constructed and then reconstructed by several editors—and so on. The text's historical setting as well as the type of literature it represents are significant details to know. The work of personally listening to and entering into the text is not wasted in the face of the historical-critical or other methods of biblical studies; it ensures that our recontextualizations are actually related to the text we have before us. In the recontextualizations we offer in this book, we do not introduce readers to a great deal of the background detail to each Gospel but focus mainly on points related to the particular section of text under consideration. We do this to make our text more manageable, but we refer readers to the many excellent commentaries available which offer such introductions.[36]

A further exercise that can be undertaken at this point is for participants to practice identifying the literal (or pre-critical) meaning of the text, undertaking a critical reading, and then contrasting the literal with a symbolic (or post-critical) reading. For example, in reading Genesis 1, a literal reading might be that "God created the world in seven days." In contrast, a symbolic reading might be that "God is the source of all life." This practice helps participants right from the beginning to appreciate that the text is open to multiple readings. However, in light of the work that has been done with the commentaries, participants should also be assisted to recognize that while the text is open to multiple meanings, not every meaning one can suggest is always meaningful or disclosive of truth. In other words, there is always critical judgment involved in interpretation.

[36]For accessible examples, see the Friendly Guides Series (Garrett); Daniel Durken, ed., *The New Collegeville Bible Commentary. New Testament* (Liturgical Press, 2009). For richer fare, see the Sacra Pagina Series (Liturgical Press) or the Anchor Yale Bible Commentaries (Bloomsbury, 2021).

The next step is to enter into dialogue with Christian tradition with regard to the meaning/s that the text has communicated or been used to communicate in history. Sometimes this will involve a dialogue between the selected text and other biblical texts. For example, if the selected text includes Gal. 3:28 ("There is no longer Jew or Greek, there is no longer slave or free, there is no longer male and female; for all of you are one in Christ Jesus"), this text might have been (and sometimes was) read by the Christian tradition in light of 1 Tim. 2:11-12 ("Let a woman learn in silence with full submission. I permit no woman to teach or to have authority over a man; she is to keep silent"). If the selected text is from Genesis 3 (the story of the fall), then in some contexts it will be important to explain that Augustine used this text to develop the doctrine of original sin—in part because of a misreading of Rom. 5:12-13 ("Therefore, just as sin came into the world through one man, and death came through sin, and so death spread to all because all have sinned" was read as " ... and so death spread to all men, through one man, *in whom all men sinned*."). It will also be necessary to explain that Jews and most Protestants have no such doctrine, even though they share the same scripture. Evidently, just as the dialogue with the biblical text requires the support of experts, dialogue with the Christian and Catholic tradition needs the support of persons highly skilled in theology. Apart from anything else, if one is going to critique particular readings of tradition, it is important to know that these readings are *actually held*. For example, limbo was never an official doctrine of the Church—which was made clear by the International Theological Commission in 2007, but perhaps not registered by many Catholics.[37] It is not enough to use the *Catechism of the Catholic Church* to navigate theological history, because the *Catechism* uses a kind of shorthand: it cannot communicate the fullness or subtlety of the history, context, and theological argumentation involved in the Church's determination of various questions.

A final step in the dialogical phase is to explore issues arising from the text in light of the current context/s. In 2019 for example, the overwhelmingly dominant international issue was the spread and control of COVID-19. A selected text might have spoken to that issue, or it might not. It is important not to force text and issue together but to explore whether there is any dialogue naturally arising between the two. For example, if the selected text were Deut. 30:19-20 ("I call heaven and earth to witness against you today that I have set before you life and death, blessings and curses. Choose life so that you and your descendants may live, loving the Lord your God, obeying him, and holding fast to him"), it might be noted with older students that this text has been used in anti-abortion campaigns by the Church. Now, three bishops in Sydney churches raised ethical concerns in August 2020

[37]International Theological Commission, *The Hope of Salvation for Infants Who Die Without Being Baptised* (Catholic Truth Society, 2007), nn. 3, 24.

about the COVID-19 vaccine being developed by Oxford University because the researchers "made use of a cell line cultured from an electively aborted human foetus."[38] In December 2020, the Congregation for the Doctrine of the Faith—the congregation of the Roman Curia responsible for safeguarding the Catholic Church's doctrine on faith and morals—issued a "Note on the Morality of using some anti-COVID-19 vaccines."[39] In this statement, the Congregation noted that while ethically derived vaccines were a preferential option, in the absence of choice, Christians were urged to consider not only their own health when deciding whether or not to be vaccinated against COVID-19, but also to consider the common good.

The final dialogue phase brings together all the work done to this point and encourages the naming of relevant issues as they arise for the participants. The group respectfully discerns together those that warrant further exploration for recontextualization. Often this will mean undertaking further research to locate supporting resources that break open different aspects of these issues.

Perform a Recontextualization

In a particular sense, it is a bit artificial to claim at this point that one is performing the recontextualization, since everything until now has been part of that process. Nevertheless, this is the time to bring that to a head and to ask: "How is the text speaking to me (or us) today?" It is important to allow time to reflect quietly on the issues in light of the biblical text, responses from the tradition, and issues arising in the contemporary context. Next, it is important to consider or discuss what emerges from those moments of reflection and to deepen the insights, testing their consonance with Christian faith as professed and exploring what such insights might mean for others. It is quite possible that multiple insights will emerge.

To show what we mean, let us consider an example. At the time of writing, the first reading for the day happened to be Jer. 7:25-28. God speaks to the prophet, Jeremiah, about the faithlessness of the chosen people, Israel:

> From the day that your ancestors came out of the land of Egypt until this day, I have persistently sent all my servants the prophets to them, day

[38]Alison Xiao, "Oxford University Coronavirus Vaccine Has 'Ethical Concerns', Sydney Archbishops Warn Followers," *ABC News* (August 24, 2020), https://www.abc.net.au/news/2020-08-24/sydney-catholic-archbishop-warns-pm-against-coronavirus-vaccine/12588578?utm_medium=content_shared&utm_source=abc_news_amp&utm_campaign=abc_news_amp&utm_content=mail.

[39]Congregation for the Doctrine of the Faith, "Note on the Morality of Using Some Anti-Covid-19 Vaccines" (December 17, 2020), https://www.vatican.va/roman_curia/congregations/cfaith/documents/rc_con_cfaith_doc_20201221_nota-vaccini-anticovid_en.html.

> after day; yet they did not listen to me, or pay attention, but they stiffened their necks. They did worse than their ancestors did.
>
> So you shall speak all these words to them, but they will not listen to you. You shall call to them, but they will not answer you. You shall say to them: This is the nation that did not obey the voice of the Lord their God, and did not accept discipline; truth has perished; it is cut off from their lips.

Here, we have quoted from our preferred translation, the NRSV Anglicised Catholic Edition, but the version in *Universalis* is the one we first listened to, and according to that translation (from the Jerusalem Bible), the last line reads "Sincerity is no more, it has vanished from their mouths." In fact, this line was actually what we found most striking about the text, which is re-emphasized by its difference from the translation we have used here. Let us assume that we have done our due diligence with the text, that we have read it to the extent that we can in the context of its times and that we have observed its use in Christian tradition over the centuries.

What was front and center in our minds as we examined this text were political issues: a senior federal cabinet minister had been accused of raping a sixteen-year-old girl in 1988. Since she never completed making a sworn statement to the police before taking her own life in 2020, her friends brought it to the attention of government. The cabinet minister emphatically denied the allegations. The prime minister declared that nothing could be done because there was no evidence to prove guilt (or at least, there is no "admissible" evidence, in the words of the police). Shortly before this revelation, a former aide to a different cabinet minister had alleged that she was raped by a colleague one night in said minister's office and claimed to have been treated unthinkingly by the (female) minister in the aftermath. This minister had been overheard calling the woman who had been raped a "lying cow." A number of other parliamentary workers then came forward to report instances of sexual assault and bullying. A workplace like no other, it became apparent that persons making such reports generally lose their jobs, for there is no proper process for dealing with these matters: ministers hire and fire their own staff, and there is no HR department. The country was divided in its opinions. In the case of the allegation concerning the senior cabinet minister, there were those who proclaimed that he had been tried by the media; since the alleged victim had passed away, there was no proof for the allegation, no way for the minister to clear his name, and no reason for him to resign. Others called for a coronial investigation of the woman's death and for the minister to step aside for its duration. Both ministers vanished on sick leave. How did the text speak to the issues in the contemporary context? Indeed, "sincerity is no more, it has vanished from their mouths."

In this light, we watched as a Royal Commission into Aged Care handed down its report. Up to a third of residents in nursing homes were found to have been abused, physically or sexually. We saw CCTV of patients being beaten and tormented by psychopathic "carers." We heard that one in six patients had malnutrition, patients were left lying in feces in their beds for many hours at a time, and chemical restraints were regularly used to control patients who are considered "difficult." And this was the forty-second investigation into aged care in the last ten years! During the COVID-19 lockdown, some nursing home patients received neither food nor drink for three days. Nursing homes refused or were advised not to transfer elderly victims to hospitals, and the infection spread like wildfire. We heard of private nursing home operators vowing to do their best, yet while patients were eventually vaccinated, no provision had been taken to vaccinate the workers. "Sincerity is no more, it has vanished from their mouths." Some people spoke of responding to COVID-19 by isolating only the elderly and vulnerable, so that those younger and needing to make a living could just get on with it. A former prime minister was reported to say: "the economic cost of lockdowns [mean] families should be allowed to consider letting elderly relatives with the coronavirus die by letting nature take its course."[40]

Did the text challenge the new context? Without our intending to portray any hint of self-righteousness in responding—of course it did, for it is we who accept and benefit from the compromises of our politicians. The text holds up a mirror to our society: "Sincerity is no more, it has vanished from their mouths." The text calls us to come to our senses, to recognize that we have not only been wilfully blind, but also that we must act to restore sincerity.

Did the contemporary context speak to the text? This it did by asserting its secularity. In the face of neither god nor heaven, the command to speak sincerely could come only from a shared humanist or rationalistic ethic. An alternative reading might be that the context revealed the hypocrisy of those who are apparently committed to the God of the text.

How does a recontextualized text challenge the Christian community? How does it challenge *us*, those engaged in the dialogue, who might bring other worldviews to the table? How does it challenge *me*? This exercise frequently opens questions that might potentially have answers but cannot easily be resolved. In the discussion and recontextualization, we need to be prepared to keep the tension open and not to rush to make the text and new context harmonious. It is possible that the dialogue will not lead to easy responses or satisfactory resolutions. We must be prepared to *dwell with* the issues arising. We must resist platitudes or pious commentary. And we must remember that *not* to respond is still to respond.

---

[40]Patrick Wintour, "Tony Abbott: Some Elderly Covid Patients Could Be Left to Die Naturally," *The Guardian* (Australia) (September 2, 2020), online.

We ask whether new understandings of the text have arisen as a result of its being placed in a new context. What insights about the context have arisen? As a result of this dialogue, what shifts have taken place in our understandings of the text and the contextual issue/s? And most importantly, how does the engagement between text and context speak to us of God—if it does? *The recontextualization is fundamentally what takes place in this dialogue.*

Evaluate the Recontextualization

The final phase in a recontextualization is its evaluation and recording, in which we recognize our responsibilities to both the text and the context. We ask: i) Does the recontextualization respect the text in its faith-context? Alternatively, does it twist or warp the text? ii) Does it respect the contemporary context/s in which the text has been placed? Alternatively, does it twist or warp the contemporary context? iii) Does it allow the text to speak powerfully in a new context? iv) Does the recontextualization challenge or interrupt the faith context? If so, how? v) Does it challenge or interrupt the contemporary context? If so, how? vi) Is it a "strong" recontextualization—will it stay with you—or a "weak" recontextualization—one that will become irrelevant quite quickly?[41] The richest recontextualization leads to lasting transformation—of text, context, and reader. However, sometimes an attempt at recontextualization will not "hold together" or achieve the intended transformation. There is often as much to learn from this failure as from success. We could ask why the text or the context seems resistant to recontextualization. Alternatively, we could ask if there is something that has been misunderstood about the text or the context or understood in too facile a way.

Once we have evaluated the recontextualization, it is ready to be documented in some way. Certainly, it is helpful to write it down, to describe the process, to try to capture the insights. But it is also possible that it can be expressed creatively: perhaps in art, poetry, music, and so on. The documentation is important not only for those who have been through the recontextualization but also for those who come late to the conversation—those who come afterward. The documentation can sometimes become a springboard for the recontextualizations that others undertake, and the process continues.

In a final step, we return to where we began—in prayer or reflection. What do I need to *do* in response to the recontextualization? Make a note of any important insights in a personal journal, and remember to return

[41]We thank Jan Bouwens for his work in developing criteria for recontextualization. See Jan Bouwens, "Recontextualizing Catholic School Identity: Five Criteria," in *Teaching and Tradition: On Their Dynamic Interaction*, ed. Jos Moons, Rudi A. te Velde, and Archibald L.H.M. van Wieringen (Brill, 2023), 150–70.

to them, often—in further reflection or prayer. Recontextualization that is transformative by necessity involves personal change, and from a Christian perspective, human beings are created to be the hands of God in the world—to change the world for the better.

The remainder of this book constitutes a series of examples of recontextualization that have taken place as part of particular experiences. While these examples are intended to inform, and might to some extent be re-implemented, the most important thing to remember is that recontextualization is usually context and time-specific. Ideally, recontextualization is not something we "do" to others but is a dialogical process in which we engage, often *with* others. In addition to a recognition of different times and contexts, variations in recontextualization depend to some extent on the hermeneutical lenses we employ as we engage in the process. If our process favors the interpretation of texts and symbols, for example, our recontextualization may yield different results than if we seek explicitly to be open to learning from other religious traditions and cultures. Being attentive to these hermeneutical (or interpretive) lenses can assist us in the process of meaning-making by enabling us continually to deepen the questions we bring to the text and context. Keeping all of these differences in mind, the examples we provide in this book might have worked for us, but they might not work for you. What you will see, however, is that within the general structure we have proposed (and which is available as a reference sheet at the back of this book), there are multiple variations possible. While our four steps involve several sub-processes, they remain four steps because those sub-processes can take different forms and emphases. They are intended to promote creativity, not to constrain it.

2

Jesus and the Woman Caught in Adultery: The Experience of Shame

In Chapter 1, we considered what it might mean to recontextualize—particularly from a (Judeo)-Christian perspective—and underscored the significance of context to understanding and interpretation. It is crucial to recognize that while we may be writing from a particular perspective, we cannot presume to know the readership of this manuscript; therefore, we cannot specify all those contexts in which it will be read. A love letter might begin its journey of delivery with every good intention, only to be delivered to the wrong address or intercepted by someone for whom it was not intended, read by a genealogist 100 years later in a family tree search or delivered to its addressee only after the sender has been killed in war. All that we, the authors, can do is to characterize our own context as best we can, although even *context* can be plural (there are two of us writing together, whose contexts are similar but by no means identical; each of us also inhabits several contexts). We quote below a text that we read from within a Christian context, perhaps on the Sunday of the fifth week of Lent in the Lectionary cycle year C, or perhaps as part of prayer in some other situation. We hear this text from within a Catholic, Christian context, and while we do not hear it as God's words, we hear it as God's Word, and we are open to finding ourselves having been affected by it as it is read and as we reflect on it. This might not be the case for our readers. We do not know where you stand: forgive us in advance if we presume too much. That said, we do our best to settle into stillness and ask for openness and insight as together we listen to a reading from the Gospel of John.

The Text: John 8:2-11

Early in the morning he came again to the temple. All the people came to him and he sat down and began to teach them. The scribes and the Pharisees brought a woman who had been caught in adultery; and making her stand before all of them, they said to him, "Teacher, this woman was caught in the very act of committing adultery. Now in the law Moses commanded us to stone such women. Now what do you say?" They said this to test him, so that they might have some charge to bring against him. Jesus bent down and wrote with his finger on the ground. When they kept on questioning him, he straightened up and said to them, "Let anyone among you who is without sin be the first to throw a stone at her." And once again he bent down and wrote on the ground. When they heard it, they went away, one by one, beginning with the elders; and Jesus was left alone with the woman standing before him. Jesus straightened up and said to her, "Woman, where are they? Has no one condemned you?" She said, "No one, sir." And Jesus said, "Neither do I condemn you. Go your way, and from now on do not sin again."

Now we listen again, even more keenly attentive to each word and phrase. We write down those words or phrases that cannot quickly be swallowed, but instead, beg to be held in the mouth and tasted more carefully, those words calling to the reader in the moment.

Reading with a Hermeneutic-phenomenological Lens

Phenomenology, as the name suggests, is the study of phenomena—but it is more than simply that. Phenomenology is the study of phenomena as they *are given* to us *in experience*, which means that we first need to take a step back and try to put aside everything we already think we know about the particular phenomenon in question. We do this in order to scrutinize the phenomenon more carefully. For example, when we are contemplating a textual phenomenon, if it is something that is well-known to us, we might not read it very carefully or even notice the details—we just assume we know what it is about. This is especially the case when reading a scriptural text, about which we frequently do not wonder or question.

To undertake a phenomenological reading, it is helpful to pretend that we have not read the passage before, and to suspend all belief or disbelief in that to which it may refer. This is called "bracketing" (more technically, the "phenomenological *epochē*"), and one phenomenologist helpfully describes it as referring to something "within quotation marks." The point of bracketing, he says, is "[to] quote our experiences, without asserting (or denying) their implicit 'claims'."[1] In reading Judeo-Christian scripture, one

---

[1]Søren Overgaard, "How to Do Things with Brackets: The Epochē Explained," *Continental Philosophy Review* 48, no. 2 (2015): 192.

brackets whether or not one believes in the truth claims that are made about scripture—either by Jews and/or Christians, or by atheists, or by anyone in between.

The second step is to undertake what is called the "phenomenological reduction." This means that we choose a particular lens through which to look at the phenomena appearing to us. We might choose a very narrowly focused lens, such as the lens that allows objects like trees and houses and bottles of wine to appear, or we might choose a very wide lens such as that of the so-called reduction to "givenness"—the reduction to whatever gives itself to perception. Using the reduction to givenness means that we see not only objects but also their symbolic nature in given networks of meaning (the bottle of wine, for example, in its shared enjoyment), and other phenomena such as entities (persons, both human or non-human, for example) and their ways of being in the world, essences, and so on, as well as other phenomena that are invisible, especially those that *resist* our gaze, perhaps appearing to the affect alone—provoking feelings or, more deeply, longer-lasting moods.

Hermeneutics is the art and science of interpretation, which might initially seem a long way from what we are doing when we try to strip things back to our perception of them in phenomenology. Nevertheless, hermeneutics relates very closely to how we perceive and understand as well as how we interpret, because we often only arrive at understanding by means of a process of interpretation. Hermeneutics bears a relation to phenomenology to the extent that in order to perceive something *as* something, we need to bring other factors into play—such as the context. This might be the physical context, or it might be the historical or literary context. If we are reading Mt. 5:29-30, in which Jesus states that eyes or hands that cause us to sin should be plucked out or cut off respectively, even advocates of a very "literalist" reading of the Bible will suddenly remember that it is all about context.[2] To undertake a hermeneutical-phenomenological reading, then, we need to

[2]The Pontifical Biblical Commission notes the distinction between the literal sense and literalist readings of scripture: "The literal sense is not to be confused with the 'literalist' sense to which fundamentalists are attached. It is not sufficient to translate a text word for word in order to obtain its literal sense. One must understand the text according to the literary conventions of the time. When a text is metaphorical, its literal sense is not that which flows immediately from a word-to-word translation (e.g. 'Let your loins be girt': Lk. 12:35), but that which corresponds to the metaphorical use of these terms ('Be ready for action'). When it is a question of a story, the literal sense does not necessarily imply belief that the facts recounted actually took place, for a story need not belong to the genre of history but be instead a work of imaginative fiction." "The literal sense of Scripture is that which has been expressed directly by the inspired human authors. Since it is the fruit of inspiration, this sense is also intended by God, as principal author. One arrives at this sense by means of a careful analysis of the text, within its literary and historical context. The principal task of exegesis is to carry out this analysis, making use of all the resources of literary and historical research, with a view to defining the literal sense of the biblical texts with the greatest possible accuracy." Pontifical Biblical Commission, *The Interpretation of the Bible in the Church* (Pauline Books, 1994), B n.1.

look very closely at what is given in the text and also be attentive to the ways in which we are always and already understanding and interpreting the significance of what appears. This is what we try to do in our reading of Jn 8:2-11.

A Hermeneutic-phenomenological Reading of John 8:2-11

It is early in the morning when Jesus comes back to the temple. Does he expect to be alone there? All the people come to him, like children, flocking to his side, asking him questions, and he responds to them by sitting down to teach.

Jesus is not up high, not on high, not at a lectern. Does he stand up when the woman enters the temple with her accusers? (He was sitting down, but later he bends down, which is harder to do if you are already sitting ...) With the interruption of the accusers the focus shifts from sitting to standing level.

Now, we do not see Jesus (or any of the other characters, in fact) in photographic detail, and yet this is a text that is in some ways all about visibility. The woman's accusers *make her stand before all of them*. That's the thing. She had been caught in the act of adultery, and they bring her and make her stand there in front of everyone. She can be seen; her intense visibility is all the more striking when she remains in so many ways invisible to us (she has no name, no features). If there is any light to be shone in this text, it is upon her, such a powerful light that it exposes her from the inside out. There is no barrier to shield her from the probing looks of the assembled people; there is no resistance to their seeing because she has been caught in her utmost intimacy. It is all there, and she is more than naked, to be seen. This is because what is typically least visible—what is largely internal to her—is somehow exteriorized by way of the shaming condemnation: she has been caught in adultery, and so we have not only her by-now-very-sordid act before us but also her feeling, no named feeling, but feeling as such, whatever feeling has motivated her liaison with this partner. In this way, the invisible woman almost burns with interior visibility, which is the essence of shame. We are not told how she feels as she stands there before them and before us, yet we see her shame. What belongs inside her, that which is most secret, is now on the outside, exposed. There is no longer a border between inside and outside to protect her; her skin is breached all over and all at once. There is no place of invisibility into which she can retreat.

(Given only in the harbor of invisibility, of course, is the woman's sexual partner. She had been caught *in the act*; ergo, they had been caught in the act together. She has been dragged here; for some reason, he remains elsewhere. He is given, but he does not appear.)

As much as this is a text about visibility, it is a text about looking. Frankly, I don't really want to look at this: it is all too much information. I don't really want to see what shames another, lest I become a *voyeur* and complicit in putting her there, lest I participate in her shaming. Are the assembled people looking? The woman is made to stand *before all of them* and her accusers highlight her visibility as they address Jesus (*Teacher, this woman was caught in the very act of committing adultery*). But are the people really *looking*? It is evident that the woman is there to be seen by them in all her heightened visibility. Perhaps they are looking. Perhaps they are less squeamish than I; perhaps they want to look; perhaps the temple has momentarily become the stadium, the Colosseum for sinners. Yet these are the people who have been drawn to Jesus. Are they looking at the woman, or are they averting their eyes?

More than that, if I look at her she confronts me with sin—not hers, but mine. There but for the grace of God …. All that remains unseen, for the most part, so easily dragged into the light (*and people loved darkness rather than light because their deeds were evil*). C. S. Lewis is right, I think, that murder begets murder because the sin gets harder and harder to hide from oneself. We don't want to look at sin, or if we do, we want to make sure it belongs to someone else and that we destroy the carrier of the infection. The woman acts as a mirror: only throwing stones will appropriately deal with what she represents to her accusers (and, ultimately, the onlookers). In the *dénoument* to the story, Jesus calls this for what it is. If anyone is prepared to look in the mirror, they may throw first.

What are we given of the accusers, these men who bring the woman to be humiliated (on her way to being stoned)? They are named in code: *scribes and Pharisees*. Their reference to the woman in their address to Jesus suggests that they look at her, but perhaps only momentarily. If they were really looking, would they be able to do this to her? Their bringing her in seems so callously done—in a sense, almost casual. They have brought her here with an end in mind, apparently, which is to catch a much bigger fish, to draw Jesus into a discussion that will trap him. The woman is merely instrumental to that end. Are they really here for the sport of shaming her, or is that incidental to the main game? Are they looking at her—do they really see *her*? Their use of her suggests instead that she remains an object to them, and not a person. Their focus is, in any case, more upon *him*, their opponent. Yet when they look at him, what do they see? What does anyone see when there is a threat? What do we see other than a threat? Not a person, certainly, but the projection of our fear, which becomes the object of our hate. In the accusers, we are given Jesus as a screen onto which is projected all their own demons. He comes to represent one who judges; who would not be afraid? Who would not be afraid that this might all lead to personal annihilation? In a text that is apparently about visibility, the accusers do not see the woman, and they do not see Jesus: all they see is themselves.

One thing is clear, which is that Jesus seems to be doing his best for most of the scene not to look at the woman. He shifts the plane of action once again; bending down, and writing on the ground, he draws the attention of the onlookers away from her. Given that he is writing on the ground, it appears that his gaze is down for much of the time (and we can say no more about this than that it serves as a point of focus). Refusing to respond to the accusers, he prolongs the awkwardness of the moment. The question—*what do you say?*—hangs there in the air, with no quick agreement from Jesus with their condemnation on the basis of the law of Moses. (Does anyone feel uncomfortable or embarrassed here? Might the onlookers feel uncomfortable because they are not quickly reassured that it is just to condemn the woman? Or might they feel uncomfortable because they think Jesus can't respond to the challenge?) In any case, the accusers get right on with it. They keep on questioning him, like children with tunnel vision for pursuing a satisfactory outcome to an issue without, apparently, seeing what else is going on around them.

When Jesus finally stands and responds, he suddenly comes sharply into narrative focus. Still we may not see him as such, but his words concentrate his person. This happens twice. He rises and speaks for the first time, with a force and an authority that is striking because of its context. The one who has placed himself at the lowest level, hands in the dirt, and who appears to be without answers, arises to speak powerfully and unambiguously. The air of unease or embarrassment around Jesus' capacity to respond is almost violently dispelled; the trap has been more than neatly avoided; the response is devastating. Jesus becomes the mirror to the accusers and to the crowd: see here your own sin; see here how you participate in the sin of the woman. The spotlight is suddenly shone upon everyone and a new sense of embarrassment arises to thicken the air once again. For all of an instant, the scene is over-exposed.

What does sin look like out in the open? We have already been shown something of the sin of the woman and her shame in her appalling visibility. The sins of the multitude are not named; all we are given to see, in fact, is the sin of their preparedness to sacrifice her without thought to their own need to repent. Yet that is enough. The givenness of sin saturates intuition in its own way: even as the sinner becomes more visible, sin is given in a kind of conceptual darkness. We are not presuming to personify it here, but only to observe how it somehow escapes rationality, emerging from and at once retreating into a depth that is unfathomable. Imaginatively, while there is—on the one hand—a kind of scale to sin, stretching from the least venial to the most mortal, there is also—on the other hand—never more than a hair's breadth between any single point on that scale and any other. It is all of a piece, which is why being confronted with sin is not only absolutely humiliating but can be truly terrifying.

The challenge given, Jesus withdraws again, returning in a downward movement to the narrative dust. The crowd dissipates, and at last the scene becomes personal. For all the obscene exposure encountered in the text thus far, there has been nothing intimate about it: for all that it evidently puts on display what is most personal, the pornographic obliterates the personal in the same move. So, finally we enter a space of real intimacy. When the crowd has gone, *Jesus* [is] *left alone with the woman standing before him.* He rises a second time and addresses her directly. *Woman, where are they? Has no one condemned you?*

Speak, Lord, your servant is listening. There is a marked contrast between Jesus' address to the woman and his earlier address to the crowd. Where that had taken the form of something like a juridical pronouncement (*let anyone among you who is without sin be the first to throw a stone at her*), his address now reflects the beginnings of a personal relationship. Jesus' address to the woman starts, not with his assessment of her or of what has taken place, but with two questions for her to answer. This effectively means that she first has to assess the situation for herself. She cannot make this assessment with her eyes downcast (have they been downcast?), but must look up and around to see that the crowd has, in fact, gone, and that no one remains to condemn her with a stone. And so, she responds: *no one, sir.* For we who see her now, who have been reluctant witnesses to her utter nakedness before, there is a dramatic shift. Suddenly she becomes more herself than she was then, in spite of the fact that we had already viewed her completely exposed, as if there were nothing more we could possibly have seen. The woman is addressed, and she responds, and she is given a dignity that is all the more profound for the way that she remains, as it were, unclothed, not hiding anything. Jesus addresses her, and she becomes herself: in Jesus' address to her she is given herself, and she responds as herself at last.

It is *as* herself in this way that the woman finds she is not rebuked by Jesus (*neither do I condemn you*) and perhaps experiences for the first time the possibility of fulfilling his otherwise seemingly impossible command: *from now on do not sin again.* The self re-given in being personally addressed by Jesus, is the self thus invested with a new dignity and enabled to respond, the self able to move forward as itself, the respons-*able* self, the self able to desire the good instead of being dissipated in sin.

Class dismissed. *Go your way* ... The narrative ends abruptly. The woman has had the offer of being transformed, and we might want to dwell with her on the great mercy she has been shown and the kindness of Jesus himself. She—and we—might wish to linger in his presence, to enjoy the moment, to enjoy *him* in her newfound identity (should she choose to accept it). Instead, just as she comes face to face with him, she is told to leave. We do not get to hold on to Jesus, to grasp him (as if we *could*), but only to remember that he has been there and to desire that he might come again. He never becomes ours. It is a severe mercy, a costly blessing. However, if we are prepared to be found in the deepest dark of our secret lives and come into the light—not only adulterers, but also inquisitors, spectators, people who have been prepared to sacrifice others to protect ourselves—the offer remains for us to become his.

Suddenly we are alone again. He is gone. We are left to ponder: at what point(s) did the heart stir, if it stirred at all?

Re-member the scene (put it back together again). Replay the moments that sparked your anger or fear, your empathy or compassion. Consider your mood—before, and after. What were the points where the narrative touched your own life, your own sexual history, perhaps, or your feelings of being over-exposed and humiliated, or being caught up with a crowd in self-righteous indignation? Where are you in the text? Stay with that a while.

Engaging in Critical Dialogue with Biblical Tradition

We call on biblical scholars to show us things about the text we might not otherwise have known. Perhaps there is something we have seen and interpreted in a twenty-first-century fashion, and before we seize it and run with it, we need to know what it might have meant in the first century. Perhaps it is not as significant as we think, or not significant in the way that we think it might be. John 8:2-11 is part of a slightly longer text that includes verses 7:53 and 8:1. We have omitted the introductory verses in our reading, however biblical scholars normally include them as a whole in discussion of Jesus and the woman caught in adultery, referring to this as the *Pericope Adulterae* (PA).

An important question about Jn 7:53–8:11 regards its provenance.[3] Most scholars agree that this whole section of text does not naturally fit into the structure and flow of John. Moreover, the PA does not appear in the earliest extant Johannine manuscripts. Why might this be the case? Some authors suggest that the story is original to John but was removed from early versions, either accidentally or because it fell out of use. Or, some contend, "the PA was removed for pious reasons by well-meaning but misinformed church leaders."[4] These scholars speculate that such "pious reasons" included objections to the sexual subject matter of the text, or the fact that Jesus does not condemn the woman for a sexual sin that elsewhere he condemns.[5] Frances Gench goes so far as to declare: "In

---

[3]See the summary in David Alan Black and Jacob N. Cerone, eds., *The Pericope of the Adulteress in Contemporary Research* (Bloomsbury, 2016).

[4]John David Punch, "The Piously Offensive," in *The Pericope of the Adulteress in Contemporary Research*, ed. David Alan Black and Jacob N. Cerone (Bloomsbury, 2016), 31.

[5]Augustine is the first known to speculate on this in writing. See Adulterous Marriages 7.6, in Augustine, *Treatises on Marriage and Other Subjects: The Good Marriage, Adulterous Marriage, Holy Virginity, Faith and Works, the Creed, Faith and the Creed*, ed. Roy Joseph Deferrari, trans. Charles T. Wilcox (Catholic University of America Press, 1955).

all likelihood, [the PA does not appear] because it was suppressed! A good case can be made that the ease with which Jesus extended mercy to an adulterous woman embarrassed the earliest Christian communities and undermined their own more severe penitential practices."[6] More recently, however, it has been argued that the suppression theory is implausible.[7]

Other scholars argue, instead, that the PA does not appear in John because it is a later text and not an authentic part of the Gospel. This is particularly the case for some Evangelical readers, for whom the PA's "absence from the earliest manuscripts renders it neither inspired nor canonical."[8]

Responding to these positions, Francis (Frank) Moloney writes: "For sound textual reasons it is universally admitted that the account of Jesus and the woman taken in adultery (7:53–8:11) does not belong to the Fourth Gospel. ..." However, he considers the PA to be part of the early Jesus tradition: "This popular ancient tradition about Jesus, which 'floated' in written Jesus material, was incorporated into various manuscripts at different places in early textual traditions, mainly in the Fourth Gospel (after 7:36; 7:44; 7:52; or 21:25), but also in Luke (after Luke 21:38)."[9] Chris Keith underlines the way in which many New Testament scholars consider the PA to be authentic, if not to John, to Jesus himself.[10] Keith gives a detailed history of the PA, maintaining that while its origin is unknown, "PA, or a version of it, circulated in the early Church from at least the second century CE." He also notes that "the earliest interpreters of PA (Ambrose, Augustine, Jerome) all read the story in John's Gospel."[11]

From our point of view, debates about the provenance of the PA remind us of the apparent contingency of scripture, even if it is maintained that Christian scripture is the product of the inspiration of the Holy Spirit. Scholars agree that the Christian Gospels reflect earlier collections of sayings and traditions of Jesus, sewn together by the Gospel authors with various narrative purposes in mind. The PA's inclusion in John actually suggests its authenticity in terms of its origins in the person of Jesus, since it is not a text

[6]Frances Taylor Gench, "John 7:53–8:11," *Interpretation* 63, no. 4 (2009): 398.

[7]See Jennifer Wright Knust, *To Cast the First Stone: The Transmission of a Gospel Story*, ed. Tommy Wasserman (Princeton University Press, 2019), 97–8, 137.

[8]Sarah Eekhoff Zylstra, "Is 'Go and Sin No More' Biblical?: If the Earliest Manuscripts of the Gospel of John Don't Include the Story of the Woman Caught in Adultery, Why Is It in Our Bibles?," *Christianity Today* 52, no. 6 (2008): 60; Knust, *To Cast the First Stone*, 49.

[9]Francis J. Moloney, *Sacra Pagina: The Gospel of John*, ed. Daniel J. Harrington, Rev. ed. (Liturgical Press, 2005).

[10]Chris Keith, "Recent and Previous Research on the Pericope Adulterae (John 7.53–8.11)," *Currents in Biblical Research* 6, no. 3 (2008): 394.

[11]Keith, "Recent and Previous Research on the Pericope Adulterae (John 7.53–8.11)," 386.

universally admired by the Church.[12] At the very least, this text takes too lenient a view of sexual sin from the point of view of some, and it is perhaps too salacious for others.[13]

The thesis that the PA has quite a history of its own, struggling to find its place in the canonical Gospels, highlights its eventual location in the Gospel of John. As Moloney writes: "As this [that is, F.M's] commentary is dedicated to an analysis of the dynamic of the Johannine narrative, John 7:53–8:11 is regarded as an intrusion." He adds: "this synoptic-like story, which does not relate to the broader context of the Gospel and interrupts the already complex thought of 7:1–8:59, disturbs the storyteller's systematic account of Jesus' presence at the feasts of 'the Jews.'"[14] In other words, the PA is an interruption to the Johannine narrative. Since it also reflects a positive engagement on the part of Jesus with a woman—no matter what her history, and in spite of women frequently being used by many men as objects either of pleasure, or humiliation, or both—the PA also enacts an interruption to the patriarchal culture of its time, resulting in a dual force of interruption.

A further observation to make about the text relates to the status of the charge of adultery as it is presented there, and the way that this has been interpreted intertextually (i.e., with regard to other teaching on adultery and marriage in 1 Cor. 7:10-11; Mk 7, 10; Mt. 5, 15, 19; and Lk. 16, 18). Jesus' lack of condemnation of the woman has often been at issue in this light (how could he possibly make an *exception* to the rule?). Holly Toensing observes that the solution to this problem is typically made in terms of Jesus' being led by his accusers into an irresolvable dilemma. "The traditional explanation, often repeated in commentaries of John's gospel over the past 40 years, suggests that if Jesus were not to condemn the woman, he would break Jewish Law; if he were to condemn the woman, he would usurp Roman power, for Jews did not have the right to try their own legal cases."[15] However, Gail O'Day explains that the accusers actually present only half the Jewish law:

---

[12]A text's distance from what the Church might have wanted to teach is one of the tests "historical Jesus" scholars use to test for the authenticity of its origins in Jesus. In other words, that the text is included in the canon in spite of potential resistance to it is evidence of the belief at the time in its authenticity. For a statement of these criteria, see David G. A. Calvert, "An Examination of the Criteria for Distinguishing the Authentic Words of Jesus," *New Testament Studies* 18, no. 2 (1972): 209–19. Scholars also apply the criterion of distance from Jewish tradition, and thus assert a "double dissimilarity" of the PA; see Carl B. Bridges, "The Canonical Status of the *Pericope Adulterae* (John 7:53–8:11)," *Stone-Campbell Journal* 11 (2008): 213–21.

[13]See Gail R. O'Day, "John 7:53–8:11: A Study in Misreading," *Journal of Biblical Literature* 111, no. 4 (1992): 639–40. See also Keith, "Recent and Previous Research on the Pericope Adulterae (John 7:53–8:11)," 99ff; Knust, *To Cast the First Stone*.

[14]Moloney, *Sacra Pagina: The Gospel of John*, 281.

[15]Holly J. Toensing, "Divine Intervention or Divine Intrusion? Jesus and the Adulteress in John's Gospel," in *Feminist Companion to John*, ed. Amy-Jill Levine (Bloomsbury, 2003).

> Both Lev 20:10 and Deut 22:22-24 advocate the death penalty for adultery, although neither specifies stoning. The two texts also prescribe death for both offenders, the man and the woman, even though the woman's accusers here speak as though the death penalty applies to the woman (note the feminine accusative plural pronouns ... [)]. The narrator's commentary in v. 6a explains why the scribes and Pharisees only speak of half the law. Their first concern is with entrapping Jesus, not with the law or justice, or even the woman.[16]

Toensing agrees with O'Day that Jesus would not have been in breach of Jewish law in refusing to condemn the woman on such a skewed charge; however, she also argues that Jesus would not have been in breach of Roman law, either.[17] This changes the nature entirely of Jesus' refusal to condemn the woman: it is not so much that Jesus needs to avoid the trap laid by the accusers, but that he resists reducing the woman to an object.

A final note about the biblical text is worthy of mention: O'Day argues that the PA is actually not primarily about the woman but is a story of Jesus' relationships with *two* addressees: the onlookers, and the woman. She reads the two parts of the text chiastically to assert: "The speeches Jesus addresses to each party reinforce the narrative of the text, that the woman and the scribes and Pharisees are equals."[18] Such a chiastic reading, however, is not universally accepted, even if her insight about the equality of personhood is true.[19]

Engaging in Dialogue with Post-Biblical Tradition

To some extent, our dialogue with the biblical tradition has also led us into dialogue with the Christian tradition more broadly. We have already mentioned, for example, that in the eyes of some early commentators, the PA is problematic because it might be seen to condone sin: the fact that the woman is not unquestionably condemned by Jesus contrasts with other teaching forbidding adultery.

One of the important threads to come out of theological debate of New Testament passages to do with adultery is the question of Catholic teaching on the indissolubility of marriage. David G. Hunter examines the scriptural evidence and observes that the historical discussion reveals a double

[16]O'Day, "John 7:53–8:11: A Study in Misreading," 632.
[17]Toensing, "Divine Intervention or Divine Intrusion?" 163 n.113.
[18]O'Day, "John 7:53–8:11: A Study in Misreading," 637.
[19]See Keith, "Recent and Previous Research on the Pericope Adulterae (John 7.53–8.11)," 395.

standard.[20] This is based on reading the Gospel parallels with regard to Jesus' prohibition of remarriage: Matthew includes reference to a teaching that husbands who divorce their wives and remarry commit adultery—except if the divorce is on the basis of adultery; Mark and Luke do not contain this addition.[21] Augustine argues that this addition constitutes authentic teaching on marriage; that is, neither husbands nor wives of adulterers may remarry. Yet Augustine's contemporary, Pollentius, and the pseudonymous writer Ambrosiaster, maintain that after a wife's dismissal for adultery, remarriage is possible for husbands.[22] Hunter, however, insists that in various texts, Augustine actually comes to doubt whether his strong commitment to the impossibility of remarriage is right.[23] We will return to this question in a moment.

In a modern example of teaching from the tradition, Archbishop Charles Chaput writes in 2015 about the story of the Woman Caught in Adultery, with a focus on the difference between justice and mercy: "In forgiving the woman, Jesus does by grace what the moral law cannot do."[24] While humans seek justice, he argues, God is able to go further than to act in accordance with justice—God is able to show mercy. At the same time, Chaput maintains that being in receipt of God's mercy requires a preparedness to be truthful and to change one's life in response. The point Chaput wishes to make is that while the woman has been forgiven by Jesus, her adulterous lifestyle is not condoned.[25] However, he makes this point in the context of a question arising at the time about divorced and remarried Catholics in Germany being able to receive communion, which is at issue in the two meetings of the Synod of Bishops on the family. He affirms Pope Francis' pastoral

[20]David G. Hunter, "Augustine's Doubts on Divorce," *Augustinian Studies* 48, no. 1 (2017): 161–82.

[21]Moloney comments: "Calling upon the data provided by 1 Corinthians 7:10-11, where Paul appears to be paraphrasing a word of Jesus, Matthew 5:32, and Luke 16:18 ('Q'), scholars are able to suggest the probable 'primitive form' of this word of Jesus that had its origins on the lips of Jesus of Nazareth during the course of his ministry … Part 1a: Everyone who divorces his wife and marries another /Part 1b: commits adultery. /Part 2a: And the one who marries a divorced woman /Part 2b: commits adultery." He then states: "Matthew must add the exception clauses to Matt 5:32 and 19:9." Francis J. Moloney, "A New Testament Hermeneutic for Divorce and Remarriage in the Catholic Tradition," *Australasian Catholic Record* 92, no. 3 (2015): 276.

[22]Augustine, *Treatises on Marriage and Other Subjects*, 27; Ambrosiaster, "Commentary on 1 Corinthians 7: 11" [366–384] in *Commentaries on Romans and 1–2 Corinthians* (InterVarsity Press, 2009), 150–1.

[23]Yet cf. Henri Crouzel, "Divorce and Remarriage in the Early Church: Some Reflections on Historical Methodology," *Communio* 41 (2014): 472–503, "Divorce et remariage dans l'Église primitive," *Nouvelle Revue Théologique* 98, no. 10 (1976): 891–917.

[24]Charles J. Chaput, "A Jubilee Year of Mercy," *First Things* 35–36 (December 2015): 33.

[25]"The Church can be truthful without being merciful, like the scribes who wished to stone the adulteress who violated the Mosaic law. But the Church cannot be merciful without being truthful. And the truth is, we are called to conversion." Chaput, "A Jubilee Year of Mercy," 36.

approach of accompanying people where they are, yet warns: "a therapeutic age tends to translate 'accompaniment' as 'thou shalt not judge,' affirming people indiscriminately as they are." He insists: "This is not mercy."[26]

When Pope Francis publishes *Amoris Laetitiae* in 2016, he deliberately leaves open a number of moral dilemmas in light of pastoral concerns. Chaput is then part of a group of five Cardinals who address a *dubia* to Pope Francis concerning paragraphs 300–305 of *Amoris Laetitiae*, questioning the legitimacy of remarried Catholics potentially being admitted to Communion, and demanding doctrinal clarity. In a related news article, the interviewer describes Chaput's position:

> John Paul II and Benedict XVI reaffirmed Church teaching that the remarried may not receive Communion, except possibly when they try to live "as brother and sister." Archbishop Chaput said that this teaching, and Jesus's prohibition of adultery, could not be changed: "It seems to me that it's impossible for us to contradict the words of Jesus, and it's also impossible for a teaching to be true 20 years ago not to be true today when it's the teachings of the pope."

In other words, Chaput challenges the Pope on the basis that Jesus has prohibited adultery, specifically in the teaching about divorce and remarriage. Moreover, he challenges Francis on the basis of a principle that the Church never contradicts its former teaching. Chaput sees the prohibition of remarriage after divorce as a moral absolute. Using the language of chapter 1 of the present text, Chaput views the ethical tradition of the Church in a universal and context-free manner: this is an example of classical consciousness.

Contrasting Chaput's position with the 2015 scriptural investigation by Moloney of the question of Jesus' prohibition of divorce and remarriage, we see that Moloney states straight up: "The revelation of God to the world is not found in either the Word of God in the Bible, or the formal teaching of the councils. It is found in both."[27] He notes that Jesus' reported words contradict the Jewish law formulated in Deut. 24:1-4.[28] Yet, Moloney observes that in 1 Corinthians 7, Paul not only affirms but also overrides Jesus' teaching in the case of believers married to unbelievers.[29] In other words, Paul modifies the Jesus tradition in order to account for the circumstances of the community at the time. Similarly tracing the ways in which Matthew also rewrites Mk 10:1-12 in response to circumstances in his community, Moloney writes:

[26]Chaput, "A Jubilee Year of Mercy," 36.
[27]Moloney, "A New Testament Hermeneutic," 271.
[28]Moloney, "A New Testament Hermeneutic," 277.
[29]Moloney, "A New Testament Hermeneutic," 279.

> Whatever the precise situation addressed by Matthew, and whatever the exact meaning he wishes to give to the word *porneia* [often translated as adultery, but having a range of meanings], the decisive matter is that he uses two sources that record the memory of Jesus' absolute prohibition of divorce and remarriage ("Q" and Mark), and he modifies both of them (Matt 5:32; 19:9). We are dealing with another moment in the developing theological and pastoral consciousness of the earliest church that quite freely and consistently accommodates a teaching of Jesus. This is a further indication within the inspired pages of our Christian Sacred Scriptures that shows the need for the church to rethink Jesus' fiercely eschatological teaching in the light of the long-term pastoral situation of the developing Christian church.[30]

Moloney takes seriously, in other words, the possibility that Church teaching is responsive to context, or better, that it evolves in an ongoing, revelatory way in relation to context. "The church does not simply look back to the identifiable words of Jesus to establish its doctrinal and moral bedrock truths: it reflects upon its biblical and ecclesial tradition in dialogue with an ever-expanding body of knowledge and experience."[31] Let us be clear that no one writing in the Christian tradition is honoring adultery. However, in the debate about Church teaching on marriage, we need to consider that in which both marriage and adultery consist.

Engaging in Dialogue with the Current Context

Any engagement with the current context is virtually impossible in a printed book, because a book is in some ways out of date before it even goes to press. Moreover, the context of the writers is not the context of the readers. From personal reflection, together with considerations of biblical and traditional insights into the PA, we perceive a number of themes emerging that could bear a relation to the contemporary context as we experience it in writing in Australia in the 2020s. Other reflections could emerge differently.

The first theme for us concerns the ways in which we perceive the woman is enabled to become fully *herself* in the presence of Jesus. This could be explored in relation to concepts of personhood, or through investigations into the experience of women or other "others" in patriarchal societies. Quite a number of studies read the PA through a feminist lens, including that of Toensing, who takes a view contrary to ours about the role of Jesus

---

[30]Moloney, "A New Testament Hermeneutic," 284.
[31]Moloney, "A New Testament Hermeneutic," 287.

in freeing the woman.[32] Issues that have arisen as part of the #MeToo movement, especially issues arising in relation to the treatment of women working within the Australian parliament, for example, could fruitfully be put in dialogue with the text of Jn 8:2-11. Brittany Higgins, the woman who alleged she was raped by a senior colleague in the office of a Cabinet Minister late one night in 2019, reflected at a women's rally on the ways in which women have no *standing* in a testosterone-fuelled universe:

> I am cognisant of all the women who continue to live in silence. The women who are faceless. /The women who don't have the mobility, the confidence or the financial means to share their truth. /Those who don't see their images and stories reflected in the media, those who are sadly no longer with us. /Those who have lost their sense of self-worth and are unable to break the silence, all of which is rooted in the shame and stigma of sexual assault.[33]

We have deliberately chosen the word *standing* here: in the legal sense, only persons who have standing—a clear relation to the case—can be party to prosecuting legal matters; in a broader sense, there are persons in the community who have standing, that is, high status or reputation. A presiding judge grants or decides who has standing. These women are granted no standing, no visible *selves*, no more reality in appearance than common objects, no more perdurance in time than in those moments in which they are bullied or beaten or possessed. Strangely enough, the accused man in the Higgins case was not named in public for many months and was sacked not long after the alleged rape, for "security reasons" that security officers nevertheless maintained did not exist. The adulterous man is given only in invisibility, which protects him rather than shames him. Higgins herself—risking all by going public—was both lauded and shamed. There were voices baying for her blood because she became drunk and was raped.

Second, the experience of shame could be examined, particularly in relation to the ways in which individuals and societies manipulate media to "shame" others. A good example in the Australian context is the case of a female New South Wales' State Premier. In October of 2020, it was revealed that this Premier had been having a long-term, secret affair with a male colleague who was the controversial subject of an investigation of the Independent Commission Against Corruption. What was striking about this event was the way in which the Premier—whose behaviors were clearly compromising—was treated by the media. Journalist Annabel Crabb

---

[32] Gench, "John 7:53–8:11"; Toensing, "Divine Intervention or Divine Intrusion?"; O'Day, "John 7:53–8:11: A Study in Misreading."

[33] "Read What Brittany Higgins Had to Say When She Spoke at the Women's March," *ABC News Online* (March 16, 2021), https://www.abc.net.au/news/2021-03-15/brittany-higgins-speech-womens-march-parliament-house-canberra/13248908.

comments on the difference between the treatment of men and women in similar situations:

> Sex (or sex-adjacent) scandals affecting women are much rarer. And the source of controversy tends to be, in almost every case, not goatishness in itself but the spectre of influence. This is the intriguing mechanics of "sex scandals" in Australian politics; for men, the assumption is that they've outsourced their thinking to a crucial organ. For women, it's assumed they've outsourced it to the bloke. /And if that bloke's dodgy, then she's very likely to contract a burning case of STD: Sexually Transmitted Disgrace.[34]

The third issue we could consider is that of human dignity, the restoration by Jesus of the dignity of a woman who has been *used* to make a point. In the PA, we see that Jesus prioritizes relationship over righteousness, refusing to participate in her shaming—resisting the temptation to make even a moral point of her. This gives us pause when it comes to thinking about how the question of remarriage and adultery has been handled in the Catholic tradition. In particular, it gives us pause when we think about how Pope Francis was asked for doctrinal certainty in *Amoris laetitiae* by a cabal of cardinals. Doctrinal certainty was requested so that everyone could be clear about who is *in* and who is *out*, so that we could make judgments about people. Yet Pope Francis is, precisely, extremely reluctant to make such judgments: "who am I to judge?" he responds when asked about the morality of homosexual relationships.

In February 2021, a scandal broke that a senior member of federal Cabinet was at the center of a historical rape allegation (this is the case to which we referred at the end of Chapter 1). Incriminating documents had been sent to several members of parliament, including the prime minister, by friends of the alleged victim, who had suicided in 2020 prior to having had her formal statement taken by police. After some weeks of speculation, the accused cabinet minister—the Attorney-General—revealed his identity. Protesting his innocence, he took medical leave. In the meantime, the prime minister, who declared that he had not actually read the documents but had simply asked the Attorney-General if he was guilty of the rape, determined that no action would be taken to investigate further. Under public pressure, a Cabinet reshuffle followed and the accused minister was given a different portfolio. He then launched a defamation suit against the national public broadcaster, which had not named him in its enquiries, but which, he alleged, had made it obvious that he was the one at the center of the scandal.

[34]Annabel Crabb, "Hot Takes on Gladys Berejiklian's 'Sex Scandal' Abound—but It's Worth Digging Deeper than the Reactions," *ABC News Online* (October 17, 2020), https://www.abc.net.au/news/2020-10-17/gladys-berejiklian-icac-sex-scandals-and-women-in-politics/12774412.

The difficulty at the heart of this case was that there is no admissible evidence available to the police to test it. After the alleged incident occurred in 1988, the victim was reluctant to report it; she had been aged just sixteen at the time and was a high-achieving student and champion debater. The trauma had continued to make itself known, however, through serious mental illness that affected her entire life. Over the years since, she had kept diaries which referred to the matter, had confided in a close friend, had disclosed it to a sexual assault counsellor, and had, in her final year of life, engaged a lawyer for whom she had written a lengthy statement describing the event. Part of her reluctance to report the incident to police was apparently her knowledge that it would destroy the minister's career. A formal complaint was finally made to New South Wales police in 2020, who sought to interview the woman for a sworn statement at her address in South Australia. However, their request to a senior officer to allow travel there during the COVID-19 pandemic was—quite strangely—denied.[35] The day before taking her own life, the woman asked that police not pursue the matter further. Believing that a grave injustice had taken place, her lawyer and her friends eventually decided to make her story public in early 2021.

The ex-Attorney-General believed himself to be hard done by, arguing that the usual burden of proof has been reversed and that he was being asked to prove his innocence, if not legally, then in the court of public opinion. The press conference at which he made his statement showed him visibly distressed, and a case could be made to say that he had been publicly shamed. He had his word of innocence accepted by the prime minister, however, and he remained in a senior role in Government until some months later, when he unexpectedly settled his suit against the Australian Broadcasting Corporation without any requirement for retraction or apology—although he publicly claimed victory.[36] Later again, he communicated his decision to retire from Parliament at the next election.

The unnamed woman also had her integrity impugned—in her case, without any hope of recourse. Public awareness of her mental illness led to the conflation of her accusation of the minister with her mental state, with several sources arguing that her accusation was delusional. Others claimed that the allegation arose from (illegitimate) psychological investigation of so-called "repressed memories"—a claim explicitly denied by her

[35]See Laura Gartry, "NSW Deputy Police Chief Denied Investigators' Request to Travel to Interview Christian Porter's Accuser in SA," *ABC News Online* (April 12, 2021), https://www.abc.net.au/news/2021-04-12/nsw-police-denied-travel-interview-christian-porter-accuser/100061776.

[36]Amanda Meade, "Christian Porter Made Two Offers to Settle ABC Defamation Case That Cost Broadcaster $780,000, Senators Told," *The Guardian Australia* (June 7, 2021), https://www.theguardian.com/media/2021/jun/07/christian-porter-made-two-offers-to-settle-abc-defamation-case-that-cost-broadcaster-780000-senators-told.

therapist.[37] While she remains nameless for the protection of her privacy, even post-mortem, the fact that published images of the woman showed her face obscured with white pixellation reminds us very much of the woman in the Gospel story. Both women are invisible and inaudible. Both women are shamed in their nakedness. Both women are used to make a very public point. The male adulterer only appears in his absence in the PA; the former Attorney-General was similarly able to walk away. For all intents and purposes, his claim that the event never happened is the last word on the matter.

In the PA, Jesus gifts the woman anew with her dignity. What do we, the public, do to enable the "redemption" of the dead woman from the indignity of history? How do we reclaim her story from the indignant defense of the Minister? How do we live with the consequences that her claim can never be tested? Why ought we to care?

How Is the Text Speaking to Me (or Us) Today?

The PA is presumably not a story about a woman falsely accused. Instead, it concerns the difference between how we treat our fellow human beings and how God treats them. No person is an object for our use. The unnamed woman stands out in the biblical tradition as one beloved of Jesus. Her enduring significance is not so much that she has been caught in an adulterous liaison and that she is forgiven (even though forgiveness is precious), but that she is envisaged by Jesus in her own, free personhood and thus enabled to become who she is.[38] In much the same way that some newer biblical editions use "The Parable of the Loving Father" to refer to what is also known as "The Parable of the Prodigal Son," perhaps the pericope of "The Woman Caught in Adultery" should really become known as "The Woman seen by Jesus as her true Self." In this way, we would hear more clearly the point that it is not sin that is the focus of God's attention but freeing the human (in)capacity for freedom and relationship. One does not have to be "good enough" for grace.

---

[37]Louise Milligan, Lucy Carter, and Lauren Day, "Sexual Assault Counsellor Says Christian Porter's Accuser Told Her of Alleged Rape Eight Years ago," *ABC News Online* (March 8, 2021), https://www.abc.net.au/news/2021-03-08/woman-told-counsellor-of-porter-rape-allegations-eight-years-ago/13221438.

[38]This point is made in O'Day, "John 7:53–8:11: A Study in Misreading," 631.

3

Jesus and the Woman with the Hemorrhage: The Experience of Abjection

In Chapter 2 we read the story of Jesus' encounter with an unnamed woman in the context of the use, abuse, and shaming of women in contemporary society. Here we turn to the story of another unnamed, biblical woman—the woman with the hemorrhage. One of the interesting things about this healing story is that it is embedded in the context of another healing, that of Jairus' daughter, a point that will become more important as we dialogue with the biblical hermeneuts. To begin, however, we seek to open ourselves to this text and how it might speak to us as we read it slowly and carefully. In order to listen more acutely, this time we will read intertextually, using the versions from each of the synoptic gospels. For those reading from within a Christian lifeworld, it may be helpful to place oneself in the context of prayer, that is, being before God or beside Christ.

The Texts: Mark 5:25-34; Matthew 9:20-22; Luke 8:43-48

Now there was a woman who had been suffering from hemorrhages for twelve years. She had endured much under many physicians, and had spent all that she had; and she was no better, but rather grew worse. She had heard about Jesus, and came up behind him in the crowd and touched his cloak, for she said, "If I but touch his clothes, I will be made well." Immediately her hemorrhage stopped; and she felt in her body that she was healed of her disease. Immediately aware that power had gone forth from him, Jesus turned about in the crowd and said, "Who touched my clothes?" And his disciples said to him, 'You see the crowd pressing in on you; how can you say, "Who touched me?"' He looked all round to see who had done it. But the woman, knowing what had happened to her, came in fear and trembling, fell down before him, and told him the whole truth. He said to her, "Daughter, your faith has made you well; go in peace, and be healed of your disease."

Then suddenly a woman who had been suffering from hemorrhages for twelve years came up behind him and touched the fringe of his cloak, for she said to herself, "If I only touch his cloak, I will be made well." Jesus turned, and seeing her he said, "Take heart, daughter; your faith has made you well." And instantly the woman was made well.

Now there was a woman who had been suffering from hemorrhages for twelve years; and though she had spent all she had on physicians, no one could cure her. She came up behind him and touched the fringe of his clothes, and immediately her hemorrhage stopped. Then Jesus asked, "Who touched me?" When all denied it, Peter said, "Master, the crowds surround you and press in on you." But Jesus said, "Someone touched me; for I noticed that power had gone out from me." When the woman saw that she could not remain hidden, she came trembling; and falling down before him, she declared in the presence of all the people why she had touched him, and how she had been immediately healed. He said to her, "Daughter, your faith has made you well; go in peace."

A Hermeneutic-phenomenological Reading of Mark 5:25-34; Matthew 9:20-22; and Luke 8:43-48

When we contemplate this scene, what is given to us?

First, we see a woman, but we see her only as she tries to remain hidden. Nameless throughout the narrative, the woman's illness makes her repellent. Even if we cannot yet see the inevitable stain of her disease on her clothes, we are given its characteristic smell, and the stigma of her uncleanliness hangs like a pall around her. While she clearly believes that Jesus can heal her, she evidently feels she can only approach him anonymously. Jostling in the crowd, her stench undoubtedly competes with all the surrounding smells of an ancient town, and she stands a chance of momentarily disguising her approach. Her healing reportedly takes place as soon as she touches [the fringe of] Jesus' clothes/cloak.

The Jesus we are given in this narrative is characterized by strangeness. The description of his feeling power having gone out from him is just plain odd to the modern ear and appears even stranger as his evident powerfulness contrasts with his apparent lack of awareness of who has touched him. If we have been educated to any degree about Jesus' context in ancient Palestine, we might see him in terms of a culture where wonder workers are relatively commonplace. His complete otherness to the contemporary mind makes him resistant to the gaze.

In Mark and Luke, however, Jesus' question brings him sharply into personal focus. *Who touched me?* Not only the woman and others in the crowd, but also we—the hearers of the narrative—are brought into the sphere of his address. The disciples' response is logical but dismissive; Jesus' insistence on the point ("someone touched me …") begins to draw him and the woman together in a different way. Her givenness in the narrative is altered at this stage: the woman comes into full view, and her selfhood erupts in her testimony: *she came trembling; and falling down before him, she declared in the presence of all the people why she had touched him, and how she had been immediately healed.* In responding to Jesus, she herself becomes visible—as one who confesses (and thus brings to manifestation) both her faith and Jesus' power to heal. At this point, we also see Jesus himself more clearly as a person, as he addresses her, not only with authority, but also with tenderness and compassion: *Daughter, your faith has made you well.* Yet with these words, Jesus declines the identity of a healer or wonder worker; he ascribes the healing to her faith, and in doing so, invites our further questioning about his identity. In almost the same moment, however, both she and we are gently dismissed from him: *go in peace.*[1]

Engaging in Critical Dialogue with Biblical Tradition

In the same way that much critical discussion of the story of the Woman Caught in Adultery revolves around what Jesus might have written in the dirt, the discussion of the haemorrhaging woman is often dominated by the mystery of her illness and the potential stigma arising from it.[2] Most commentators conclude that the bleeding from which the woman suffers has a gynecological origin and that it renders her impure—and thus cut off

[1]This description first appeared in Robyn Horner, "A Phenomenology of Revelation: Contemporary Encounters with Saint Ignatius Loyola," in *The Challenge of God*, ed. Colby Dickinson, Hugh Miller, and Kathleen McNutt (Bloomsbury, 2019), 69–85.

[2]In our discussion of this text, we are particularly thankful to our colleague, Dr. Janine Luttick, for sharing her work: Janine Luttick, *Purity, Anti-Judaism and Contemporary Biblical Interpretation* (Master of Arts in Religion and Theology, Monash University, 2012). See also Janine Luttick, *Jairus' Daughter and the Female Body in Mark* (Society of Biblical Literature, 2023).

from Jewish society.[3] Nevertheless, it is clear that such bleeding is not part of the woman's normal menstrual cycle. The story is, thus, usually read in light of Lev. 15:25: "If a woman has a discharge of blood for many days, not at the time of her impurity, or if she has a discharge beyond the time of her impurity, for all the days of the discharge she shall continue in uncleanness; as in the days of her impurity, she shall be unclean."[4]

While the source of bleeding is not certain, there is a logic to the gynecological assumption: the modesty of the description is suggestive; moreover, it could reasonably be assumed that any *other* sort of bleeding would either have been linked to a disease that would have killed the woman long before or might more readily have been stemmed before twelve years had elapsed.[5] On the point of her isolation, however, using the pericope to argue against the oppressive nature of Jewish purity laws perpetuates a history of Christian, anti-Semitic criticism.[6] It is not necessary to insist that the purity laws mean that the woman is cut off from all human society. To be clear, on the basis of the Masoretic (traditional Hebrew) text of Leviticus, a menstruating woman (*niddah*) "communicates impurity *by being touched*" whereas a woman with an irregular flow of blood (*zavah*) does not. Neither the niddah nor the zavah "[communicate] impurity *by touching*."[7] This means that bleeding women are not cut off from society, as some Christian scholars argue. At the same time, anyone who has menstruated knows how anti-social the odor of menstrual blood can become. There is a point, then, to discussion about stigma and the potential isolation of the woman for the twelve years of her infirmity, even if it is not related to impurity as such.

If purity laws remain in the frame, a second scholarly thematic around the story concerns the courage of the woman in flouting them by touching Jesus. Yet, if the woman does not actually contaminate by touching or being touched, this theme is nonsensical. More likely, the courage of the woman is depicted in her going out in public, where she risks others being offended by

---

[3]See, for example, Marla J. Selvidge, "Mark 5:25-34 and Leviticus 15:19-20: A Reaction to Restrictive Purity Regulations," *Journal of Biblical Literature* 103, no. 4 (1984): 619–23. See also Frank Moloney "This ailment renders her ritually impure at all times, unable to play an active life in the community of Israel (see Lev 15:25; m. *Zabim* 5:1, 6). Her impurity places her 'outside' the chosen people of God." Francis J. Moloney, *The Gospel of Mark: A Commentary* (Baker Academic, 2012), 79.

[4]Selvidge, "Mark 5:25-34 and Leviticus 15:19-20" 619.

[5]"The Greek reads literally 'being with a flowing of blood' (*rysei haimatos*) ... [T]his phrase appears in Lev 15:19 for menstrual bleeding and in 15:25 for other unspecified forms of vaginal bleeding." John R. Donahue, *Sacra Pagina: The Gospel of Mark* (Liturgical Press, 2005), 191.

[6]See Charlotte Elisheva Fonrobert, *Menstrual Purity: Rabbinic and Christian Reconstructions of Biblical Gender* (Stanford University Press, 2000), 193; Amy-Jill Levine, "Discharging Responsibility: Matthean Jesus, Biblical Law, and Hemorrhaging Woman," in *Feminist Companion to Matthew*, ed. Amy-Jill Levine and Marianne Blickenstaff (Bloomsbury, 2001), 77.

[7]Fonrobert, *Menstrual Purity*, 193–5. Emphasis added for clarity.

her smell and by the inevitable stains on her clothing. And this means that a third theme, which is the alleged flouting by Jesus of those same purity laws, again makes no sense.[8] Part of the significance of the action of Jesus in the text is not his flouting of purity laws so much as his preparedness to address the woman in a familiar, even familial way ("daughter").[9] Not only is she a woman—and thus socially inferior—but she is also a woman who is potentially very unpleasant to be near. It is one thing to love God in the face of the other; it is quite another thing altogether when one has to overcome a psychological resistance to difference as well as that visceral resistance which is apparent in an involuntary reaction of disgust. Yet, Jesus addresses the woman as part of his family.[10]

In terms of synoptic intertextuality, Chris L. de Wet notes that only Matthew has Jesus turn around and see the woman prior to healing her. "Matthew appears to save Jesus the embarrassment of someone 'stealing' a miracle from him, as some ancient interpreters saw it. In Mark and Luke, the initiative and agency remain fully with the woman, while in Matthew Jesus remains in control."[11] Shelly Rambo argues that the trauma of the woman's twelve years of bleeding cannot be expressed in words, but only physically, through touch. Jesus witnesses to this trauma in the physical communication of his power. "Faith … is presented within the context of a bodily exchange; it is not dependent on a verbal proclamation to some truth. Jesus models a necessary and corresponding movement as he testifies to the persistence and power of spirit, both human and divine."[12]

Of further significance is the way in which Matthew and Luke speak not only of Jesus "clothes" or "cloak" (Greek ἱματίου—garment) but also of the fringes on this piece of clothing. It is likely that Jesus is wearing fringes (Hebrew *tzitzit*) on each corner of his outermost garment, which would have been typical for a committed Jewish man (cf. Nu 15:37-41). The woman's touching of the fringes highlights Jesus' identity as a Jew, and more particularly, his connection to God. In other words, it highlights the woman's faith in God to heal.

There are a number of other features of the text that are closely connected with its cultural and sociological contexts. There is an emphasis on "power" apparently leaking from Jesus—no doubt in parallel with the way that the woman's blood distressingly "leaks." The idea of palpable healing power

---

[8]The two points are noted in Levine, "Discharging Responsibility," 71.

[9]Donahue, *Sacra Pagina: The Gospel of Mark*, 193. Note, however, that Donahue's reading highlights the thematic we have already observed, that is, ritual purity.

[10]Moloney refers to the section running from Mk 3:7 to 6:6a as "Jesus and His New Family" to indicate the types of relationships Jesus forms there. Moloney, *Mark: A Commentary*.

[11]Chris L. de Wet, "John Chrysostom on the Healing of the Woman with a Flow of Blood: Exegesis, Tradition, and Anti-Judaism," *Journal of Early Christian History* 9, no. 2 (2019): 7–8.

[12]Shelly Rambo, "Trauma and Faith: Reading the Narrative of the Hemorrhaging Woman," *International Journal of Practical Theology* 13, no. 2 (2009): 253.

makes Jesus reminiscent of a *theios anēr*. John R. Donahue explains: "The idea of healing through touch is very common in the Hellenistic world, since healers were thought to be figures of power. This narrative is often invoked to undergird the view that the Markan Jesus is a Hellenistic *theios anēr*, a semi-divine figure gifted with supernatural powers."[13] Donahue also emphasizes the links between healing and salvation: "The translation retains 'saved' for *sōthēsomai* in order to preserve the notion of 'rescue' from illness and possible death and to highlight the linkage with the surrounding narrative (vv. 23, 35)."[14] He underscores that the woman is undoubtedly close to death after twelve years of bleeding and sees her touching of Jesus as an event of physical as well as spiritual salvation. The motif of "fear and trembling" to describe the woman's approach to Jesus can be linked to many other biblical texts where the protagonists approach God.[15] However, we should not assume that fear and trembling relate to any shame in being before Jesus: as Rambo points out, it "can equally suggest an experience of divine presence, a *theophany*."[16] In other words, the woman's approach in fear and trembling is further recognition of Jesus' divinity.[17]

It is somewhat artificial to treat the story of the Woman with the Hemorrhage in isolation from the story with respect to which it provides an interruption: the narrative of the Raising of Jairus' Daughter.[18] There are many parallels between the two stories that work together in the sequence of the whole narrative.[19] The stories are thematically linked by small details such as the observation that Jairus' daughter is twelve years old, and the woman has endured twelve years of bleeding.[20] The strongest parallels are

[13]Donahue, *Sacra Pagina: The Gospel of Mark*, 192. Note the comments about the contemporary lack of consensus about the figure of the *theios anēr*, by Andrew J. Kelley, "Miracles, Jesus, and Identity: A History of Research Regarding Jesus and Miracles with Special Attention to the Gospel of Mark," *Currents in Biblical Research* 13, no. 1 (2014): 85.

[14]Donahue, *Sacra Pagina: The Gospel of Mark*, 192.

[15]Donahue, *Sacra Pagina: The Gospel of Mark*, 193; Moloney, *Mark: A Commentary*, 80.

[16]Rambo, "Trauma and Faith," 247.

[17]Raymond E. Brown, *An Introduction to the New Testament: The Abridged Edition*, ed. Marion L. Soards (Yale University Press, 2016), 48.

[18]As Moloney notes, this is a typically Markan "sandwich" construction. Moloney, *Mark: A Commentary*, 79.

[19]"Though self-contained narratives, the two stories are carefully woven together. Both deal with women in life-threatening situations, and both women are called 'daughter' (5:22, 34). Both women are explicitly or implicitly hoping for salvation or rescue from their situation (5:23, *sōth*; 5:28, *sōthēsomai*). In both narratives 'faith' is important; the woman's faith is praised (5:34) and Jairus is encouraged to have faith (5:36). In both narratives misunderstanding of Jesus' power (5:31, 40) is followed by its dramatic manifestation (5:34, 42)." Donahue, *Sacra Pagina: The Gospel of Mark*, 198.

[20]Donahue asserts that the Woman with the Hemorrhage is childless and the young girl who has died will similarly be childless, that is, that they are linked by their inability to bring life. While it is culturally distinctive that the hemorrhaging women is out in public on her own, there is no certainty that she has not had children. Donahue, *Sacra Pagina: The Gospel of Mark*, 199.

arguably the themes of the power of faith and the importance of touch.[21] In both stories, death is seen to be a crisis to which only Jesus can respond. The Raising of Jairus' Daughter contextualizes the story of the Woman with the Hemorrhage, but we are removing it from that context in order to recontextualize it—an action that is deliberate but not without loss.

Engaging in Dialogue with Post-Biblical Tradition

One of the themes to emerge in the Christian discussion of the story of the Woman with the Hemorrhage is that of how to "deal with" bleeding women in the new context of the Church.[22] Christian writers in history frequently maintain that menstruating women are unclean and should not come to the church. Dionysius of Alexandria writes: "Menstruous women ought not to come to the Holy Table, or touch the Holy of Holies, nor to churches, but pray elsewhere."[23] His medieval commentator, Theodore Balsamon, observes that this comment is made directly in relation to the biblical story of the Woman with the Hemorrhage.[24] The teaching that women who are menstruating should be excluded from Eucharist is affirmed by the fourth-century Synod of Laodicea: "The altar must not be approached by women."[25] In the same

[21]Moloney, *Mark: A Commentary*, 81–2.

[22]The discussion here is largely guided by William E. Phipps, "The Menstrual Taboo in the Judeo-Christian Tradition," *Journal of Religion and Health* 19, no. 4 (1980): 298–303; Doris M. Kieser, "The Female Body in Catholic Theology: Menstruation, Reproduction, and Autonomy," *Horizons* 44, no. 1 (2017): 1–27; Fonrobert, *Menstrual Purity*.

[23]Dionysius, "The Letter of the Blessed Dionysius, the Archbishop of Alexandria to Basilides the Bishop," in *A Select Library of the Nicene and Post-Nicene Fathers*, ed. Philip Schaff and Henry Wace, vol. 14, 2 (1900; Wipf and Stock, 2022), 1099. Note Charlotte Fonrobert's identification of the non-application of Jewish purity laws to Christian women in the *Didascalia*, and her reading of this Dionysian text: "Whereas the Didascalia tried to convince women in its community to partake in the Eucharist while they are menstruating, Dionysius attempts to keep them away from it, as well as from the altar and the church altogether. Again the woman with the twelve-year flow of blood is representative of any woman who has her menstruation. But now she becomes exemplary for barely having touched Jesus, since in fact she never touched Jesus' body, and her touch is not really any touch at all. The priestly terminology and regulation of Leviticus has sunk into oblivion. The rhetoric is a different one, and in a way a more misogynistic one, because Dionysius is no longer arguing about the validity or abolishment of a tradition, be it legal or practical. Rather, he seems to consider menstruation as essentially and inherently forbidding, so much so that the very question about it should be regarded as superfluous, so much so that 'good' women, pious women, would never even get such a horrendous idea as to partake in the Eucharist 'in such a condition'." Fonrobert, *Menstrual Purity*, 196–7.

[24]Dionysius, "The Letter of the Blessed Dionysius, the Archbishop of Alexandria to Basilides the Bishop," 247.

[25]Synod of Laodicea, Canon XLIV, in *Nicene and Post-Nicene Fathers*, ed. Philip Schaff and Henry Wace, series II, vol. 14 (Christian Classics Ethereal Library, 2009), 244.

century, Jerome writes: "Nothing is more unclean than a menstruating woman, who makes unclean whatever she touches."[26] Thomas Aquinas later affirms Jerome's teaching that menstruating women cannot have intercourse because any children conceived during that time would have birth defects.[27] All the same, Thomas allows that if a woman is bleeding at a time other than her period, intercourse is licit, since, he argues, this does not affect the conception of children and since otherwise "the husband would have to abstain for always."[28] There are two exceptions to this historical Christian approach to women and gynecological bleeding: the unknown author of the third century *Didascalia*, who polemically argues that Christians do not have to keep the Jewish purity laws; and Pope Gregory the Great, who argues in a letter to Bishop Augustine of Canterbury that since Jesus fully accepts the woman with the hemorrhage, menstruating women can be part of the Eucharist.[29]

Doris Keiser argues that in the Middle Ages "the focus [with regard to women] shifted from menstrual purity to virginal purity."[30] The Church's thinking of sexuality is too large a topic to be considered in the present text, although it is obviously not without consequence for our discussion—we are evidently looking at a far more complex phenomenon than just attitudes toward menstruation. We simply note, then, that attitudes within the institutional Church toward women on the sanctuary remain largely negative until the present day, and that there is an argument that this has, in part, to do with menstruation. The 1917 *Code of Canon Law* states: "The minister serving at Mass should not be a woman unless, in the absence of a man, for a just cause, it is so arranged that the woman respond from afar and by no means approach the altar" (813.2). This reflects the rule that lay people are not allowed to be on the sanctuary, although it is a rule able to be modified for men or boys who wear the appropriate vestments. In section 7 of the 1972 document *Ministeria Quaedem*, Paul VI is open to the possibility of lay ministers, although he maintains the rule of not allowing women on the sanctuary: "In accordance with the ancient tradition of the

[26]*Commentary on Zechariah*, in Jerome, *Commentaries on the Twelve Prophets. Volume 2* [406], ed. Thomas P. Scheck (IVP Academic, 2017).

[27]Amy-Jill Levine draws our attention to other bizarre beliefs: "Isidore of Seville, … records in his *Etimologias* 11.1.141 that menstrual blood causes fruits not to germinate, wine to sour, plants to parch, trees to lose their fruit, iron to be corroded, bronze to turn black, and dogs to become rabid if they eat anything that has come into contact with it." Levine, "Discharging Responsibility," 82.

[28]Thomas Aquinas, *Summa Theologica*, trans. Fathers of the English Dominican Province (Benziger Bros., 1911-1920), Supplement q. 64 a. 3.

[29]Alistair C. Stewart, *The Didascalia Apostolorum* [3rd Century], *An English Version* 1 (Brepols, 2009), 254. Gregory the Great, "Letter LXIV to Augustine, Bishop of the Angli," in *Nicene and Post-Nicene Fathers*, ed. Philip Schaff, series II, vol. 13 (Christian Classics Ethereal Library, 2009), 185.

[30]Kieser, "The Female Body in Catholic Theology," 13.

Church, institution to the ministries of reader and acolyte is reserved to men."[31] It is most famously Leonard Swidler who argues that this "ancient tradition" is fundamentally about the uncleanliness of menstruating women and their potential to contaminate the sacred space.[32] The 1983 *Code of Canon Law* is more inclusive, giving bishops discretion to allow women to serve as lectors and acolytes although not to be installed permanently in these roles. Yet, it is an inclusivity that is still dependent on one man's personal view amongst a range of views, so it is not really inclusivity at all.

In 2015, there are still those who consider it inappropriate to have women on the sanctuary, which is fundamentally understood to be a man's domain. As Raymond Cardinal Burke explains in an interview with the blogsite, *The New Emangelization: Drawing Men to Jesus Christ and His Catholic Church*:

> The Church [has become] very feminized. Women are wonderful, of course. They respond very naturally to the invitation to be active in the Church. Apart from the priest, the sanctuary has become full of women. The activities in the parish and even the liturgy have been influenced by women and become so feminine in many places that men do not want to get involved.[33]

It is certainly not clear that the source of this misogyny is menstruation—later comments on the blog try to emphasize that the Cardinal is merely lamenting the loss of men to the Church—but as we have seen, negative views about women being on the sanctuary have risen historically, at least in part, by means of an understanding that women's bodies are fundamentally unclean. It is hard to read the Cardinal's comments without reflecting on the question of why the sanctuary must be a place for men alone.

In 2021, Pope Francis makes a change to Canon Law that puts the matter beyond doubt insofar as participation of women in the ministries of reader and acolyte (and thus, their rightful presence on the sanctuary) is concerned. With the exception of Holy Orders, he argues, ministries in the Church are "based on the common condition of being baptized and the royal priesthood received in the Sacrament of Baptism." He goes on to state: "Canon 230 § 1 of the Code of Canon Law shall in future have the following formulation: 'Lay

---

[31]Pope Paul VI, *Ministeria Quaedem* (Libreria Editrice Vaticana, 1972), Apostolic Letter issued Motu Proprio.

[32]Leonard Swidler, *Jesus Was a Feminist: What the Gospels Reveal About His Revolutionary Perspective* (Sheed and Ward, 2007), 26.

[33]"Cardinal Raymond Leo Burke on the Catholic 'Man-Crisis' and What to Do About It," The New Emangelisation, https://www.newemangelization.com/uncategorized/cardinal-raymond-leo-burke-on-the-catholic-man-crisis-and-what-to-do-about-it/, accessed March 26, 2020.

persons who possess the age and qualifications established by decree of the conference of bishops can be admitted on a stable basis through the prescribed liturgical rite to the ministries of lector and acolyte'."[34] Putting to one side what is *not* being addressed here, however, one has to ask in light of the sexual abuse crisis whether this long overdue change comes too late to save the institutional Church from itself.

There is an irony in the fact that much of Christian tradition both embraces the blood taboo that is part of Jewish law and simultaneously claims to supersede it. There is a deeper irony—and great poignancy—in the fact that as Christian women rightly appeal to Jesus in light of his compassionate response to the bleeding woman, this is often at the expense of Jewish culture and practice, even as this is heterogenously understood by Jewish people themselves.[35]

Engaging in Dialogue with the Current Context

There are many ways in which the story of the Woman with the Hemorrhage potentially speaks to contemporary culture, and vice versa. Limited as we are by the fixed context of a print publication, we follow but one thread of the story that has been striking to us, putting many others to one side. We have already seen that the story of the bleeding woman potentially challenges the tradition of the Church insofar as it has lived out its patriarchal history at odds with the person of Jesus, who always responds in the Gospel to those who are in need. It is a commonplace to speak of this: Jesus mixes with sinners, the poor, and those who are rejected by society. Lest we sound prosaic, let us recall the power of the words of Isaiah as they resound in Luke's Gospel:

> "The Spirit of the Lord is upon me, because he has anointed me to bring good news to the poor. He has sent me to proclaim release to the captives and recovery of sight to the blind, to let the oppressed go free … "
>
> (4:18)

> And he answered them, "Go and tell John what you have seen and heard: the blind receive their sight, the lame walk, the lepers are cleansed, the deaf hear, the dead are raised, the poor have good news brought to them …"
>
> (7:22)

[34]Pope Francis, "Spiritus Domini", Apostolic Letter issued Motu Proprio (January 10, 2021), https://www.vatican.va/content/francesco/en/motu_proprio/documents/papa-francesco-motu-proprio-20210110_spiritus-domini.html.

[35]Levine, "Discharging Responsibility," 80.

Jesus' mission is framed by his *response*, by his *responsibility* to the poor no matter how they manifest. Jesus' mission is one of radical *inclusion*. Those things that leave us open to the prejudice of others are not barriers to loving relationship with God. The leaking, uncontrollable messiness, and overpowering odor of vaginal bleeding are not reflected in the face of Jesus at the approach of the woman and in his response to her. To be clear, while the text is silent on his exact expression, the warmth and intimacy of his response exclude this possibility. What she has battled to keep *hidden*, thus, is able to come to light without shame, and he reflects her dignity. Helen Prejean speaks of her own presence to the men she has accompanied to the death chamber in much the same way.[36] She remarks in an interview:

> He could see where I was ... And he looked at me, and I knew then he had seen my face. He knew I was there—one person in that crowd of people that believed in his dignity and did not want to see him die, that love there at the end ... It's just pure presence like when you're at the death of anyone. You're not making long speeches. It's—there's nothing to say. You look at my face. I'll be the face of Christ for you. It's pure presence, and that's what it is.

Research by Carla Pascoe reveals that many women have felt and still feel embarrassed by menstruation, meaning that the desperate need to hide it is a common attitude.[37] This is true even though menstrual technology has made vaginal bleeding easier to hide:

> Most women concur that technological improvements in menstrual products and disposal services have made it easier to manage menstruation in public. But this "liberation" has not constituted an acknowledgement that menstruation is a natural function of the female body. Women have been emancipated only in the narrow sense that sophisticated technologies ease the burden of abiding by menstrual etiquette by facilitating a greater invisibility ...

She continues:

> Modern products have not enabled women to embrace or accept menstruation, but rather to deny its very existence. We have learnt to regard

[36]Helen Prejean, "Sister Helen Prejean on Witnessing Executions: 'I Couldn't Let Them Die Alone'," interview by Terry Gross, *Fresh Air (Religion)* (August 14, 2020), https://www.npr.org/2020/08/14/902522133/sister-helen-prejean-on-witnessing-executions-i-couldn-t-let-them-die-alone.

[37]Carla Pascoe, "A 'Discreet Dance': Technologies of Menstrual Management in Australian Public Toilets During the Twentieth Century," *Women's History Review* 24, no. 2 (2015): 234–51; Carla Pascoe, "Silence and the History of Menstruation," *Oral History Association of Australia Journal* 29 (2007): 28–33.

> the non-bleeding male body as the norm. Technological developments in menstrual management may have changed understandings of menstruation, but they did not eradicate the sense the women are striving towards a bloodless feminine ideal. [38]

The #bloodnormal campaign was an attempt by manufacturers of "sanitary" or "feminine hygiene" products to advertise by means of the normalization of menstruation. One of the most interesting aspects of this campaign is the type and the extent of the responses it generated. In Australia, in 2019, "Ad Standards, which handles complaints against the advertising industry, received more than 600 objections to the advert, and has dismissed all of them. A number of people argued that showing period blood was 'disgusting'."[39]

Disgust is often used in daily discourse to describe feelings that do not actually come close to what it signifies. The OED defines the noun "disgust" as "a feeling of revulsion or strong disapproval aroused by something unpleasant or offensive." One can imagine that those complaining about the #bloodnormal advertisement, however, really did mean to use the word "disgust." Writer Eleanor Morgan goes further, linking menstruation with what Julia Kristeva calls "the abject," that is, not a "definable" object, but what has no border and thus threatens the dissolution of the subject.[40] "The abject," writes Kristeva, "draws me toward the place where meaning collapses."[41] Menstrual blood is a "polluting object," which "stands for the danger issuing from within the identity."[42] Commenting on Leviticus, Kristeva notes that "any secretion or discharge, anything that leaks out of the feminine or masculine body defiles."[43] Leakage subjects the subject to a lack of control, to a bodiliness that asserts itself despite one's best efforts and threatens to engulf all rationality.

While it might be possible for middle-class women in the Western world to free themselves from the visibility and stench of the taboo, this is not possible for the majority of women. Indigenous women, poor women, immigrant women—these women usually do not have the liberty of hiding in plain sight while they are menstruating. A flurry of news stories has

---

[38]Pascoe, "A 'Discreet Dance'," 247.

[39]Mary Lloyd, "Depicting Blood During Libra Commercial Does Not Breach Ethics Code, Watchdog Rules," *ABC News Online* (September 18, 2019), https://www.abc.net.au/news/2019-09-18/as-standards-rule-on-period-blood-after-complaints-over-libra-ad/11521530.

[40]Eleanor Morgan, *Hormonal: A Conversation About Women's Bodies, Mental Health and Why We Need to Be Heard* (Hachette, 2019).

[41]Julia Kristeva, *Powers of Horror: An Essay on Abjection*, trans. Leon S. Roudiez (Columbia University Press, 1982), 2.

[42]Kristeva, *Powers of Horror*, 71.

[43]Kristeva, *Powers of Horror*, 102.

emerged in recent years describing the circumstances of women who suffer menstrual exclusion. In parts of Nepal, for example, women are shamed and banished from the family home during menstruation, made to live in *chhaupadi goth* (huts, stables, or caves). This frequently leads to their death, either by cold, the onset of disease, animal attack, or the inhalation of smoke from fires lit to keep the cold at bay. [44] A lack of knowledge about or capacity to pay for adequate menstrual products leaves many girls feeling unable to attend school during their period. In New South Wales, "a survey of 659 menstruating students aged 10–18 years old has found one in five are too embarrassed to go to school when they have their period."[45] Menstruation can be particularly difficult for isolated indigenous women, who lack access to resources and frequently experience inadequate privacy: "Wendy Anders, an Arrente woman from Central Australia, said talking about menstruation was a taboo topic. 'It's a very shame thing in Aboriginal communities,' she said."[46] Similarly, throughout much of Africa and the developing world, menstrual health is seen to be a challenge which impacts success in school and thus impedes the progress of women in societies.[47] Resources on this issue abound. It is not difficult to use them across the school curriculum to engage in dialogue with the biblical story; the real question is the extent to which the dialogue is enabled both to make meaning of the context and to make meaning of the Christian story. It would be easy to lose the Christian story in the abundant stories from the context.

---

[44]"Temporarily living in an unhygienic livestock shed or traditional *Chhau* shed increases the likelihood of diarrhea and dehydration, hypothermia, reproductive tract and urinary tract infections. Moreover, the mental health of women and girls is impacted by feelings of abandonment, insecurity, guilt, and humiliation for being 'impure' and 'untouchable'. Worse still, deaths have been reported from poisonous snake and scorpion bites as well as wild animal attacks on women and girls residing in menstrual exile sheds." Prabisha Amatya, Saruna Ghimire, Karen E. Callahan, Binaya Kumar Baral, and Krishna C. Poudel, "Practice and Lived Experience of Menstrual Exiles (Chhaupadi) Among Adolescent Girls in Far-Western Nepal," *PloS one* 13, no. 12 (December 10, 2018): e0208260, doi:10.1371/journal.pone.0208260. See also Rojita Adhikari, "Bringing an End to Deadly 'Menstrual Huts' Is Proving Difficult in Nepal," *British Medical Journal (Clinical research ed.)* 368 m536 (February 14, 2020), doi:10.1136/bmj.m536vol.

[45]"Girls Are Staying Away from School When They Have Their Period, Research Shows," ABC News Online, Australian Broadcasting Corporation, updated Tuesday April 27, 2021, https://www.abc.net.au/news/2021-04-27/girls-staying-away-from-school-because-of-period-research/100098630, accessed June 7, 2021.

[46]Emma Haskin, "Fighting Shame and Challenges of Menstruation in Isolated Australian communities," *ABC News Online* (February 20, 2020), https://www.abc.net.au/news/2020-02-20/fighting-the-shame-of-menstruation-in-remote-communities/11963334.

[47]Siri Tellier and Maria Hyttel, *Menstrual Health Management in East and Southern Africa: A Review Paper* (2018), https://esaro.unfpa.org/en/publications/menstrual-health-management-east-and-southern-africa-review-paper.

How Is the Text Speaking to Me (or Us) Today?

The narrative of the Woman with the Hemorrhage is a powerful story because it brings to light so much that is hidden, in contrast with a Christ who is revealed to be not omniscient or in control (in Mark and Luke), but who responds to human persons with compassion and love. From a Christian perspective, the story reveals deep-seated prejudices: the Church has often demonstrated itself to be anti-Semitic, and as fundamentally and almost irresolvably misogynist and patriarchal. Having been shown another way in the person of Christ, the Church often chooses to act entirely against this way. All Christians stand accused.

In the 1999 International Theological Commission (ITC) document, *Memory and Reconciliation: The Church and the Faults of the Past*, there is no small irony that a distinction is drawn between "the holiness of the Church" and "the holiness in the Church." Led by Josef Cardinal Ratzinger at the time (the future Pope Benedict XVI), the ITC articulates the paradox that the Church is both perfect (of God) and imperfect (because there are people in the Church who are sinful).[48] It is precisely this paradox that highlights the incapacity of the Church to change or to express genuine sorrow or remorse. Without a theological recognition that the Church itself can be wrong, that it can be flawed because it is fundamentally a human society, that it is not an earthly anticipation of heaven and thus that sin relates not just to individuals in the Church but also to particular ways of being Church (which mean the fact that it is clerical, authoritarian, secretive, exclusive, patriarchal, and so on), there is no addressing the ways in which it fails to speak and live out of Christ.[49]

As we saw in the previous chapter, the PA also calls us to recognize that to be overwhelmed, undone, or shamed by our bodiliness is not unusual, but that to be a body is perfectly acceptable. To be a body, of course, opens onto death: not only a dying of embarrassment or shame, but a death addressed by Jesus through the double narrative of Jairus' daughter and the bleeding woman. There is no ground on which to stand when one is faced with abjection, but there is the ongoing presence of God's affirmation of dignity and love. For those who do not believe in such a God, the story yet confirms the value of the work of sharing this dignity. It is good to be a body, and it is right to accept it and to enable others to accept it as well.

---

[48]International Theological Commission, *Memory and Reconciliation: The Church and the Faults of the Past* (Paulist, 1999), n. 3.2.

[49]Brian P. Flanagan, "Can the Church Be Both Holy and Sinful?" *America* (October 22, 2018).

4

Jesus Stills a Storm: The Experience of Hell

In Chapters 2 and 3, we engaged with what is often hidden in plain sight: the burning body of shame, which is frequently the experience of women. The present chapter continues to engage with the experience of bodiliness; this time, however, we engage with it in terms of the agonizing paralysis of terror. To borrow and reapply the words of Emmanuel Levinas, we could say that terror "amounts to an impossibility of being what one is."[1] What is there to do when being oneself becomes impossible?

The Text: Mark 4:35-41

On that day, when evening had come, he said to them, "Let us go across to the other side." And leaving the crowd behind, they took him with them in the boat, just as he was. Other boats were with him. A great windstorm arose, and the waves beat into the boat, so that the boat was already being swamped. But he was in the stern, asleep on the cushion; and they woke him up and said to him, "Teacher, do you not care that we are perishing?" He woke up and rebuked the wind, and said to the sea, "Peace! Be still!" Then the wind ceased, and there was a dead calm. He said to them, "Why are you afraid? Have you still no faith?" And they were filled with great awe and said to one another, "Who then is this, that even the wind and the sea obey him?"

---

[1]Emmanuel Levinas, *On Escape: De l'évasion*, trans. Bettina Bergo (Stanford University Press, 2003), 66.

A Hermeneutic-phenomenological Reading of Mark 4:35-41

The sun is falling below the western horizon, but it is still hot, especially with the crowd milling about. Jesus suggests they go across to the far side of the lake, and without pausing to collect anything ("just as he was"), they wade into the cool water as far as their knees before clambering over the gunwales and into the boats. Someone stays in the water holding the bow until each boat is ready to be pushed out into deeper water and turned around, and then the last person climbs in near the stern to grasp the helm. Meanwhile, a single sail is hoisted for each boat, and they flap lazily in the breeze. The noise of the crowd fades as the boats get out further, pushed along slowly by the gentle wind. With the sun glittering on the water, it is a scene of calm and close companionship. Jesus is no sailor and trusts the fishers amongst them to take charge of the journey. Tired after the long day of teaching, he succumbs to the gentle movement of the boat on the slight seas, lies down under the stern deck, and falls asleep.

No one notices the storm clouds gathering overhead until suddenly it goes dark and the temperature drops. The wind picks up, and the sea becomes rough. As the force of the storm increases, waves randomly crash over the bows and wet the voyagers right through. Water starts to collect in the bottom of Jesus' boat, and no matter how quickly the sailors work to bail it out, it threatens to overwhelm the vulnerable craft. The person at the helm loses all control of the steering and everyone is thrown about wildly. The boat rolls unpredictably from one side to the other, while simultaneously pitching violently as each wave crest is awkwardly mounted and the boat falls down into the deep troughs on the other side, so deep that the waves before and behind seem like great walls of water and it is impossible to see even the other boats nearby. Stomachs churn as the altitude unpredictably and frequently changes. Some of the less experienced voyagers vomit into the boat, too fearful to lean over the side lest they be tossed into the churning mass of the sea. Sheets of lightning menace close by, bringing the extent of the danger into full view, while the noise of thunder explodes in their ears and threatens to crack the very timbers of the boat. They hang on tightly, desperate not to be ejected from their vessel—tiny island of relative safety—and into the raging waters around them. Fear tenses their muscles and knots in their throats. If it were possible to think about it, it would probably be fear of death, fear of drowning and disappearing without a trace, fear of finding themselves alone and in the dark and being unable to resist the water flowing into their lungs. But it is not possible to think, and the experience is more terror than fear. Terror is overwhelming. Time *cannot pass*, because while terror screams that the experience is intolerable and *must* stop, it *does not stop*. It *cannot be endured* but is suspended in a now that is oblivious to a past and finds no comfort in a future toward which it must be moving.

Desperate prayers are mentally murmured and promises made to a God who seems completely absent from the chaos.

How can he possibly remain asleep there? Who could sleep through this mayhem? Granted that the stern enjoys a slight advantage in stability, who could remain on a cushion while the boat is being tossed around like a beetle at the mercy of a cat? Someone thinks to wake up Jesus, whose sleep is an affront to their terror ("'Teacher, do you not care that we are perishing?'").

> And he rebukes the wind and orders the sea: "Peace! Be still!"
> The wind ceases, and there is a dead calm.
> And Jesus says to them, "Why are you afraid? Have you still no faith?"

Wait. Roll back a bit.

We have missed something. How could he possibly remain asleep there? *Who could even remain on a cushion while the boat is being tossed around like a beetle at the mercy of a cat?*

That's it, there's the clue. This is not a recollection of being in a boat at all. They're terrified by their situation, whatever it may be, yet he seems completely unaffected by it. A word from him, and all cause for terror ceases. He speaks to them as if they are children: "Why are you afraid? Have you still no faith?"—Isn't that a bit invalidating of their experience? First, he sleeps through (he appears oblivious to) their crippling terror. They feel completely at the mercy of the storm and unable to escape it, and they panic. Once called upon, and by his voice alone, he resolves the source of the terror. And finally, he asks why they didn't know better than to give into it. Well, in fact, faith is not primarily a question of knowing (theoretically believing) as a question of trusting—a trust that is constituted in relationship with him—and complete trust is not easy because it involves a particular type of surrender of the locus of control. The disciples have not been able to *remain* in his love for them (Jn 15: 9) but have reverted when challenged by the storm to former patterns of thinking and behaving. They experience such terror because they have not yet been able to trust him completely. What the disciples do not know is that by accepting Jesus' complete love and care for them, they will cease to be afraid.

Engaging in Critical Dialogue with Biblical Tradition

What is the significance of the Stilling of the Storm story? Since we are reading it in the context of the book of Mark, we will start with how the Markan author has incorporated this story into the Gospel and what it might mean there. If we ask when the Gospel of Mark was authored and the circumstances that perhaps motivated its development, we find that the fears and tribulations of the early Christian community were likely in the background. Donahue argues that most scholars consider Mark to have been written in approximately 70 CE, a time when Christians were undergoing major persecution in Rome after the great fire of 64 CE. He writes: "the shadow of the cross, opposition from powerful leaders, divisions among Jesus' followers, persecutions, and betrayals—all these themes in Mark's Gospel would have been especially meaningful to an early Christian community that had suffered for the name of Jesus and was expecting even more suffering."[2] The image of terrified disciples in a storm-tossed boat would resonate strongly in that community.

How does the Markan author intend verses 4:35-41 to be understood? Using the language of Catholic biblical interpretation, what is the 'literal' meaning of this text? If we turn to the Pontifical Biblical Commission for further guidance, we read that the literal sense is "that which has been expressed directly by the inspired human authors" and that discerning the literal sense is "by means of a careful analysis of the text, within its literary and historical context."[3] The Commission distinguishes between literal and literalist interpretations (it observes that fundamentalist interpreters understand "literal interpretation as 'naively literalist interpretation'").[4] In other words, a "literal" reading does not necessarily imply that the biblical writer is relating or referring to an eye-witness account of an historical or empirical event. Discerning the "literal" sense of a text might involve recognizing clues in the text that give license to a reader to interpret the text otherwise. While "other-than-literal" senses are identified in the document, it is possible for the biblical text to have more than one sense, including a deeper literal sense: "a human author can intend to refer at one and the same time to more than one level of reality." Moreover, "even when a human utterance appears to have only one meaning, divine inspiration can guide the expression in such a way as to create more than one meaning" and (in the context of an example, Jn 11:50) "[the] two aspects belong, both of them, to the literal sense, for they are both made clear by the context." The Commission emphasizes that the example "[provides] a warning against adopting too narrow a conception of the inspired text's literal sense."[5]

Let us try, first, to interpret Mark's telling of the story as an historical account. How are we to picture the boat and Jesus' sleeping within it? What about the other details in the text? Do they ring true as historic events in the context? With regard to the boat, we are helped in imagining this detail

[2]Donahue, *Sacra Pagina: The Gospel of Mark*, 54.

[3]Pontifical Biblical Commission, *The Interpretation of the Bible in the Church*, II.B.1. See also Daniel J. Harrington, *How Do Catholics Read the Bible?* (Rowman & Littlefield, 2005), chapter 7.

[4]Pontifical Biblical Commission, *Interpretation*, I.F.

[5]Pontifical Biblical Commission, *Interpretation*, I.F.; II.B.1.

by archaeological finds of the "Sea of Galilee" (or "Kinneret") boat together with a boat mosaic uncovered at Magdala-Taricheae. The fishing boat recovered from the first century is some 9 metres in length and 2.4 metres at its widest point. Its original depth is estimated to be 1.2 metres and its draught is shallow.[6] Reconstructive work suggests that as a fishing boat, a deck would have been required at the rear to support the weight of the net.[7] Donahue imagines Jesus asleep on this deck.[8] This image is supported by the suggestion that the "cushion" refers to something on which the helmsman normally sat. Archaeologist Shelley Wachsmann argues, however, that it would have been too exposed and too difficult for a person to sleep on top of the deck, especially given that the helmsman sat there and likely used oars for steering. It would have been more comfortable to sleep *under* the rear deck, perhaps using sand bags—often used for ballast, and probably stored there—as a head-rest.[9] In either case, and as is evident in our phenomenological reading of the Stilling of the Storm pericope, it is hard to imagine that anyone could remain undisturbed by the commotion of such a storm and the pitching and rolling of such a boat in it.[10] Moreover, anyone under the rear deck would quickly have become wet. If the cold and the violent, unpredictable motion did not wake that person, they would have been at risk of drowning as the waves crashed over the boat and began to fill it. The setting of the story, however, is realistic. As John P. Meier observes, "no one questions the historical fact that Jesus crossed the Sea of Galilee in a boat with his disciples and probably did so with some frequency. Nor does anyone question the existence of frequent violent storms that suddenly descend upon the basin-like Sea of Galilee from the surrounding mountains, especially from the south."[11] So, while the context of the story is probably typical of situations in which Jesus found himself, the detail of his sleeping in the boat does not suggest that Mark is describing an historical event. Of course, there is the presentation of a miracle and the dialogue with the disciples at the end of the passage still to consider. Yet even these events do not do away with the problem of the sleeping Jesus if the text is understood in a historical way. While Mk 4:35-41 is clearly an example of a nature miracle, it appears that the story might not have been written as a recollection but as a kind of allegory.

---

[6]Shelley Wachsmann, *The Sea of Galilee Boat: An Extraordinary 2000-year-old Discovery* (Plenum, 1995), 135.

[7]Wachsmann, *Sea of Galilee Boat*, 326.

[8]Donahue, *Sacra Pagina: The Gospel of Mark*, 174.

[9]Wachsmann, *Sea of Galilee Boat*, 326–8.

[10]This is a source of skepticism with regard to the historicity of the story. See O. Lamar Cope, *Matthew: A Scribe Trained for the Kingdom of Heaven* (Catholic Biblical Association of America, 1976), 97. Quoted in Alistair I. Wilson, "In the Same Boat? Jonah and Jesus as Wave-Beaten Heralds," *In die skriflig* 55, no. 1 (2021): 2.

[11]John P. Meier, *A Marginal Jew: Rethinking the Historical Jesus*, vol. 2 (Yale University Press, 1994), 933.

The theme of God having control over storms is common in the Bible.[12] As such, the Stilling of the Storm pericope is often viewed through an intertextual lens—principally, Jon. 1:4-17, where once Jonah is aboard the ship, "the LORD hurled a great wind upon the sea, and such a mighty storm came upon the sea that the ship threatened to break up. Then the mariners were afraid, and each cried to his god" (Jon. 1:4-5a). In the meantime, Jonah goes to sleep. The ship's captain wakes Jonah and cries: "What are you doing sound asleep? Get up, call on your god! Perhaps the god will spare us a thought so that we do not perish." After Jonah eventually identifies himself to the sailors as the probable cause for the storm, and they have tried their best to reach land, the sailors "[pick] Jonah up and [throw] him into the sea; and the sea [ceases] its raging. Then the men [fear] the LORD even more" (1:15-16). The parallels are obvious. Fear for their lives in each case transmutes to awe for what God has done. What is particularly distinctive, however, is that where it seems reasonable that people on boats during severe storms should fear for their lives, Jesus seems surprised by the fear of the disciples.[13] We could read Jesus' response—"Why are you afraid? Have you still no faith?"—as a reproach. Wendy Cotter reads it, more softly, as a sign of Jesus' concern and care for the disciples. The disciples do not yet know or understand what Jesus knows and understands; they need never have feared while he was with them.[14] As Michael Fallon points out, in Mark, "Jesus does not contrast faith with doubt but with fear."[15]

Misunderstanding by the disciples is a strong theme in Mark's Gospel, culminating at the half-way point with the Transfiguration story, where Peter confesses Jesus' identity as the Christ.[16] Yet even after Peter's recognition, the disciples still misunderstand that the path of Jesus is one of suffering—as we discover in the second half of the Gospel.[17] The theme of constant misunderstanding by the disciples is emphasized by many Markan commentators. "Again and again throughout the narrative, the disciples fail to understand Jesus (4.40-41; 5.31; 6.37, 51-52; 7.18; 8.4, 16-21, 32-33; 9.5-6, 19, 32; 10.13, 23-24, 32; 14.37-41)." Michal Beth Dinkler suggests that we make best sense of the theme of misunderstanding "if it is read as an instantiation of the social rejection that Jesus experiences throughout the story and, therefore, as a form of his suffering."[18]

---

[12]For example, Pss 65:7; 89:9; 107:29.

[13]Unlike Jonah, Jesus responds obediently. See Wilson, "In the same boat?" 5–6.

[14]Wendy Cotter, *The Christ of the Miracle Stories: Portrait Through Encounter* (Brill, 2010), 211–2.

[15]Michael Fallon, *The Gospel According to St Mark: An Introductory Commentary*, 2nd ed. (Chevalier, 2009), 110.

[16]See Frank J. Matera, *New Testament Christology* (Westminster John Knox, 1999).

[17]Donahue, *Sacra Pagina: The Gospel of Mark*, 176.

[18]Michal Beth Dinkler, "Suffering, Misunderstanding, and Suffering Misunderstanding: The Markan Misunderstanding Motif as a Form of Jesus' Suffering," *Journal for the Study of the New Testament* 38, no. 3 (2016): 322.

Many scholars read the purpose of the Stilling of the Storm pericope—like other miracle stories—as the demonstration of divine power and authority.[19] Although Cotter accepts that the narrative can be read as a manifestation of God's power in Jesus, her primary thesis is that "the revelation of that power was only on account of the disciples' panic. It is only Jesus' love for them that causes him to manifest his authority in this way and sternly rebuke the wind and sea, calling for a restoration of calm, for the sake of the unknowing disciples."[20]

One of the issues biblical scholars typically examine is what a gospel author is trying to say by situating a pericope at a particular point in their narrative. Kathleen M. Fisher and Urban C. von Wahlde maintain that greater focus in reading Mark should rest on the interpretation of the literary grouping of miracles in 4:35-5:43.[21] They argue that there are common elements in each of these miracles. Each displays: "the quality of the spectacular"; a contrast between the reaction of the witnesses and Jesus' understanding of the situation; a "[manifestation] of the power of Jesus overcoming the grip of the devil in the world"; and establishing that Jesus reveals God's power in all dimensions of life.[22] While this reading clearly emphasizes the pre-eminence of God's power in Jesus and focuses attention on the outcome, it is important to underscore the reference to a contrast between the attitudes of the witnesses and that of Jesus. It is common in miracle stories about Jesus for this to be the case; the key to understanding miracles in the gospels (which the witnesses do not grasp) is usually not the miraculous deed as such but the relationship with Jesus that unfolds.

The reading above would support the miracles in 4:35-5:43 being interpreted as a block. Timothy Milinovich disagrees, repeating the common understanding with respect to Mark that "the relationship of the storm pericope to its surrounding contexts is primarily transitional: it is understood to link together the localized ministry on the Western side of the Sea of Galilee in 1:15-4:34 with the progressively wider proclamation eastward."[23] Commenting on the Lucan version of the story, Louise J. Lawrence notes that "the 'journey to the other side' of the lake ... is a journey towards alien territory (characterized by unclean pigs, tombs, chaos and madness) but it is also ultimately a journey which is paradigmatic of the founding/liberation

[19]"For Mark these stories serve to recognize Jesus' identity (4:41; 5:7,19–20), to portray his possession of power (4:39; 5:30), and to foreshadow Jesus' gift of eternal life (5:23,42)." Brown, *An Introduction to the New Testament*, 48.

[20]Cotter, *The Christ of the Miracle Stories*, 214.

[21]Kathleen M. Fisher and Urban C. von Wahlde, "The Miracles of Mark 4:35–5:43: Their Meaning and Function in the Gospel Framework," *Biblical Theology Bulletin* 11, no. 1 (1981): 13.

[22]Fisher and von Wahlde, "The Miracles of Mark 4:35–5:43," 13–15.

[23]Timothy Milinovich, "The Parable of the Storm: Instruction and Demonstration in Mark 4:1–41," *Biblical Theology Bulletin* 45, no. 2 (2015): 88–9.

of a community."[24] It is important to remember that while the Sea of Galilee is also referred to as a lake, this should not imply that it is anything less than a small sea: the journey to the other side often involves heading off without being able to see the destination, some 13 kilometres away. While the "transitional" explanation helps to connect the Storm pericope to the other miracles, Milinovich argues for the promotion of a greater coherence between verses 1-34 of Chapter 4 and verses 35-41. In other words, he suggests that the miracle story at the end of Chapter 4 should be read together with the parables that immediately precede it instead of the miracles that follow it. He argues this on the basis of a narrative-critical reading that determines "an instruction-demonstration pattern that is seen in four other instances in Mark ...." This pattern amounts to a period of public teaching followed by confirmation of Jesus' authority in a miracle.[25] Milinovich reinforces his argument by the examination of significant terms or phrases used throughout Chapter 4. One of these terms is "boat" (πλοῖον), which thematically links 4:1 with 4:35 and enables us to read "just as he was" as a reminder that Jesus was already in the boat at the point of setting off for the other side.[26] Milinovitch's interpretation emphasizes that Chapter 4 forms a whole, which once again underscores the theme of misunderstanding: while Jesus has taught using several parables, the disciples do not yet understand what Jesus' teaching means. This is despite the fact that "even the sea obey[s] him."[27]

Study of the Markan text reveals that it is reliant on much pre-existing material. Meier hypothesizes that the miracle stories in Mk 4:35-5:43 perhaps "[represent] a pre-Marcan collection ... that formed something of a didactic cycle in early Christian tradition."[28] This could support the idea that the miracles are meant to be read together, although the detail added by the Markan author about the boat in 4:1 supports Milinovitch's theory that Mark wants the prior parables and the miracle to cohere. Meier notes the sheer volume of miracle material in the Gospels and uses the criterion of "multiple attestation of sources and forms" to argue that some of the biblical pericopes recounting miracles come from the earliest Jesus tradition and cannot be considered inventions of the early Church.[29] However, he also observes that the criterion of multiple attestation does not apply to the nature miracles, and even claims the category of "nature

---

[24]Louise J. Lawrence, "'The Stilling of the Sea' and the Imagination of Place in a Cornish Fishing Village," *Expository times* 120, no. 4 (2009): 174.

[25]Milinovich, "The Parable of the Storm," 89.

[26]Some scholars suggest that "just as he was" is Mark's addition to the original pericope and is intended to signal Mark's narrative clarification that Jesus was already teaching from within a boat (Mk 4:1). Cotter, *The Christ of the Miracle Stories*, 199.

[27]Milinovich, "The Parable of the Storm," 97.

[28]Meier, *A Marginal Jew*, Vol. 2, 924.

[29]Meier, *A Marginal Jew*, Vol. 2, 618–20.

miracle" itself is inappropriate.[30] Recategorizing the Stilling of the Storm as a "rescue miracle," Meier maintains that it is found only in one gospel story, one source and one literary form.[31] He thus associates the miracle under consideration here with the tradition of the early Church and not with the earliest Jesus tradition.[32] Further, he argues, "most of the so-called 'nature miracles' pose grave problems for anyone trying to establish some historical basis for them."[33] Graham H. Twelftree lists a number of relevant issues with regard to the nature miracles:

> [O]nly the disciples appear to be aware of them, their support in the arguably authentic sayings of Jesus is limited or non-existent, they are not mentioned in the summaries of Jesus' miraculous activity, they are flush with Old Testament motifs as well as beliefs and practices of the early church, and, most problematic, they have, it is argued, few if any analogies with which to help assess their veracity.[34]

It is intriguing that in Craig S. Keener's account of miracles more broadly through history, those miracles he reports as being attested to after the early first century are typically miracles of healing and exorcisms, but not nature miracles.[35]

In an earlier chapter, we observed Jesus "perform" a miracle but made no specific comment on it *as* a miracle (the woman with the hemorrhage was healed when she touched Jesus). In this chapter, we need to make some broader reference to the question of miracles as such, because they can be a significant barrier to contemporary religious belief. David Hume famously defined miracles as violations of the laws of nature, and this is a popular understanding in our times that would seem to be exemplified in the Stilling of the Storm narrative.[36] In his recent philosophical work on miracles, David Basinger observes two features generally ascribed to them: that

---

[30]Meier, *A Marginal Jew*, Vol. 2, 877–8.

[31]Meier, *A Marginal Jew*, Vol. 2, 878.

[32]"Our examination of Mark's redactional theology in the text, the heavy presence of OT themes and phrases serving a surprisingly high christology of the church, the similarity all this bears to the walking on the water, the lack of multiple attestation of the miracle, and the miracle's continuity with the miracle tradition of the early church rather than the miracle tradition that has a claim to go back to Jesus' public ministry oblige us to conclude that the more probable opinion—though not an absolutely certain one—is that the stilling of the storm is a product of early Christian theology." Meier, *A Marginal Jew*, Vol. 2, 933.

[33]Meier, *A Marginal Jew*, Vol. 2, 879.

[34]Graham H. Twelftree, "The Miraculous in the New Testament: Current Research and Issues," *Currents in Biblical Research* 12, no. 3 (2014): 331.

[35]Craig S. Keener, *Miracles: The Credibility of the New Testament Accounts* (Baker Academic, 2011), chapter 10.

[36]David Hume, Lewis Amherst Selby-Bigge, and Peter H. Nidditch, *David Hume: A Treatise of Human Nature*, 2nd ed. (Oxford University Press, 1978), X, i, 90n. This argument has been brought into question. See David Basinger, *Miracles* (Cambridge University Press, 2018), 19.

they are unusual or exceptional in some way (and not violations of the laws of nature, a theory that has been strongly brought into question subsequent to Hume), and that some kind of divine cause is attributed to them. To these features, he adds a third—that miracles must be, in principle, observable phenomena.[37] This definition means that the Stilling of the Storm fits conceptually the pattern of a miracle, presuming that the historicity of the narrative can be demonstrated.

However, this does not help us in our dialogue with biblical scholars on the Storm pericope, partly because biblical scholars do not always make a judgment on the possibility or even historicity of miraculous events, but instead, on the historicity of the text, how miracles might have been understood at the time and how they can be understood in the context of the overall narrative. Meier writes, for example:

> I do not claim to be able to decide the theological question of whether particular extraordinary deeds done by Jesus were actually miracles, i.e., direct acts of God accomplishing what no ordinary human being could accomplish. As I have indicated, I think that such a judgment ("this particular act is a miracle performed directly by God") goes beyond what any historian can legitimately assert within the limits of his or her own discipline.[38]

With respect to the historicity of miraculous events in the Bible, it is simply impossible to respond, or at least, one can respond either with belief or disbelief in their historicity, but neither of these approaches is productive or even helpful for persons struggling to understand who Jesus is today. Instead, as Eric Eve notes: "What we should not do is to approach [the miracles of Jesus] with a predetermined attitude either of naïve credulity or of dogmatic scepticism. Reading critically means reading with discernment, questioning what we read, and being open to different possibilities about both meaning and truth."[39]

It is important, then, to consider the kind of worldview that would embrace the possibility of miracles in first-century Palestine. At the time of Jesus, itinerant wonder-workers were part of everyday life; although the similarity with Jesus is there, it can also be argued, however, that Jesus is distinct from these persons in a number of ways.[40] Jesus behaves not as a magician or pagan wonder-worker, but—if we refer only to the healing

---

[37]Basinger, *Miracles*, 17. See also the discussion about defining miracles in Twelftree, "The Miraculous in the New Testament."

[38]See Meier, *A Marginal Jew*, Vol. 2, 617; reprinted in John P. Meier, "5.7 The Historicity of Jesus' Miracles: The Global Question, 1994," in *Jesusforschung in vier Jahrhunderten*, ed. Zager Werner (De Gruyter, 2014), 473.

[39]Eric Eve, *The Healer from Nazareth: Jesus' Miracles in Historical Context* (SPCK, 2009), 1.

[40]Géza Vermès, *Jesus the Jew: A Historian's Reading of the Gospels* (Collins, 1973), 58–82.

miracles for a moment—from within an understanding of health common to his Jewish contemporaries, where both sickness and healing have their source in God.[41] From a twenty-first-century perspective there is not only "faith" but also an extraordinary vulnerability on display here, in which the precariousness of life is bound up in an enchanted worldview where God alone is responsible for illness and its consequences in recovery or death.[42] Yet, from within the worldview of those times—as within many communities who live in contexts of complete powerlessness today—miracles make sense. Having authority over nature is not unheard of in the wider ancient world and communicates within that worldview a connection with divinity.[43]

While Meier refers to the literary form of the "miracle story," Cotter argues that these pericopes take the form, not of miracle stories as such, but of anecdotes (and it is well to be reminded at this point that the New Testament refers not so much to miracles but to "mighty deeds").[44] The anecdote, Cotter insists, is a common literary form in the first century, whereas the "miracle story" is not.[45] In other words, what we might refer to as the miracle stories were not conceived in exactly the same way by the Gospel writers or even in the tradition that they inherited and shaped. As one of their purposes, anecdotes serve as "*exempla*, stories that provide some virtue to be admired and imitated."[46] Cotter proposes that the anecdotes about Jesus are used both to tell us something about who Jesus is and to exemplify how his followers should respond to people who are often difficult or needy in some way. Thus,

---

[41]Kelley, "Miracles, Jesus, and Identity," 85–90. On the context, see also José Antonio Pagola, *Jesus: An Historical Approximation*, 4th ed. (Convivium, 2009), 161–9; Meier, *A Marginal Jew*, Vol. 2, chapter 8. The main distinction Meier identifies between Jesus and magicians or wonder-workers is that "at least implicitly, the context of miracles in the Gospels is one of faith, trust, or discipleship" (542). Moreover: "in cases where faith or some other personal attitude is implicit in Mark, it tends to be made explicit in the revisions of Matthew and Luke" (543). Further, "negative statements [about culpability in not believing in Jesus after witnessing a miracle] in John, Mark, Matthew, and Luke arise from a positive presupposition that pervades the Four Gospels: all the miracles of Jesus aim at bringing people to faith, repentance, and discipleship ... Even the short miracle stories and the summaries of Jesus' miracles are brought within an overarching context: the interrelationship between Jesus and the recipients of his miracles" (544).

[42]With respect to "enchantment," we do not use this word pejoratively, but in the sense that it is understood by Charles Taylor in *A Secular Age*. Vatican News, "Pope at Urbi et orbi: Full Text of His Meditation," Vatican City (March 27, 2020).

[43]See Cotter, *The Christ of the Miracle Stories*, 230.

[44]Meier, *A Marginal Jew*, Vol. 2, 646. "There is no word as such for 'miracle' in the Bible. It speaks only of 'signs,' 'wonders,' 'portents,' 'works of power,' or simply 'works.'" See also Richard P. McBrien, *Catholicism*, Rev. and updated ed. (CollinsDove, 1994), 339.

[45]Cotter, *The Christ of the Miracle Stories*, 14.

[46]Cotter, *The Christ of the Miracle Stories*, 5.

> the encounter [between Jesus and the petitioner], is not simply a vehicle to hurry us to the amazing miraculous action at all. Rather, ... the narrator, having caught the listener's attention with the presence of these bold petitioners, now illustrates Jesus' view of them and his response. It is in this response by Jesus that the would-be follower would find the *exempla*.[47]

The *exempla* demonstrates both that Jesus listens and responds to people in need with respect and empathy, and that the quality of faith shows itself unexpectedly in people who are often social outcasts.[48]

Engaging in Dialogue with Post-Biblical Tradition

There is no doubt that many within the Christian tradition have, through history, believed miracles to have taken place not only in Jesus' time but also up to and including in their own times. Jim Harrison argues that widespread scholarly skepticism with regard to the historicity of the nature miracles in the Gospels is misplaced. Against Meier, he maintains that these miracles belong to the earliest Jesus tradition and can be considered even today to be historical occurrences.[49] From a slightly different critical perspective, Keener questions whether the academic dismissal of the historicity of miracles reveals a deep prejudice against certain types of experience. He asks whether ruling out reports of miracles is based on "philosophic assumptions about what is possible for intelligent people in other cultures and eras to believe that they have seen." This is in spite of whether miracles are interpreted using "naturalistic or supernatural terms."[50] Keener argues that "many other cultures and some religious subcultures within our culture provide

---

[47]Cotter, *The Christ of the Miracle Stories*, 7.
[48]Cotter, *The Christ of the Miracle Stories*, 8.
[49]Jim Harrison, "Modern Scholarship and the 'Nature' Miracles: A Defense of Their Historicity and Affirmation of Jesus' Deity," *Reformed Theological Review* 72, no. 2 (2013), https://rtrjournal.org/index.php/RTR/article/view/48. With regard to extra-biblical accounts, Keener notes: "in ancient stories, Pythagoras and Empedocles reportedly calmed storms. Various ancient figures also reportedly walked on water: Orion, a son of Poseidon; Xerxes, who thereby displayed a divine power; Pythagoras; and a Hyperborean magician." Keener, *Miracles: Credibility*, 483. However, Keener also observes that such stories usually appear much later than the life of the person involved. Nevertheless, he writes: "Given the abundance of eyewitness claims to what we consider nature miracles, there is no reason to doubt that eyewitnesses in Jesus's day could have made similar claims in which they believed. ... [While these accounts] often stretch the credibility of a nontheistic or nonsupernatural paradigm ... the stronger examples cumulatively invite open-minded hearers to consider the hypothesis of supernatural causation" (492).
[50]Keener, *Miracles: Credibility*, 79.

better paradigms for a sympathetic reading of the Gospels' claims than our dominant Western academic paradigms do."[51]

Belief in the occurrence of miracles is the fundamental but not always uncritical position of the Catholic Church.[52] Certainly, it is belief in the miracles of the incarnation and resurrection (which, we would argue, are of a different order to other miracles reported in the New Testament) that is understood to be central to Christian faith. Moreover, it is not always the case in the tradition that the miracles in the New Testament are to be read quasi-historically. And this, indeed, is what happened in our phenomenological reading, above—we stumbled over a clue in the story where the author signaled that they were not talking about Jesus being asleep in a real boat at all. Moreover, this realization brought us to recognize something more profound than wind and waves being brought to a halt: what the disciples do not know is that by accepting Jesus' complete love and care for them, they will cease to be afraid.

Finding allegorical meaning in the Markan text in this way is common in the history of the Church: for example, it is found in Augustine's Sermon LXIII on the Stilling of the Storm. He urges his audience not to allow their faith to go to sleep: "[I] take occasion thereby to exhort you, that against the tempest and waves of this world, faith sleep not in your hearts." He explains: "the sailors are the souls passing over the world in wood. That ship also was a figure of the Church. And all, individually indeed are temples of God, and his own heart is the vessel in which each sails; nor can he suffer shipwreck, if his thoughts are only good." Believers will find themselves in a tempest. They will experience insults and feel anger and easily become shipwrecked, with Christ asleep in their hearts because of their forgetfulness. Augustine exhorts them to let go of their anger, find forgiveness, and "return to the repose of [their] hearts[s]. Christ hath commanded the sea, tranquillity is restored."[53]

We find other figurative uses of the Stilling narrative in history. In the third century, for example, Athanasius focuses not on the weakness of

---

[51]Keener, *Miracles: Credibility*, 80.

[52]This is affirmed in Vatican I Council, *Dei filius: Dogmatic Constitution on the Catholic Faith* (Libreria Editrice Vaticana, 1870), chapter 3, sections 4–5. Disbelief in miracles is condemned in Pope Pius X, *Lamentabili sane: Syllabus Condemning the Errors of the Modernists* (Libreria Editrice Vaticana 1907), n. 28. *Lumen gentium*, from Vatican II, affirms that miracles show the reign of God has broken through on earth (n. 5). The *Catechism* focuses on the idea that miracles reinforce belief in God's revelation in Christ. *Catechism of the Catholic Church* (Libreria Editrice Vaticana, 1993, as updated), nn. 156, 548.

[53]St. Augustine, "Sermon on the Mount; Harmony of the Gospels; Homilies on the Gospels," in *Nicene and Post-Nicene Fathers*, Philip Schaff ed., vol. 6 (Christian Classics Ethereal Library, 1987). See also Augustine's Commentary on John, XI:1-54, 19 in Philip Schaff, ed., *Nicene and Post-Nicene Fathers*, vol. 7, *St. Augustine: Homilies on the Gospel of John; Homilies on the First Epistle of John; Soliloquies* (Christian Classics Ethereal Library, 1987), 457.

the disciples in the storm, but on their wisdom in remaining with Jesus in the boat:

> By [sin] the fool is wrecked, as by the waves of the sea, being led away and enticed by his fleshly pleasures ... For where there is sagacity, there the Word, who is the Pilot of souls, is with the vessel ... The disciples since they were wise, and therefore remained with the Lord, although the sea was agitated, and the ship covered with the waves, for there was a storm, and the wind was contrary, ... fell not away. For they awoke the Word, Who was sailing with them, and immediately the sea became smooth at the command of its Lord, and they were saved.[54]

Preaching on marriage, Aelred of Rievaulx in the eleventh century recalls the image of the boat together with the metaphor of crossing over to the other side: "the profession [of faith] in Christ's cross during this life is a boat and by this boat a person can cross over to Christ."[55] George Herbert personalizes the boat as the Christian in the opening stanza of "The Bag":

> Away despair! my gracious Lord doth heare.
> Though windes and waves assault my keel,
> He doth preserve it: he doth steer,
> Ev'n when the boat seems most to reel.
> Storms are the triumph of his art:
> Well may he close his eyes, but not his heart.

Pope Francis provides another interpretation of Mk 4:35-41 when he delivers the *Urbi et Orbi* blessing for the world during COVID-19 in 2020:

> For weeks now it has been evening. Thick darkness has gathered over our squares, our streets and our cities; it has taken over our lives, filling everything with a deafening silence and a distressing void, that stops everything as it passes by; we feel it in the air, we notice in people's gestures, their glances give them away. We find ourselves afraid and lost. Like the disciples in the Gospel we were caught off guard by an unexpected, turbulent storm. We have realized that we are on the same boat, all of us fragile and disoriented, but at the same time important and needed, all of us called to row together, each of us in need of comforting the other. On this boat ... are all of us. Just like those disciples, who spoke anxiously with one voice, saying "We are

---

[54]Athanasius, Festal Letter XIX.6, in Philip Schaff, ed., *Nicene and Post-Nicene Fathers*, vol. 4, Athanasius: Select Works and Letters (Christian Classics Ethereal Library, 1887).

[55]Theodore Berkeley and M. Basil Pennington, *Aelred of Rievaulx: The Liturgical Sermons*, Cistercian Fathers 58 (Cistercian, 2001), sermon 22 section 4, cited in Marie Anne Mayeski, "'Like a Boat Is Marriage': Aelred on Marriage as a Christian Way of Life," *Theological Studies* 70, no. 1 (2009): 92–108.

perishing" (v. 38), so we too have realized that we cannot go on thinking of ourselves, but only together can we do this.[56]

Instead of focusing on individual faith, Pope Francis focuses on the role of community in what is, effectively, his recontextualization of the story. "Embracing the cross," he maintains "... means finding the courage to create spaces where everyone can recognize that they are called, and to allow new forms of hospitality, fraternity and solidarity. By his cross we have been saved in order to embrace hope and let it strengthen and sustain all measures and all possible avenues for helping us protect ourselves and others." In light of these examples, it is possible to affirm the miracle stories as true without presuming that a literal*ist* reading reflects an accurate grasp of what the biblical author intended.[57]

None of this commentary is actually decisive, however, for the person who wants to ask whether the miracles ascribed to Jesus "really happened." We argue that a more useful approach is to bracket the question of causality altogether where it comes to miracles. By this we mean that we should describe miracles as "events." If we use the language of phenomenology, events are happenings that appear without clear cause and are so excessive in quality that they cannot be grasped as such.[58] Events can be appreciated as extraordinary because they are radically singular and transform the lives of those affected by them or bearing witness to them.[59] Miracle stories are events that are recounted in order to show something about who Jesus is—whether that is within a circumscribed oral or literary context or with reference to an apparently historical one. So, asking whether the miracles ascribed to Jesus "really happened" is, perhaps, the wrong question, because it means that we are missing the point.[60]

---

[56]Vatican News, "Pope at Urbi et orbi."

[57]Dulles recalls Augustine's Tractates on the Gospel of John 24 in this regard: "Let us interrogate the miracles themselves, what they tell us about Christ: for they have a tongue of their own, if they can be understood. For since Christ is Himself the Word of God, even the act of the Word is a word to us." Avery Dulles, "Symbol, Myth, and the Biblical Revelation," *Theological Studies* 27, no. 1 (1966): 3 n. 3.

[58]Robyn Horner, *The Experience of God: A Phenomenology of Revelation* (Cambridge University Press, 2022), 104–7. This does not preclude, of course, that one risks reading them as ways in which God has engaged with the world. "Risk" here highlights that one has made a commitment despite the sort of evidence demanded by a secularist. A secularist, in fact, takes a risk in the opposite direction.

[59]See Claude Romano, *Event and World*, trans. Shane Mackinlay (Fordham University Press, 2009), 30.

[60]The exception, of course, is the matter of Jesus' resurrection, since on this matter Christian faith stands or falls. Yet it is commonly agreed by theologians that the resurrection is an "eschatological" rather than a historical event. By this, it is meant that the resurrection takes place outside history. There is no attempt to describe the resurrection in the Bible, but only the (ambiguous) evidence of the Empty Tomb tradition and the testimony to Jesus' post-resurrection appearances.

Engaging in Dialogue with the Current Context

A common understanding of Mk 4:35-41—certainly common in those we can find readily on the internet—is that when we are in times of trouble, God is with us, and we do not need to be afraid. Yet this message can appear glib. In its generalization it lacks something of the lived experience of real fear. Being in a boat on the sea in a violent storm is terrifying. In a striking experiment, Lawrence uses the spiritual exercise of the "imagination of place" in an attempt to enhance the reading of Luke's version of the Storm story by the community of a fishing village in Britain. Reflection by the group turns to the tragic loss of the crew of a local lifeboat in 1981, called out at night to rescue a ship during a hurricane. She records: "One participant within the group commented how the stilling of the storm was a hard narrative to digest by families bereaved through perils encountered on the sea." The participant recalls "how the current coxswain of the lifeboat, himself the son of one of the members of the crew that lost their lives ... had stated that when they answer emergency calls 'we need someone who believes for us'." In the community reading of the story, "the sleeping stranger in the boat, who exercises divine power and mastery over the unruly elements and the community meeting in his name, is such an advocate."[61]

We have already noted that in situations of great peril, time can sometimes seem to stand still: a person in this setting desires nothing more than that the terrifying situation will cease, and yet it remains. This can be described as a kind of hell. It is *intolerable* and yet *must be tolerated* at the same time. Emmanuel Levinas' description of nausea is evocative in this way, although it refers to an instance where what is unendurable affects us from the inside instead of from without:

> There is in nausea a refusal to remain there, an effort to get out. Yet this effort is always already characterized as desperate: in any case, it is so for any attempt to act or to think. And this despair, this fact of being riveted, constitutes all the anxiety of nausea. In nausea—which amounts to an impossibility of being what one is—we are at the same time riveted to ourselves, enclosed in a tight circle that smothers. We are there, and there is nothing more to be done, or anything to add to this fact than we have been entirely delivered up, that everything is consumed: this is the very experience of pure being.[62]

As another example of where time stands still in suffering, we could think of Jean-Paul Sartre's portrait of hell in *Huis Clos* ("In Camera," translated

[61]Lawrence, "'The Stilling of the Sea'," 175.
[62]Levinas, *On Escape*, 66.

into English as *No Exit*).[63] Sartre famously depicts hell as "other people"; in the play, hell is the situation of being enclosed in a windowless room with others whose severe judgments of us are our only means of judging ourselves.[64] It is living, as the character Garcin explains, "with one's eyes open all the time" and where the lights are never turned off. As the characters disabuse themselves of the notion that hell is where they are to be tortured by demons, Inez realizes: "You'll see how simple it is. Childishly simple. Obviously there aren't any physical torments—you agree, don't you? And yet we're in hell. And no one else will come here. We'll stay in this room together, the three of us, for ever and ever ... each of us will act as torturer of the two others."[65] Although Inez uses the language of time (hell is "for ever and ever"), we suggest that hell is eternal, a now where time does not pass.

While there are other situations we could perhaps describe as hell, we have chosen in this instance to recontextualize the Stilling of the Storm narrative in the context of the contemporary "epidemic" of mental illness. In fact, there are many mental illnesses, with many consequences in individual and communal lives, and with many people suffering not just from one mental illness but also comorbid afflictions. We are used to hearing about the prevalence of depression and anxiety, and we do not in any sense wish to diminish their traumatic significance. Here, and with a warning that what follows will be challenging and potentially triggering, we consider the situation of persons suffering from borderline personality disorder (BPD). In this examination, we make use of the recently published memoir of Marsha M. Linehan, a research psychologist who has developed an effective

[63]Jean-Paul Sartre, *No Exit and Three Other Plays* (Vintage International Series, [1944] 2015), 4.

[64]"What I wanted to say was that hell is other people. But 'hell is other people' has always been understood. It has been thought that what I meant by that was that our relations with other people are always poisoned, that they are invariably hellish relations. But what I really mean is something totally different. I mean that if relations with someone else are twisted, vitiated, then that other person can only be hell. Why? Because other people are basically the most important means we have in ourselves for our own knowledge of ourselves. When we think this about ourselves, when we try to know ourselves, basically we use the knowledge of us which other people already have. We judge ourselves with the means other people have and have given us for judging ourselves. Into whatever I say about myself someone else's judgment always enters. Into whatever I feel within myself someone else's judgment always enters. Which means that if my relations are bad, I am situating myself in a total dependence on someone else. And then I am indeed in hell. And there are a vast number of people in the world who are in hell because they are too dependent on the judgment of other people." Sartre, *No Exit*, 26; Jean-Paul Sartre, Michel Contat, and Michel Rybalk, eds., *Sartre on Theater* (Quartet Books/Random House, 1976), 199.

[65]Sartre, *No Exit*, 10.

treatment for BPD, "dialectical behavioural therapy" (DBT).[66] What was unknown until relatively recently is that Linehan suffered from BPD herself, describing it frequently as hell, and dedicating her life to "helping others to get out of hell."[67]

BPD is a frequently misunderstood illness. For a start, there is nothing "borderline" about it, except that in the days when psychiatrists were first trying to characterize it, it seemed to be a condition on the border between what they understood as psychosis and what they understood as neurosis.[68] Much more important is the recognition that it is a disorder of the personality, which means that it affects how one conceives one's identity and how one relates to others.[69] Persons with BPD are diagnosed when they meet at least five of nine criteria set out in the *Diagnostic and Statistical Manual of Mental Disorders* [DSM], currently published in its fifth edition. BPD is defined there as: "A pervasive pattern of instability of interpersonal relationships, self-image, and affects, and marked impulsivity, beginning by early adulthood and present in a variety of contexts."[70] The nine criteria listed in the DSM-V-TR are:

1. Frantic efforts to avoid real or imagined abandonment.
2. A pattern of unstable and intense interpersonal relationships characterized by alternating between extremes of idealization and devaluation.
3. Identity disturbance: markedly and persistently unstable self-image or sense of self.
4. Impulsivity in at least two areas that are potentially self-damaging (e.g., spending, sex, substance abuse, reckless driving, binge eating).
5. Recurrent suicidal behavior, gestures, or threats, or self-mutilating behavior.
6. Affective instability due to a marked reactivity of mood (e.g., intense episodic dysphoria, irritability, or anxiety usually lasting a few hours and only rarely more than a few days).

[66]The originally published work is Marsha Linehan, *Cognitive-Behavioral Treatment of Borderline Personality Disorder* (Guilford, 1993). On the efficacy of DBT, see the systematic review: Patrick T. Panos, John W. Jackson, Omar Hasan, and Angelea Panos, "Meta-Analysis and Systematic Review Assessing the Efficacy of Dialectical Behavior Therapy (DBT)," *Research on Social Work Practice* 24, no. 2 (2014): 222.
[67]"I made a promise to God, a vow, that I would get myself out of hell—and that once I did, I would find a way to get others out of hell, too." Marsha M. Linehan, *Building a Life Worth Living: A Memoir* (Penguin Random House, 2020), 6.
[68]Linehan, *Cognitive-Behavioral Treatment of BPD*, 5.
[69]Peter Tarr, "Understanding Borderline Personality Disorder: Q & A with Anthony C. Ruocco," *Brain and Behaviour* (May 2022): 21.
[70]American Psychiatric Association, *Diagnostic and Statistical Manual of Mental Disorders: DSM-5-TR*, 5th ed. (American Psychiatric Association, 2022), F60.63.

7 Chronic feelings of emptiness.
8 Inappropriate, intense anger or difficulty controlling anger (e.g., frequent displays of temper, constant anger, recurrent physical fights).
9 Transient, stress-related paranoid ideation or severe dissociative symptoms.

Looking closely at the criteria, we are perhaps able to imagine a second reason why BPD is so frequently misunderstood. Some of the behaviors associated with BPD (frantic efforts to avoid abandonment; unstable relationships that alternate between extremes; impulsivity; suicidality; self harm, and so on) can easily be misinterpreted by others as attempts to manipulate or seek attention, when, in fact, they arise out of a genuine and constantly experienced terror.[71] Misinterpretation of BPD symptoms is experienced as intensely invalidating by those who suffer from it.[72] Fundamentally, the person with BPD has no capacity to regulate emotion. As Linehan describes it, "For these clients, it was as if they didn't have emotional skin. As if they had suffered from third-degree burns all over their body. Even the lightest touch was excruciatingly painful."[73] Of all mental illnesses, sufferers of BPD have one of the highest rates of suicide (approximately 10 percent).[74]

The list of characteristics from DSM-V does not really give a sense of what living with BPD is like, which is why it can be helpful to engage with the experience of a sufferer. While there are a number of works that open onto this experience—either written by survivors or containing their collected perspectives—it is useful to have the meta-level reflection on the experience of BPD that Linehan's memoir provides.[75] Linehan describes her school years as relatively unremarkable, except that she is intelligent and

---

[71]See Maaria Koivisto, Tarja Melartin, and Sari Lindeman, "Self-invalidation in Borderline Personality Disorder: A Content Analysis of Patients' Verbalizations," *Psychotherapy Research* 32, no. 7 (2022): 932; Karlen R. Barr, Mahlie Jewell, Michelle L. Townsend, and Brin F. S. Grenyer, "Living with Personality Disorder and Seeking Mental Health Treatment: Patients and Family Members Reflect on their Experiences," *Borderline Personality Disorder and Emotion Dysregulation* 7, no. 1 (2020): 4, 7; Sharon Lawn, Janne McMahon, and Sara Zabeen, *Foundations for Change* (Private Mental Health Consumer Carer Network Australia, 2017), 9; Craig W. LeCroy and Jane Holschuh, *First Person Accounts of Mental Illness and Recovery* (Wiley, 2012), 199.

[72]Fiona Donald, Cameron Duff, Katherine Lawrence, Jillian Broadbear, and Sathya Rao, "Clinician Perspectives on Recovery and Borderline Personality Disorder," *The Journal of Mental Health Training, Education, and Practice* 12, no. 3 (2017): 204.

[73]Linehan, *Building a Life Worth Living*, 219.

[74]Edward Chesney, Guy M. Goodwin, and Seena Fazel, "Risks of All-Cause and Suicide Mortality in Mental Disorders: A Meta-Review," *World Psychiatry* 13, no. 2 (Jun 2014): 153–60; Alexander L. Chapman, "Borderline Personality Disorder and Emotion Dysregulation," *Development and Psychopathology* 31, no. 3 (2019): 1144.

[75]See, for example, Rachel Reiland, *Get Me Out of Here: My Recovery from Borderline Personality Disorder* (Hazelden, 2004); LeCroy, Holschuh, and LeCroy, *First Person Accounts of Mental Illness.*

sociable.[76] She also describes a felt sense of difference, and an incapacity to live up to the expectations of her mother and to fit into her family.[77] Toward the end of her schooling, she remembers: "Somehow I lost all ability to regulate not only my emotions but my behavior as well … It was an alarmingly rapid and complete descent into hell." Linehan is admitted to a private psychiatric hospital, the Institute of Living, where she remains—against her will—for two years.

> I did not know what had happened to me. No one knew. My experience at the institute was one of descending into hell, an out-of-control storm of emotional torture and absolute anguish. There was no escape. "God, where are you?" I whispered each day, but got no answer. I find the pain and turmoil hard to describe. How do you adequately describe what it is like being in hell? You can't. You can only feel it, experience it. And I did. I felt this inside myself, and it came out finally as suicidal behavior.[78]

She further describes her experience as "drowning in an ocean of self-loathing and shame, … feeling unloved and unlovable, … [feeling] indescribable emotional agony, so much that I wanted to be dead."[79] Through Linehan's eyes, we begin to see that suicide is less a choice than a compulsion, because there appears no other way to stop the all-consuming experience of suffering.

> The suicidal person is like someone trapped in a small room with high walls that are stark white. The room has no lights or windows. The room is hot and humid, and the boiling heat of the floor of hell is excruciatingly painful. The person searches for a door out to a life worth living, but cannot find it. Scratching and clawing on the walls do no good. Screaming and banging bring no help. Falling to the floor and trying to shut down and feel nothing brings no relief. Praying to God and all the saints one knows brings no salvation. The room is so painful that enduring it for even a moment longer appears impossible; any exit will

---

[76]Linehan, *Building a Life Worth Living*, 6.

[77]The etiology of BPD is presently unknown, although it is hypothesized that there are genetic as well as environmental factors. It has been connected to childhood trauma, but this is not always the case. "Broadly, an invalidating rearing environment may play an important role in socializing the vulnerable child's emotion regulation tendencies, shaping increasing emotional lability and dysregulation, culminating in the development of maladaptive coping behaviors that often begin to appear in adolescence (e.g. [Non-suicidal Self-Injury], suicidal behavior, and substance use). In addition, inadequate or delayed development of various social cognitive capacities and adaptive stress response may further contribute to [Emotional Dysregulation] and serious behavioral problems among adolescents. These behavioral problems, in turn, contribute to and predict the development of BPD." Chapman, "Borderline Personality Disorder," 1150.

[78]Linehan, *Building a Life Worth Living*, 6–7.

[79]Linehan, *Building a Life Worth Living*, 18.

> do. The only door out the individual can find is the door of suicide. The urge to open it is great indeed.[80]

As she says, "the desire to commit suicide ... has at its base a belief that life cannot or will not improve."

Linehan's vow to get out of hell and to find a way to rescue others from it has occupied her entire life. Motivated by this vow, after she gets out of hospital she initially pursues part of the long educational path to becoming a psychiatrist before realizing that becoming a clinical research psychologist in an academic institution will enable her to reach her goal more readily. Over the course of her illness, her life, and her research, she isolates the development of four sets of skills she perceives to be essential to the treatment of BPD: mindfulness, interpersonal effectiveness, emotional regulation, and distress tolerance. These become the skills taught in group DBT sessions as part of a larger program for the patient that includes individual psychotherapy as well as managed phone support from the therapist.[81] In addition, she requires that each individual psychotherapist works as part of a larger team, in order to avoid burnout. This highlights both the degree of difficulty of working with sufferers of BPD and the importance of the patient's relationship with the therapist as the place where trust, reliability, and consistency in relationships are learned. Like the coxswain on the village lifeboat, "we need someone who believes for us." Instead of stigmatizing BPD, Linehan encourages her student clinicians to become deeply compassionate to those who suffer from it. In fact, she goes so far as to emphasize the power of love as transformative:

> If you are with someone who is in hell, keep loving them, because in the end it will be transformative. They are like someone walking in a mist. They don't see the mist, and you may not see it, either. They don't see that they are getting wet. But if they have a pail for water, you put it out in the mist. Each moment of love adds to the mist, adds to the water in the pail. By itself, each moment of love may not be enough. But ultimately the pail fills and the person who has been in hell will be able to drink that water of love and be transformed. I know. I have been there. I have drunk from that pail.[82]

Linehan admits that the path out of hell is immensely difficult for the patient, because it involves coming to an acceptance of the pain that characterizes

---

[80]Linehan, *Building a Life Worth Living*, 24.

[81]Linehan, *Cognitive-Behavioral Treatment of BPD*, 144; Marsha M. Linehan and Chelsey R. Wilks, "The Course and Evolution of Dialectical Behavior Therapy," *American Journal of Psychotherapy* 69, no. 2 (2015): 103. See also Alexander L. Chapman and Katherine L. Dixon-Gordon, *Dialectical Behavior Therapy* (American Psychological Association, 2020), 66.

[82]Linehan, *Building a Life Worth Living*, 101.

the present as well as holding to the possibility of change in the future. Rediscovering the dynamic of time is part of the dialectic.[83]

> The bottom line is that if you are in hell, the only way out is to go through a period of sustained misery. Misery is, of course, much better than hell, but it is painful nonetheless. By refusing to accept the misery that it takes to climb out of hell, you end up falling back into hell repeatedly, only to have to start over and over again.[84]

At the same time, Linehan herself is testament to the potential that persons suffering from BPD can be healed.

How Is the Text Speaking to Me (or Us) Today?

The dialogue between the Stilling of the Storm narrative and the hell that is the experience of BPD could easily be appropriated as a recontextualization where Jesus is taken to be the therapist who descends into hell to save the patient who lives there (and thus performs a miracle). This would, however, be missing our point and minimizing the significance of the dialogue with contemporary experience (See! Just trust in Jesus and all your problems will be solved!). Far from transposing the miracle into contemporary categories, as it were, we seek to use the experience of the BPD patient to explore the nature of hell. In a doctrinal sense, hell is the absence of God. In this recontextualization we come to sit alongside the person who is terrified, for whom God is completely absent. This is not about explaining to the terrified person that God does not abandon us, but about sharing their experience—to the extent that it is possible—and learning to be compassionate and loving.

[83]"Dialectical strategies stress the creative tensions generated by contradictory emotions and oppositional thought patterns, values, and behavioral strategies, both within the person and in the person-environment system." Linehan, *Cognitive-Behavioral Treatment of BPD*, 201.
[84]Marsha Linehan, *DBT Skills Training Manual*, 2nd ed. (Guilford, 2015), 461.

5

Jesus and the Death of Lazarus: The Experiences of Grief and Compassion

In Chapter 4, we explored the experience of terror, of finding oneself in a hell which *is* the experience of oneself and from which it is thus seemingly impossible to escape. We turn, now, to a different kind of pain, which emerges in the experience of grief. For some, grief may actually begin as a type of hell, or even continue in that way for some time. Yet, grief has its own rhythms that do not quite match the experience of being suffocatingly "riveted to ourselves." Grief can well up without warning and overwhelm us. The tears that find their way out in spite of our best efforts to keep a veneer of self-control express the utter force of grief, which subsides in plaintive cries and moans until it comes to rest in an exhausted silence. We are spent. As the French say with a sublime onomatopoeia when it is uttered forcefully, we are *épuisées* (epɥize).

The Text: John 11:1-44

Now a certain man was ill, Lazarus of Bethany, the village of Mary and her sister Martha. Mary was the one who anointed the Lord with perfume and wiped his feet with her hair; her brother Lazarus was ill. So the sisters sent a message to Jesus, "Lord, he whom you love is ill." But when Jesus heard it, he said, "This illness does not lead to death; rather it is for God's glory, so that the Son of God may be glorified through it." Accordingly, though Jesus loved Martha and her sister and Lazarus, after having heard that Lazarus was ill, he stayed two days longer in the place where he was.

Then after this he said to the disciples, "Let us go to Judea again." The disciples said to him, "Rabbi, the Jews were just now trying to stone you, and are you going there again?" Jesus answered, "Are there not twelve hours of daylight? Those who walk during the day do not stumble, because they see the light of this world. But those who walk at night stumble, because the light is not in them." After saying this, he told them, "Our friend Lazarus has fallen asleep, but I am going there to awaken him." The disciples said to him, "Lord, if he has fallen asleep, he will be all right." Jesus, however, had been speaking about his death, but they thought that he was referring merely to sleep. Then Jesus told them plainly, "Lazarus is dead. For your sake I am glad I was not there, so that you may believe. But let us go to him." Thomas, who was called the Twin, said to his fellow-disciples, "Let us also go, that we may die with him."

When Jesus arrived, he found that Lazarus had already been in the tomb for four days. Now Bethany was near Jerusalem, some two miles away, and many of the Jews had come to Martha and Mary to console them about their brother. When Martha heard that Jesus was coming, she went and met him, while Mary stayed at home. Martha said to Jesus, "Lord, if you had been here, my brother would not have died. But even now I know that God will give you whatever you ask of him." Jesus said to her, "Your brother will rise again." Martha said to him, "I know that he will rise again in the resurrection on the last day." Jesus said to her, "I am the resurrection and the life. Those who believe in me, even though they die, will live, and everyone who lives and believes in me will never die. Do you believe this?" She said to him, "Yes, Lord, I believe that you are the Messiah, the Son of God, the one coming into the world."

When she had said this, she went back and called her sister Mary, and told her privately, "The Teacher is here and is calling for you." And when she heard it, she got up quickly and went to him. Now Jesus had not yet come to the village, but was still at the place where Martha had met him. The Jews who were with her in the house, consoling her, saw Mary get up quickly and go out. They followed her because they thought that she was going to the tomb to weep there. When Mary came where Jesus was and saw him, she knelt at his feet and said to him, "Lord, if you had been here, my brother would not have died." When Jesus saw her weeping, and the Jews who came with her also weeping, he was greatly disturbed in spirit and deeply moved. He said, "Where have you laid him?" They said to him, "Lord, come and see." Jesus began to weep. So the Jews said, "See how he loved him!" But some of them said, "Could not he who opened the eyes of the blind man have kept this man from dying?"

Then Jesus, again greatly disturbed, came to the tomb. It was a cave, and a stone was lying against it. Jesus said, "Take away the stone." Martha, the sister of the dead man, said to him, "Lord, already there is a stench because he has been dead for four days." Jesus said to her, "Did I not tell you that if you believed, you would see the glory of God?" So they took away the stone. And Jesus looked upwards and said, "Father, I thank you for having heard me. I knew that you always hear me, but I have said this for the sake of the crowd standing here, so that they may believe that you sent me." When he had said this, he cried with a loud voice, "Lazarus, come out!" The dead man came out, his hands and feet bound with strips of cloth, and his face wrapped in a cloth. Jesus said to them, "Unbind him, and let him go."

Undertaking Ignatian Colloquy

Having listened to the text, we engage in direct address to Jesus on the cross. As we noted in Chapter 1, this type of prayer is called a colloquy ("I speak to God as my heart is moved"), and normally it would be undertaken individually and spontaneously. Here, evidently, we have to show "one we prepared earlier." Anyone—believer or not—can participate in it.

Ignatian Colloquy in Light of John 11:1-44

I have never really imagined that you had friends. Of course, there are the disciples, but somehow I don't really think of them as your friends—not really. There is always a distance between them and you, something they can't share, like the burden in Gethsemane. They fall asleep—I get that they are just exhausted—but they can't seem to stay with you in that space when you confess that you don't want to die. Maybe it is just too singular: you can't tell them, or they can't hear what it feels like to be facing death straight on. What does it mean to say, "I don't want to die," when you know that you will die very soon? What does it mean to hear someone say that and try to respond?

In any case, apart from "the disciple whom Jesus loved," we don't know a lot about your very personal life, until John tells us about your love for the Bethany trio: "The sisters sent word to Jesus, 'Lord, the one you love is sick'"; "Jesus loved Martha and her sister and Lazarus."[1] It seems to me that you and they are intimately connected in a way we don't see so much with the twelve men who apparently follow you everywhere. Mary and Martha and Lazarus are your friends; there is something deep and distinctive about your relationship with them, a love that goes beyond any concept of the universal love we are assured at Sunday School that you have for each of us. And come to think of it, I think the very reassurance of universal love is sometimes what makes it hard to believe in your love of us, because it can sound as though you don't love any one of us as individuals. Do you not

[1]Elizabeth Schrader wonders about who these people are. She hypothesizes that Martha is a later addition to the text, and that Mary of Bethany is actually Mary Magdalene, so that our story is about Mary and Lazarus only. Elizabeth Schrader, "Was Martha of Bethany Added to the Fourth Gospel in the Second Century?" *The Harvard Theological Review* 110, no. 3 (2017): 360–92. This issue is raised again in Mary L. Coloe, *John 11-21* (Liturgical Press, 2021).

have love for each person such as they are, instead of as an example of the collective?

We can only wonder about the times you spent with Mary and Martha and Lazarus—apart from that story where you apparently favor Mary for having "taken the better part" in sitting and listening to you instead of worrying about being hospitable in the other sense—about the times around the table together, with a rough red and good food and the kind of connectedness that flows in those moments and seems like a foretaste of heaven. You really love them. Is there a you that is more relaxed and open when you are not being a public person? Maybe I have been imagining you as "God in a body" after all, despite my intellectual resistance. Or, perhaps I have thought that the kind of detachment we see in some of your dealings with others ("go your way"; "do not touch me") was the way you were with everyone. Perhaps I have unwittingly come up with an image of you as the paradigm of a celibate religious who had no "particular friends" in order to be mobile and "free" and available as the world needed. Yet you, too, love. In person.

Precisely because we are like you, then, we love in person, and so we grieve.

> Walking to-day by a cottage I shed tears
> When I remembered how once I had walked there
> With my friends who are mortal and dead. Years
> Little had healed the wound that was laid bare.
> "Out little spear that stabs!" I, fool, believed
> I had outgrown the local, unique sting,
> I had transmuted wholly (I was deceived)
> Into Love universal the lov'd thing.[2]

That very particular, sudden, and searing pain never goes away. And yet, love can still be spoken rightly in the present tense, and in the very speaking of the present, there is already a future that draws together all that has already been.

If we return to the moment you're told that Lazarus is sick, you stay away from your friends like they're contagious. I just don't get this. You don't go to them before he dies, but only after he is dead and buried. When you finally arrive, you don't even go to the house but wait for the sisters to meet you individually outside the village. Martha might be stoic and faithful, but when Mary comes to you, she is in tears. And straight away when each of them sees you, John has each of them call you out on your absence: "Lord, if you had been here, my brother would not have died."

---

[2]C. S. Lewis, "Scazons," in C. S. Lewis, *Poems*, Reissue ed. (HarperOne, 2017). Copyright © C.S. Lewis Pte. Ltd. Extract reprinted with permission.

Let's just sit with that for a moment. If you had come when they had called for you, things apparently could have been different, but you stayed away. If I had called on you to come to me like this, you would not have performed some miraculous, death-defying cure. I knew always and already that you would let death take its course. I have such little faith—I was never even going to ask for a miracle.

So, we don't know what you are doing during all that time when Mary and Martha and Lazarus are waiting for you to turn up. John has you explain that Lazarus' death is for God's glory and the glorification of the Son, but we don't know what you are doing during those days. If you love Mary and Martha—if you love Lazarus—why do you stay away? How can you not want to be there when he is facing death and when they are there, suspended in anticipated grief, waiting for the last breath between life and death, waiting for it to happen or to have happened? I remember the sound of the last exhalation, and from then on, it was always so many minutes, or hours, or days—since. It has always seemed obscene that time should pass after death. "Stop all the clocks."[3] I so wanted to remain close to—to hold onto—the boundary of living. Why do you avoid being there? Why don't you do what I want you to do, what any reasonable person would expect you to do, which is to go to them when they really need you? It's like you don't feel anything. What tasks remain for you to do while you wait these two more days? Do you do some extra teaching or healings or exorcisms? If you love him, why don't you stop him from dying in the first place? And it's all very well to say that he is just asleep, like you say of Jairus' daughter, but that's actually not a very nice thing to say. It's a euphemism, but it can make us afraid to go to sleep lest we never wake again. And *you* might be able to say it and mean it because apparently *you* can call the dead back to life, but that doesn't happen very often, and even if it does, there will remain a time for these people to die again. So, Mary and Martha and Lazarus have to go through this *twice*?

We finally see you feel something when you encounter Mary. "When Jesus saw her weeping, and the Jews who had come along with her also weeping, he was deeply moved in spirit and troubled." I have always been drawn to this passage, but it is less than straightforward, I know. Frank says the Greek text actually means that you are angry, so it is actually not the good kind of "deeply moved and troubled" I am drawn to when I hear the text in English but the bad kind of "deeply moved and troubled" that is normally hidden from me in the Greek. He says you're angry because neither Mary nor "the Jews" get the whole point of you being here. Frank says that they

[3]The reference is to the poem "Stop all the clocks, cut off the telephone," by W. H. Auden.

wouldn't be crying if they believed in your reason for coming.[4] (Sounds a bit like—"*I'll give you something to cry about!*") Maybe.

So, you're angry, then. A few words emerge from you in an attempt to regain some semblance of sympathy or self-control: "where have they laid him?" And then, it seems you begin to feel the grief to the extent that suddenly *it feels you*, such is the force of the cry that begins in an inarticulate groan and sweeps all through and over and around you, so that it is like being pushed under water and, losing all sense of orientation, fighting hopelessly to find your feet as you are tossed and driven repeatedly into a hard floor of sand. All of this force of feeling explodes and is recorded as the shortest verse in the Bible: "Jesus wept." I have to stay here with you in this weeping; I cannot and do not want to go on. I don't want to roll forward to the miracle of your raising Lazarus, because actually I don't think that's the most important part of the story. I am just stuck here with you in tears out of the real pain of death and the agony of that gulf of separation.

There's this weird kind of thing where people say, well, Jesus can't have cried out of grief here in John's Gospel, because he knows that quick as a wink, he can bring Lazarus back from the dead! Apparently, the Johannine author is thinking about the pre-existent Word all this time. Instead, I am thinking about you feeling the searing pain of being cut off from Lazarus, whom you love, and cut off from his love of you. And even more, your heart seems to be breaking for Mary. You can't *not* cry, because her heart is torn to pieces and so is yours. Tears beget real tears here, not the wailing of the culturally-conformist mourners—as John casts "the Jews" at this point—but the tears that well up and overflow when the grief is truly shared. When you see her crying, it overtakes you, and you just can't help the tears that rise up and take you hostage. John then has Mary fall at your feet. I wonder if this is not because she has faith in you (as Frank says) or because she is petitioning you (as Mary Coloe suggests) but because her grief provokes her utter collapse.[5] I am going beyond what is given in the text here, but I can't help thinking that—first-century Jewish mores aside—you then lean down to her and put your arms around her. There are times when I wish you would throw your arms around me and hold me forever. Sometimes I imagine that you do. Not because I want to possess you uniquely, but because if you genuinely love me, your heart breaks with my grief, too.

In the name of the Father and of the Son, and of the Spirit, who intercedes "with sighs too deep for words" (Rom. 8:26).

---

[4]Francis J. Moloney, *Signs and Shadows: Reading John 5-12* (Fortress, 1996), 166–7.
[5]Coloe, *John 11-21*, 44, 17.

Engaging in Critical Dialogue with Biblical Tradition

In our consideration of the story of the Woman Caught in Adultery, we did not address in any detail the wider context of the Gospel of John, except to say the Adultery story is a late addition to the work and interrupts the flow of the text in its eventual location there. When we read John's Gospel, we become aware of its entirely different style and tone from the Synoptics. Clearly, in John's Gospel we are looking at something emergent from a profound theological development that takes longer to mature than the writings of the Synoptics. Some scholars suggest that the Fourth Gospel was written as early as the year 90 CE; others speculate that it does not appear before the year 120. To see something of the growth of theological maturity evident in John, we need only reflect on the different starting points for each Gospel. Mark (approximately 66–73 CE) begins with Jesus as an adult. The two other synoptics seek to trace his human inheritance and Jewish legitimacy back further: Luke (approximately 75-85 CE) provides an infancy narrative that links Jesus to the line of Jewish priests extending back to Aaron; Matthew (also approximately 75-85 CE) provides a genealogy that traces Jesus all the way back to Abraham. The writer of John, however, outdoes all three in seeking to reach back to the creation of the world: "In the beginning was the Word, and the Word was with God, and the Word was God. He was in the beginning with God. All things came into being through him, and without him not one thing came into being" (Jn 1:1-3). For John, God speaks God's Word (or Wisdom) in flesh in the God-human, Jesus.

John's Gospel can be divided into four main sections: the Prologue (1:1-18); the so-called Book of Signs (1:19-12:50); the Book of Glory (the Easter events) (13:1-20:29) and a conclusion (20:30-31), with an epilogue (chapter 21) most likely to have been added later.[6] Our present text is taken from the Book of Signs; in fact, it forms part of the conclusion to that section, with the focus shifting toward the death of Jesus which is to come.[7] This is important to note because it provides a basis for the way that scholars interpret Jesus' demeanor and feelings in the Lazarus story.

In our engagement with this text, we do not move beyond verse 35. This is not because we want to avoid questions about the raising of Lazarus, but because our *lectio* has brought us to focus on this point: "Jesus began to weep" (or, in most translations, "Jesus wept"). There are a number of issues on which we must touch. First, we must make some reference to the Johannine characterization of the Jews since this occurs in the context of the weeping. Moloney argues that the Gospel writer's use of this epithet—

---

[6]Moloney, *Sacra Pagina: The Gospel of John*, 43–4.
[7]Moloney, *Sacra Pagina: The Gospel of John*, 44.

which has been read in history in a derogatory sense—does not actually refer to the Jewish people but to "those characters in the story who have made up their minds about Jesus."[8] By describing the Jews in this way, he insists: "The conflicts between Jesus and 'the Jews' are more the reflection of a Christological debate at the end of the first century than a record of encounters between Jesus and his fellow Israelites in the thirties of that century. *They do not accurately report the experience of the historical Jesus.*"[9] Apart from anything else, Jesus is Jewish and many of his early followers are also Jews—it would make no sense even on that level to identify the Jews as the Jewish people as such. Of course, whether or not the author of John intended to be derogatory does not alter the fact that the text is readily heard and understood in this way.[10]

In their exegesis of the Lazarus story, many scholars begin with the obvious question of why Jesus does not immediately go to Bethany upon hearing the message from Mary and Martha. The Johannine writer provides a ready response: "But when Jesus heard it, he said, 'This illness does not lead to death; rather it is for God's glory, so that the Son of God may be glorified through it'." Stephen Voorwinde rearticulates this explanation more helpfully than others in terms of Jesus' being reliant for his decision, not on his own will, but on the will of the Father. [11] Voorwinde does so in the context of examining Jesus' love for Lazarus, a love that is not simply "divine" but deeply human.[12] So, far from Jesus' not caring about Lazarus' fate and the anxieties of Mary and Martha, it is in spite of his own love for them that he stays away. Insightfully, Brendan Byrne foreshadows a reading of Jesus' tears by pointing out that in the Lazarus pericope, we

---

[8]Moloney, *Sacra Pagina: The Gospel of John*, 31.

[9]Moloney, *Sacra Pagina: The Gospel of John*, 31. Italics original. See also Raimo Hakola, *Identity Matters: John, the Jews, and Jewishness* (Brill, 2005), 15.

[10]Adele Reinhartz describes herself as "A Jewish student of this Gospel" and writes: "I confess my discomfort with the quotation marks around 'the Jews' and all they imply. This discomfort has its origin, no doubt, in my own initial encounters with this text, in which each Johannine usage of the term *Jew* felt like a slap in the face." Adele Reinhartz, "'Jews' and Jews in the Fourth Gospel," in *Anti-Judaism and the Fourth Gospel*, ed. Reimund Bieringer, Didier Pollefeyt, and Frederique Vandecasteele-Vanneuville (Westminster John Knox, 2001), 213. Thanks to our colleague Gina Bernasconi for leading us to this comment. For background, see *The Bible, the Jews, and the Death of Jesus: A Collection of Catholic Documents* (United States Conference of Catholic Bishops, 2004); Hakola, *Identity Matters*, 5–9; Ruth Sheridan, *Retelling Scripture: "The Jews" and the Scriptural Citations in John 1:19-12:15*, vol. 110 (Brill, 2012), 235–6, 243; Amy-Jill Levine, *The Misunderstood Jew: The Church and the Scandal of the Jewish Jesus* (HarperOne, 2007), 105; Australian Catholic Bishops Conference, *Walking Together: Catholics with Jews in the Australian Context* (2023).

[11]Stephen Voorwinde, *Jesus' Emotions in the Fourth Gospel: Human or Divine?* (T & T Clark, 2005), 159.

[12]Voorwinde, *Jesus' Emotions*, 156.

(and Jesus) are brought to the point of facing starkly "the incompatibility or compatibility ... between (God's love) and (God's) letting people die."[13]

In the context of the imminent conclusion of the Book of Signs in John, the dialogue with the disciples about how Jesus understands Lazarus' death (Jn 11:11-14) is seen to foreshadow Jesus' own death, which is emphasized as the disciples contemplate the risks of returning to Judea. Since Bethany is close to Jerusalem, the risk to Jesus in going there is very great (which is why when he reaches Bethany, he does not enter the village but remains outside it).[14] Yet, the disciples continue to misunderstand the purpose of Jesus' mission. This is exemplified in the words of Thomas, who seems to think that by going to Bethany, Jesus has decided to confront his accusers (which will lead to the glorious death of Jesus and of those disciples who accompany him) instead of Jesus' being prepared to give glory to God.[15] The theme of misunderstanding is strong, as it is in other places in John's Gospel and, as we have seen in another chapter of the present text, with reference to the Gospel of Mark.

It is the continued misunderstanding of Jesus' purpose that Moloney and others identify behind the powerful emotions (being "deeply moved and troubled") that Jesus feels as he engages with Mary.[16] Moloney even goes so far as to say that Jesus' weeping is from exasperation rather than compassion or grief.[17] Of two motivations commonly given to explain Jesus' being troubled (or angry), Moloney argues for the unbelief of those with whom Jesus engages, while Voorwinde argues that it is anger at the prospect of Jesus' own impending death.[18] Voorwinde adds:

> it is ... an oversimplification to understand the emotions of Jesus at this point as "a fearful perturbation." There are also overtones of sorrow and the sense of being torn between a strong sense of indignation and a grief that will openly express itself in the shedding of tears. Perhaps the sense of the words is best conveyed in the translation "he was distressed."[19]

Byrne similarly maintains that Jesus is "torn between two conflicting emotions": "empathy with those who weep for Lazarus" as well as a

[13]Brendan Byrne, *Lazarus: A Contemporary Reading of John 11:1-46* (Society of St. Paul, 1991), 50.
[14]Byrne, *Lazarus*, 58; Voorwinde, *Jesus' Emotions*, 147.
[15]Moloney, *Sacra Pagina: The Gospel of John*, 348.
[16]See the note given in the Colloquy, above, from Moloney, *Signs and Shadows*, 166–7.
[17]Moloney, *Signs and Shadows*, 169. It seems Maloney here opts for a Bultmannian reading. See Richard Schenk, "And Jesus Wept," in *Reading John with St. Thomas Aquinas: Theological Exegesis and Speculative Theology*, ed. Michael Dauphinais and Matthew Levering (Catholic University of America Press, 2005), 223–4.
[18]Voorwinde, *Jesus' Emotions*, 177.
[19]Voorwinde, *Jesus' Emotions*, 181.

"shrinking from death that is part of human nature."[20] In contrast, Sandra Schneiders argues that Jesus' weeping is a sharing in Mary's grief.[21] To us, this empathic weeping is fundamental. One grieves more profoundly in the sharing of grief—and Jesus wept.

Engaging in Dialogue with Post-Biblical Tradition

During the Ignatian Colloquy, we noted a problem with interpreting the phrase "deeply moved and troubled."[22] This was because the Greek has a more critical sense than we could hear in the English translation. However, this phrase—together with the reference to Jesus' weeping—raises another important issue that has its roots in ancient philosophy: feelings (often referred to as passions, but what we presently call emotions) are frequently seen in a negative light, and contrasted with the soundness of reason.[23] While amongst the ancient philosophers, different schools gave different advice concerning the place of emotions—including grief—Stoicism is typically held up as a preeminent example of a philosophy that sees the overcoming of emotions as central to life's ultimate success.[24] The extent to which Greek and Roman philosophy influences the shaping of Christian thought more generally, but especially on the passions, is a matter of some debate.[25] Nevertheless, Johannes Brachtendorf argues that "in both antiquity and the medieval period, *passio*'s etymological link to suffering [Greek *pathos*, Latin *passio, affectus, turbatio, peturbatio*] gave it a negative connotation."[26] This

---

[20]Byrne, *Lazarus*, 72–3.

[21]Sandra M. Schneiders, "Death in the Community of Eternal Life. History, Theology, and Spirituality in John 11," *Interpretation* 41, no. 1 (1987): 54.

[22]Note the translation of the Greek *tarásso* as "to shake, trouble, or stir up" in Schenk, "And Jesus Wept," 220–1.

[23]John T. Fitzgerald, *Passions and Moral Progress in Greco-Roman Thought* (Routledge, 2008), 2–6. We note that approaches to emotion in the ancient world are varied, however, even amongst the Stoics. See, for example, David Armstrong's discussion of the Epicureans in Fitzgerald, *Passions and Moral Progress*, chapter 5; Richard Sorabji, *Emotion and Peace of Mind: From Stoic Agitation to Christian Temptation* (Oxford University Press, 2000).

[24]Fitzgerald, *Passions and Moral Progress*, 15; Sorabji, *Emotion and Peace of Mind*, 7.

[25]Paul L. Gavrilyuk, *The Suffering of the Impassible God: The Dialectics of Patristic Thought* (Oxford University Press, 2004).

[26]Johannes Brachtendorf, "'Et lacrymatus est Jesus': The Sorrow of Jesus in the Teaching of Augustine and Aquinas on the Affections," *Augustinian Studies* 48, no. 1–2 (2017): 228; Fitzgerald, *Passions and Moral Progress*, 5. On the terminology: "The medieval nomenclature of emotions in Latin was multiple and variegated, including terms from *motus animi/animae* to *perturbatio*, from *affectus* and *affectio* to *passio*, from *inclinatio* to *primus motus* ... '[E]motion' refers to a phenomenon that is both cognitive and affective—an idea that has always been present in medieval reflections about affectivity." Damien Boquet and Piroska Nagy, "Medieval Sciences of Emotions During the Eleventh to Thirteenth Centuries: An Intellectual History," *Osiris (Bruges)* 31, no. 1 (2016): 23–4.

issue has important implications for how we think about John's presentation of Jesus in chapter 11.

Classical theism—a theological position committed to doctrines such as God's impassibility (that is, God's not being able to suffer or to experience pain or emotion)—raises difficulties with respect to how to understand the person of Jesus as both divine and human, and the ways in which Jesus' divine and human natures interact (the *communicatio idiomatum*). From the perspective of Jesus' divinity, this has prompted questions such as whether God suffered in Jesus (Patripassianism) or whether Jesus actually suffered at all (Docetism). From the perspective of his humanity, the negative evaluation of Jesus' emotions prompts the consideration of whether Jesus actually represents the fulfillment of what it means to be human, or whether, if he does, suffering is really an imperfection. Commenting on passages in John 11–13 and Matthew 26, Brachtendorf explains:

> in the medieval period, this disturbance [*turbatio*] was taken to be sorrow. The Gospels accentuate sorrow by attributing this emotion in particular to Jesus. In doing so, they stand in stark contrast to the Stoic doctrine according to which the wise person is never sorrowful. If even the Son of God, who became a man, can experience sorrow, then sorrow cannot be completely irreconcilable with human perfection.[27]

Key to appreciating each of these problems is that to experience passion is to be affected by something beyond the self and, thus, to be vulnerable and not in control. For the classical theist, this would be seen as a threat both to God's omnipotence (all-powerfulness) and God's immutability (being unchanging).

Paul Gavrilyuk argues that with respect to the question of divine impassibility, the relationship between the "God of the Bible"—who is often described as exhibiting very human emotions—and Greek philosophy is not as straightforward in the patristic writings as has sometimes been thought.[28] He maintains that many contemporary responses to the problem of divine impassibility, which tend toward theorizing a suffering God, overlook important nuances in the Patristic literature that balance a thinking of divine impassibility. Gavrilyuk argues:

> Divine compassion presupposes both impassibility and passibility. It is the main contention of the patristic understanding of the incarnation that God, remaining fully divine, became human, accepted the limitations of human existence, subjected himself to voluntary suffering for the salvation of the world and triumphed over sin, death, and corruption in the end.

[27]Brachtendorf, "'Et lacrymatus est Jesus'," 227. See, in contrast, Thomas Aquinas, *Commentary on the Gospel of John*, 12, lect. 5, n. 1652, quoted in Schenk, "And Jesus Wept," 231.
[28]Gavrilyuk, *Suffering of the Impassible*, 3.

> God is impassible inasmuch as he is able to conquer suffering and he is passible inasmuch as he is able to suffer in and through human nature.[29]

This argument depends on an interpretation of compassion that does not mean "to suffer with" the sufferer in exactly the same way that the sufferer suffers. While the compassionate person might suffer, it is a suffering that is entered into voluntarily and which is not at the mercy of that suffering.[30] Gavrilyuk thus makes the claim that a compassionate person can remain impassible to the extent that they are able to manage their compassionate response in order to help the one who suffers.[31] Lest it seem that he is trying to have it both ways, we also note Gavrilyuk's finer argument that in Patristic theology, "divine impassibility functioned as an *apophatic qualifier* of all divine emotions and served to rule out those passions and experiences that were unbecoming of the divine nature."[32]

Gavrilyuk steps his readers through the way that the problem of impassibility is dealt with in the Christological controversies of the first five centuries of the Church, namely, the positions emerging in Docetism (which emphasized the Son's divinity to the extent that in suffering, the Son could only *appear* to be human), Patripassianism (which emphasized the unity of the Father and the Son to the extent that the Father suffered along with the Son), Arianism (which emphasized that the suffering of the Son precluded his full identification with the divine Father) and Nestorianism (which emphasized two "subjects" in Christ, one human, and one divine, and ascribed the suffering to the human).[33] He lauds the determinative contribution of Cyril of Alexandria, who argues that as a single "subject," God chooses to become incarnate and suffer *in that incarnation*. This is a theology of *kenosis* (self-emptying).

The biblical foundation of the theology of kenosis is principally found in Phil. 2:6-7: "though [Christ Jesus] was in the form [*μορφή*, *morphē*] of

---

[29]Gavrilyuk, *Suffering of the Impassible*, 11.

[30]In a similar vein, with regard to compassion in the work of Hugh of St Victor: "'Co-suffering' here renders Hugh's '*compassio*', which could, of course, also be translated as 'compassion'. But 'compassion', especially since the middle of the 17th century, is used with a dizzying array of meanings, which may or may not be consonant with Hugh's meaning. The woodenly literal 'co-suffering' is nevertheless useful in forming a contrasting parallel with 'suffering', used consistently here to render Hugh's '*passio*'. Frequently, Hugh relates '*passio*' to '*compassio*' in various ways, which is more apparent in translation when these are rendered 'suffering' and 'co-suffering' respectively. Nonetheless, 'cosuffering' risks collapsing the distinction between the one who suffers and the one who is affected psychically by it. With all this in mind, I sometimes render *compassio* as 'co-suffering' and sometimes as 'compassion', despite its attendant ambiguities." Boyd Taylor Coolman, "Hugh of St. Victor on 'Jesus Wept': Compassion as Ideal Humanitas," *Theological Studies* 69, no. 3 (2008): 535.

[31]Gavrilyuk, *Suffering of the Impassible*, 8–11.

[32]Gavrilyuk, *Suffering of the Impassible*, 16.

[33]Gavrilyuk, *Suffering of the Impassible*, 16–19.

God,/ [he] did not regard equality with God/ as something to be exploited,/ but emptied himself,/ taking the form of a slave." Biblical scholar Gordon D. Fee asks whether we are to interpret this passage literally or metaphorically. "Did he literally 'empty himself *of something*' when he took the form of a slave? Or did he metaphorically 'make himself nothing' by assuming the form of a slave, in becoming human?" Conducting a linguistic analysis, Fee suggests that it refers to the way Christ emptied himself and should be read metaphorically in the sense of he "made himself nothing."[34] Taking a completely contrasting, philosophical approach, Stephen T. Davis reads *kenosis* in a classically theistic way and in terms of the *communicatio idiomatum*. Davis argues that the divine *kenosis* in becoming human involves giving up any divine properties that would be inconsistent with being human (as well as any human properties that would be inconsistent with being divine). This would mean, for example, that the God-human, Jesus Christ, would be neither omniscient, omnipotent, or impassible, for example, nor sinful.[35] Davis claims that whether or not this makes sense, however, is dependent on whether one reads those divine properties in a "strong" or a "soft" sense. A strong sense would interpret those properties absolutely, whereas a soft sense would place the emphasis on God's consistency and choice to act in particular ways, which would involve accepting "the doctrine that God is not fickle, capricious, mercurial, or moody; God's holy and benevolent nature remains ever and eternally the same; God is faithful in keeping God's promises; God's aims and intentions for human beings do not change."[36] We suggest the Philippians passage reads more clearly as "although [the Word of God] showed who God is,/ [the Word] did not regard being equal to God/ as something to hold onto at all costs,/ but let go [of this divine visibility] completely,/ becoming visible [instead] as a slave."[37] On this reading, we see that it is the divine Word (God's self-expression) who voluntarily becomes incarnate (as Christ Jesus) and becomes the subject of the suffering. Oliver Davies qualifies the meaning of this letting-go, or "self-dispossession" of *kenosis* to include the element of risk: "Where ... the self *allows itself to be put at risk for the sake of the other*, it can be described as *kenotic*." Moreover, he makes very clear the relationship between compassion and *kenosis*: "The highest expression of this cognitive,

[34]Gordon D. Fee, "The New Testament and Kenosis Christology," in *Exploring Kenotic Christology: The Self-Emptying of God*, ed. C. Stephen Evans (Regent College, 2010), 33.

[35]Stephen T. David, "Is Kenosis Orthodox?" in *Exploring Kenotic Christology*, 118. There is an inherent flaw in this reasoning, since being finite could not be attributed to God.

[36]David, "Is Kenosis Orthodox?" 136–7.

[37]We have been greatly assisted in reading this passage by the analysis in Markus Bockmuehl, "'The Form of God' (Phil. 2:6) Variations on a Theme of Jewish Mysticism," *Journal of Theological Studies* 48, no. 1 (1997): 1–23.

affective and volitional displacement of the self for the sake of the other is compassion."[38]

So, we return to John's presentation of Jesus in chapter 11. How has this been understood at different points in Christian tradition? We begin with Augustine, writing in the fourth and fifth centuries. We noted earlier that in the most extreme position of the Stoics, reason is entirely absent from the passions. In contrast, Augustine presents Jesus' being troubled as entirely in accordance with his (divine) will, which is in accord with rationality.[39] As Brachtendorf observes: "Whereas humans in their infirmity are affected externally and experience passions—often against their will—Christ is always the master of his passions."[40] Yet, it is sometimes right for human beings to be affected by sorrow, especially in the light of sin.[41] Augustine's own slow reckoning with grief in the *Confessions* shows a transformation from his believing that grief reveals a misguided affection for those other than God in Book 4 to his understanding that the tears of grief are valid and important—even if he chooses to indulge in them only before God and not in the company of others:

> Now, all at once, I had lost her, and I found comfort in weeping in your sight, about her and for her, about myself and for myself. The tears that I had been holding in I now set free to flow as much as they would, a flood that bore up my heart so that it rested upon them. For it was your ears that heard my weeping, not the ears of any human being who would twist the meaning of my tears to suit his own pride.[42]

Augustine interprets Jesus' weeping as a model to emulate: "For why did Christ weep, but to teach man to weep?"[43] The example of Jesus' weeping can also bring consolation to those who weep.[44] According to Augustine, however—as for many commentators on John—Christ weeps in light of

[38]Oliver Davies, *A Theology of Compassion: Metaphysics of Difference and the Renewal of Tradition* (William B. Eerdmans, 2003), xxi [emphasis added], 32. In the introduction from which we quote "self-dispossession," Davies actually refers to "the self-dispossession of compassion" and not "the self-dispossession of kenosis," which suggests that he actually identifies compassion and *kenosis*.

[39]Noting that the Word has taken on human nature entirely, Augustine explains that "The soul and flesh of Christ is one person with the Word of God, one Christ. And by this [Word] wherein resided the supreme power, was infirmity made use of at the beck of His will; and in this way 'He troubled Himself'." Augustine, Commentary on John, in *Christian Classics Ethereal Library*, series 1, volume 7, ed. Philip Shaff (Christian Classics Ethereal Library, 2009) XI:1-54, 18.

[40]Brachtendorf, "'Et lacrymatus est Jesus'," 241.

[41]Augustine, Commentary on John XI:1-54, 19.

[42]Augustine, *The Confessions* [397], ed. and trans. Thomas Williams (Hackett, 2019), 12.33, 160.

[43]Augustine, Commentary on John XI:1-54, 18–19.

[44]Augustine, Commentary on John XII:27-36, 3.

his own impending death. He also weeps because he is sorrowful for weak persons who do not understand his mission and may be condemned.[45] Finally, in commenting on John's presentation of Jesus' soul being troubled in chapter 12, Augustine argues that it is a matter of a strong versus a weak will: "He has taught you here what to think of, what to say, on whom to call, in whom to hope, and whose will, as sure and divine, to prefer to your own, which is human and weak."[46] None of these positions suggests that in Augustine's understanding, Jesus weeps either in sorrow for Lazarus or in compassion for Mary.

Writing in the first half of the twelfth century, Abbot Bernard of Clairvaux writes of his grief for his brother Gerard in Sermon 26 of the *Sermons on the Song of Songs*.[47] It is striking that Bernard, like Augustine in some ways, feels initial reticence about showing his grief through tears before others lest it be interpreted as a loss of faith.[48] He describes celebrating Gerard's funeral and holding back his tears: "While others wept, I, as you could not but see, followed with dry eyes in the wake of the cruel bier, stood with dry eyes at the grave side till the last solemn funeral rite was performed." Poignantly, as he performs these rites, others cry with "pity" (or "compassion"): "The eyes that beheld me were filled with tears, and the wonder was that I did not weep, since all took pity, not so much on him who had gone as on me who had lost him. Who would not be moved, even with iron for a heart, at seeing me there living on without my Gerard." Yet, eventually the pain (both physical and emotional) of holding back his tears builds to a point where Bernard can bear it no longer:

> With all the force of faith that I could muster I resisted my feelings, striving, against my will, not to be vainly upset by what is but our natural destiny, a debt that all must pay by the law of our condition, by the command of God and his just judgment; the God we must fear because it is he who strikes, his will we must accept. Since then all the time I have forced myself to refrain from much weeping, though inwardly much troubled and sad. I could control my tears but could not control my sadness; in the Scripture's words: "I was troubled and did not speak." But the sorrow that I suppressed struck deeper roots within, growing all the

---

[45]Brachtendorf, "'Et lacrymatus est Jesus'," 242–3.

[46]Augustine, Commentary on John XII:27-36, 3.Trans. modified.

[47]Bernard of Clairvaux, *Sermons on the Song of Songs* [1138] (Fig Classic Series, 2013), 1520, 1522.

[48]Bernard of Clairvaux, *Sermons on the Song of Songs*, II.3. "Thus emotion, born unintentionally, involved the movement of the rational soul and was potentially controlled by reason, and so, ultimately, by the will. Irrepressible emotions fell within the realm of moral responsibility, since the soul was to step in to repress them if inappropriate. In this way, the weakness of nature coming from the malediction of original sin was transformed into an individual failure of reason, which was to exercise responsibility over the emotions." Boquet and Nagy, "Medieval Sciences of Emotions," 328.

> more bitter, I realized, because it found no outlet. I confess, I am beaten. All that I endure within must needs issue forth. But let it be poured out before the eyes of my sons, who, knowing my misfortune, will look with kindness on my mourning and afford more sweet sympathy.[49]

The use of the words "pity" (*miseracordia*) and "sympathy" (*compassio*) with respect to his community in Bernard's text is striking, and in modern English, we might think of "empathy" as appropriate to this context. Empathy, however, is not a medieval concept.

Juanita Feros Ruys helpfully explains the meaning components of empathy:

> Empathy is a cognitive-affective complex, meaning that it includes, and is indeed prompted by, a cognitive component in which the subject willingly undertakes the perspective of another. This is then closely allied with an affective component, in which the subject uses the perspective of the other to consider his or her own likely emotional response should he or she be in the other's situation and to feel those emotions in some form and to some extent—this feeling component can be termed "sympathy."[50]

Ruys goes on to explain that "there are three key Latin terms which capture aspects of this cognitive-affective complex: *misericordia, clementia,* and *compassio. Misericordia* ... translates most accurately as 'pity'," which includes the sense of its needing to be deserved.[51] *Clementia*, with its legal overtones, is well captured by its modern English equivalent, "clemency." "Of the three key Latin terms," Ruys determines, "only *compassio* captures the interaction of judgment and feeling entailed by the term 'empathy'."[52]

Now, it happens that Bernard's contemporary, Hugh of St Victor, reads the story of the raising of Lazarus in John 11 as an example of Jesus' compassion.[53] In an examination of the theme of compassion in Hugh, Boyd Taylor Coolman argues that compassion can be defined as "affective

---

[49]Bernard of Clairvaux, *Sermons on the Song of Songs*, II.3. Commenting on the constructed nature of the text, Anna Harrison nevertheless writes: "in SC 26 Bernard is striving to paint himself as (and maybe to become) the man he believes he ought to be—for God and for others: a man who responds to the death of another with grief that sounds the depths of his emotional attachment to the deceased but does not compromise his faith. In so doing, Bernard sculpted a lesson about grief to pass on to others." Anna Harrison, "'Jesus Wept': Mourning as Imitation of Christ in Bernard's Sermon Twenty-Six on the Song of Songs," *Cistercian Studies Quarterly* 48, no. 4 (2013): 441.

[50]Juanita Feros Ruys, "Carnal Compassion: Peter Abelard's Conflicted Approach to Empathy," in *The Intellectual Dynamism of the High Middle Ages*, ed. Clare Monagle (Amsterdam University Press, 2021), 26.

[51]Ruys, "Carnal Compassion," 26.

[52]Ruys, "Carnal Compassion," 27.

[53]Coolman, "Hugh of St. Victor on 'Jesus Wept'."

participation in the experience of another."[54] Analyzing Hugh's *De quatuor voluntatibus in Christo libellus* (*A Little Book on the Four Wills in Christ*), Coolman explains how Hugh works out theologically the possibility that Christ—while divine and human—can feel authentic compassion. This is a complex analysis. Coolman clarifies that for Hugh, the divine will in Christ is that he must die in order to restore justice. Hugh then divides the human will into three components: the *secundum rationem* ("rational human will," which agrees with the divine judgment), the *secundem pietatem* ("a compassionate, psychosomatic response to the evil that befalls another"), and the *secundem carnem* ("according to the flesh"—"the body's natural, even instinctive, resistance to physical suffering").[55] The *secundem pietatam* can be identified in Hugh not only as *compassio* but also as the *mentis pietas*, the "will of tender pity." This will of tender pity is also linked in Hugh to *misericordiam* ("the feeling of heart-wretchedness"), which reflects Jesus' desire that no one be condemned.[56] "In contrast to traditional attempts to account for Jesus' fear of death," Coolman writes, "which are typically motivated by the commentator's anxiety over this emotion in Jesus, it is in fact Hugh's high estimation of compassion as the proper and signature feature of Jesus' humanity that prompts him not only to make christological sense of Jesus' tears, but also to hold up Jesus as exemplar of such human affectivity."[57] Once again, however, we see that Hugh relates Jesus' compassion to humanity more generally, instead of to Mary more particularly.

We pointed out earlier that the description of Jesus in John 11 just prior to his weeping includes his being "deeply moved and troubled." Analyzing this section and the following chapters of John in Thomas Aquinas' *Commentary* on John's Gospel, Richard Schenk writes that Thomas consistently interprets *turbatio* as *tristitia* (sadness, or sorrow).[58] According to Brachendorf, *tristia* "belongs to the highest intensity level of the primary desirous passions" and has "the gravest somatic effects."[59] Of the *Commentary* on John 11, Schenk writes: "Thomas does not read Christ's anger as directed against those who are mourning; quite to the contrary, Thomas sees the mourning of the Jews with Martha and Mary as commendable and the mourning of Jesus throughout these chapters as parenetic."[60] Shenck identifies five features of

[54]Coolman, "Hugh of St. Victor on 'Jesus Wept'," 531.
[55]Coolman, "Hugh of St. Victor on 'Jesus Wept'," 238, 533–5.
[56]Coolman, "Hugh of St. Victor on 'Jesus Wept'," 537–8, 540ff.
[57]Coolman, "Hugh of St. Victor on 'Jesus Wept'," 532–3. On Hugh's influence on Thomas Aquinas, see Paul Gondreau, *The Passions of Christ's Soul in the Theology of St. Thomas Aquinas* (University of Scranton Press, 2009), 73–6.
[58]Schenk, "And Jesus Wept," 221. Schenk observes that some exegetes resist the idea that Jesus' tears equate to sadness, which means that it is difficult to interpret them, especially if the prior disturbance is interpreted as anger (223).
[59]Brachtendorf, "'Et lacrymatus est Jesus'," 235.
[60]Schenk, "And Jesus Wept," 226–7.

the fact and significance of Jesus' sadness for Thomas: that it is sadness about human death; that it is appropriate in the context of Jesus' mourning (for Lazarus and with Mary); that Jesus' sadness demonstrates his profound humanity (Thomas supports the doctrine that Christ only suffers precisely as human); that Jesus shows not only love for Lazarus but also love and thus saving intent for all humanity; and finally, that we are to emulate Jesus' mourning, which is proportionate and in accord with reason (contra the Stoics).[61] Jean-Pierre Torrell notes: "curiously, Aquinas never speaks of compassion or pity with respect to Christ, even though [Thomas] clearly defines it as a kind of sorrow over an evil that befalls another."[62] However, in Thomas' *Commentary*, we read:

> Christ experiences a certain weakness in his human affections, becoming disturbed over the death of Lazarus. We read, "*he was deeply moved in spirit and troubled himself.*"
>
> In regard to this disturbance, we should note his compassion; secondly, his discernment; and thirdly, his power. There is compassion (*pietatem*) for a right reason, for one is rightly troubled by the sadness and the evils which afflict others.[63]

So, Thomas does, indeed, speak of Christ's compassion—if we adopt this translation of *pietatem*. We could take the general reference to "others" to include Mary. While Schenk identifies that Jesus' compassion is for Lazarus in his death and Mary in her mourning, his reference to number 1537 does not actually identify them as the *subjects* of Jesus' compassion: "Next, our Lord reveals his emotion with tears; the Evangelist says, '*he wept*'. Now his tears did not flow from necessity, but out of compassion and for a purpose. Christ was a well-spring of compassion, and he wept in order to show us that it is not blameworthy to weep out of compassion ...." Again, it could be inferred from the context that Jesus' compassion arises in relation to Mary. That his sorrow is directed toward Lazarus is implied in number 1538: "The Evangelist infers that some sympathize with Christ's affection when he says, '*So the Jews said*', after Christ showed his affections by his words and tears, '*See how he loved him*!': for love is especially manifested when people are afflicted."

While there are other commentaries on John 11 or Jesus' weeping extant in history, we turn now for sake of contrast to a contemporary

---

[61]Schenk, "And Jesus Wept," 227–34. See also Thomas Aquinas, *Summa Theologiae*, III. q.35. a.6.

[62]Jean-Pierre Torrell in his preface to Gondreau, *Passions of Christ's Soul*, 13. Note Gondreau's reference to the absence of pity in Aquinas' analysis of Christ's passions (403).

[63]Thomas Aquinas, *Commentary on the Gospel of John, Books 6-12*, trans. Fabian Larcher and James A. Weishelpl, with an Introduction by Daniel A. Keating and Matthew Levering (Catholic University of America Press, 2010), vol. 2, lecture 5, nn. 1532 and 1533.

theological understanding of Jesus' passions, particularly with respect to the vexed question of divine suffering. As Gavrilyuk observes, there are many twentieth-century examples of "theopaschism," that is, theological positions committed to the suffering of God the Father as well as God the Son.[64] With a novel twist, contemporary theologian and philosopher Emmanuel Falque argues that through the death of Christ Jesus, God the Father *also* experiences suffering. First, Falque observes the suffering of God incarnate, who alone, as divine, is capable of transforming human suffering:

> We then come to understand, through the person of the suffering Christ, the cry born from a feeling of being totally abandoned, a feeling that goes so far as a "rupture of the flesh," so that the Other in him (his Father), who is also with him, takes upon himself the burden of insurmountable corruptibility and makes it pass into the incorruptible glory of the resurrection.[65]

Next, Falque points out as a corollary the divine suffering that arises from the death of the incarnate Word: "Surely the God of Christians is precisely and paradoxically a God who, in his Son, to say the least, *dies*."[66] Evidently (and contra Patripassianism) God the Father does not suffer by dying on the cross. "On the contrary," Falque argues, "[God the Father] suffers all the more from the death of the Son, since *he himself* does not die."[67] We may choose to address this divine suffering in a way that Gavrilyuk might sanction: God suffers not because God is inherently vulnerable but because God chooses to enter into vulnerability. Falque then quotes Gustave Martelet to explain further the dimensions of divine suffering:

> The Son has become so completely man that he is capable henceforth of experiencing in his flesh (the worst of) the human, and *to make Him from whom he came encounter it*. Having become one of us, *he is empowered by his humanity to disclose to the Father, in a way that is not simply divine but also human*, this tragedy that is truly ours and that is above all only ours.[68]

---

[64]Ronald Goetz claims: "A list of modern theopaschite thinkers would include Barth, Berdyaev, Bonhoeffer, Brunner, Cobb, Cone and liberation theologians generally, Küng, Moltmann, Reinhold Niebuhr, Pannenberg, Ruether and feminist theologians generally, Temple, Teilhard and Unamuno." Ronald Goetz, "The Suffering God: The Rise of a New Orthodoxy," *Christian Century* (April 16, 1986).

[65]Emmanuel Falque, *The Guide to Gethsemane*, trans. George Hughes (Fordham University Press, 1999/2019), 2.

[66]Falque, *Guide*, 44.

[67]Falque, *Guide*, 63.

[68]Gustave Martelet, quoted with Falque's bracketed insertion to the text in Falque, *Guide*, 77. Emphasis added.

The power of Falque's Christological analysis of suffering should not go unnoticed: first, in electing to become human, the Word enters into human suffering in a way that only the divine can transform and heal; second, that same election enables God the Creator to encounter the pain of separation and death; and third, the suffering of grief, as a human reality, is fully made known to God.[69]

Engaging in Dialogue with the Current Context

In our reading of John 11 we have focused on experiences of grief and compassion. Evidently, in a believing context, God's engagement with the reality of human pain and suffering speaks powerfully to the trauma of grief. Yet, in a non-believing context—in a world where there is no meaning beyond what presents itself in everyday life—what kinds of meaning might be drawn from a reflection on Jesus' encounter with Mary after Lazarus' death? In several of the commentaries on John 11, we saw Jesus' emotion understood to be motivated by judgment rather than compassion. What other situations are open to both these interpretations? Where is compassion called for over moral judgment?

Hannah Gadsby is an Australian comedian whose 2017 stage show, *Nanette*, was recorded and released as a video by Netflix in 2018. In *Nanette*, Gadsby discloses how she struggled to come to a positive sense of her identity as gay. Gadsby grew up on the Australian island state of Tasmania, where homosexuality was illegal until 1997. For the ten years prior to this and further law reforms in 1999, Tasmanian public debate on homosexuality was vitriolic. She writes:

> Seventy percent of the people … I lived amongst … believe that homosexuality should be … a criminal act. Seventy percent of the people who raised me, who loved me, who I trusted, believed that homosexuality was a sin, that homosexuals were heinous, sub-human pedophiles. Seventy percent. By the time I identified as being gay, it was too late. I was already homophobic, and you do not get to just flick a switch on that. No, what you do is you internalize that homophobia and you learn to hate yourself. Hate yourself to the core. I sat soaking in shame … in the closet, for ten years. Because the closet can only stop you from being seen. It is not shame-proof. When you soak a child in shame, they cannot develop the neurological pathways that carry thought … you know, carry thoughts of self-worth. They can't do that. Self-hatred is only ever a seed

[69]Falque has extended this into a Trinitarian model where the Spirit is the force that drives or propels or energizes the incarnation. See Emmanuel Falque, "Trinitarian Kenosis and the Limits of Phenomenology," *Revista portuguesa de filosofia* 76, no. 2–3 (2020): 891.

> planted from outside in. But when you do that to a child, it becomes a weed so thick, and it grows so fast, the child doesn't know any different. It becomes … as natural as gravity. When I came out of the closet, I didn't have any jokes. The only thing I knew how to do was to be invisible and hate myself. It took me ten years to understand I was allowed to take up space in the world.[70]

There was a particular poignancy to the timing of the appearance of *Nanette*. In 2016, the right-leaning Australian government determined that the only way to resolve pressure for law reform to allow same-sex marriage was to hold a national plebiscite in 2017. This meant that the focus of campaigning, for or against, would allow much of the vitriol exemplified in the Tasmanian debate in the 1990s to be re-aired. In a 2016 Facebook post, Gadsby warned:

> I don't care about marriage equality for myself because I do not have an aptitude for relationships. The reason I care about this is because I don't want young kids to hear the kind of horrific bile I was forced to listen to in the 1990s when Tasmania debated on whether to legalise homosexuality. For many, the debate was theatre. For me, it made me hate myself so deeply I have never been able to develop an aptitude for relationships.
>
> In the mid nineties I was the age when I should have been learning how to be vulnerable, how to handle a broken heart, how to deal with rejection and how to deal with all the other great silly things about young love which help pave the way to the more substantial adult version. But instead I learnt how to close myself off and rot quietly in self-hatred. I learnt this because I learnt that I was subhuman during a debate where only the most horrible voices and ideas were amplified by the media. These voices also gave permission for others to tell me that I was less than them, with looks, words and on one occasion, violence.[71]

In *Nanette*, we learn that Gadsby was raped by a man who initially thought she was another man flirting with his girlfriend. Having started to move away from Gadsby with his girlfriend, the man suddenly realized Gadsby was a lesbian. He returned to her and committed the rape as part of a violent assault: "He beat the shit out of me and nobody stopped him. I didn't report him to the police. And I didn't take myself to hospital. And I should have. But I didn't, because that's all I thought I was worth. That's what happens

[70]Madeleine Parry and Jon Olb, *Hannah Gadsby: Nanette* (Netflix, 2018), Video.

[71]Hannah Gadsby, Facebook (August 24, 2016), https://www.facebook.com/hannahgadsbycomedy/posts/oh-hey-guys-this-plebiscite-thing-is-a-very-bad-idea-the-very-idea-of-an-ongoing/10154475124958000/.

when you soak one child in shame and give permission to another to hate." Most telling of all is that Gadsby reveals: "I'm still ashamed of who I am. Not intellectually. But, right there, I still have shame."

It is likely that relatively few people who commented in public or in private about the plebiscite and the kinds of rights that should be afforded to gay people have ever reflected on what Gadsby expresses as extreme self-loathing. Quite possibly, many imagine that to be gay is to make "a lifestyle choice" and, subsequently, to encounter prejudice. Gadsby's articulation of her ongoing sense of shame about who she is—a shame based on a judgment of homosexuality that she has absorbed almost from the cradle—discloses a much more nuanced understanding of her situation. She cannot help but be brought to admit her sexual identity, and therefore, she cannot help but agree with those who will judge her to be shameful. To be herself, she must hate herself, and therein self-destruct. As she observes in *Nanette*:

> I paid dearly for a lesson that nobody seems to have wanted to learn. And this is bigger ... than homosexuality. This is about how we conduct debate in public about sensitive things. It's toxic, it's juvenile, it's destructive. We think it's more important to be right than it is to appeal to the humanity of people we disagree with. Ignorance will always walk amongst us because we will never know all of the things.

And Jesus wept.

How Is the Text Speaking to Me (or Us) Today?

Return to the text and reread it. Bring the scene of Mary and Jesus before you. Where do you recognize that scene in your life? What emotions does it arouse in you? How does the text speak to your experiences of grief? How does the text speak to your need for compassion? How does it speak to your desire to be compassionate? Remember the story of the woman caught in adultery in Chapter 2 and the making visible of her shame. Think about the story of Zaccheus in Luke 19 and the social judgment of tax collectors in the previous chapter of Luke. Reflect on the experience of the man born blind, healed by Jesus in John 9, in a society where disability was frequently considered punishment for sin ("'Rabbi, who sinned, this man or his parents, that he was born blind?'"). Return to the situation of the woman who bled continuously, considered in Chapter 3 of the present text. Jesus is often drawn to people who feel shame. Feeling shame often prevents individuals from becoming who they are. Consider the ways that societies punish people for being poor, for being of color, for having chronic disease, for not fitting into an idealized schema where there is only male or female, for representing weakness. Remember the words of Pope Francis when he is asked about homosexuality: "Who am I to judge?"[72] Reflect on what the German bishops have done in advocating blessings for same-sex unions and the offering of communion to the divorced and remarried.[73] Where is your compassion needed?

[72]"Pope Francis: Who Am I to Judge Gay People?" *BBC News* (London) July 29, 2013, https://www.bbc.com/news/world-europe-23489702.

[73]"German Catholic Bishops Back Blessings For Same-Sex Couples," *Deutsche Welle* (March 10, 2023), https://www.dw.com/en/german-catholic-bishops-back-blessings-for-same-sex-couples/a-64950775; "Bishops Give Blessing to Communion for Remarried," *Deutsche Welle* (February 1, 2017).

6

Jesus Turns the Tables: The Experience of Anger

In Chapter 5, we saw that it has been difficult for theology to think about the possibility of Jesus experiencing emotion. If we needed to do a lot of work to make grief and compassion possible for Jesus, so too will we need to exercise ourselves with the subject of the present chapter, which is Jesus' experience of anger. Anger is an emotion which often bears a judgment. It is an example of an emotion that screams being out of control and impacting negatively and perhaps unfairly on those who are on the other end of it. Anger often requires an apology. So, it is even more difficult for us to consider what place it has in the life of Jesus, "gentle Jesus, meek and mild." Can anger be okay? Does it have a legitimate place in human relationships? And, more frighteningly, do we not often remember the times we have been told that God will be angry with us for what we have done?

The Text: John 2:13-19

The Passover of the Jews was near, and Jesus went up to Jerusalem. In the temple he found people selling cattle, sheep, and doves, and the money-changers seated at their tables. Making a whip of cords, he drove all of them out of the temple, both the sheep and the cattle. He also poured out the coins of the money-changers and overturned their tables. He told those who were selling the doves, "Take these things out of here! Stop making my Father's house a market-place!" His disciples remembered that it was written, "Zeal for your house will consume me." The Jews then said to him, "What sign can you show us for doing this?" Jesus answered them, "Destroy this temple, and in three days I will raise it up."

The Role of the Imagination in Prayer

There is a long history in the Christian tradition of the use of imagination in prayer, and it is particularly central in Ignatian spirituality. David Fleming writes that as one moves through the Spiritual Exercises "the imagination becomes a tool to help us know and love God."[1] Praying in this way, he says, "teaches us things about Jesus that we would not learn through scripture study or theological reflection. It allows the person of Christ to penetrate into places that the intellect does not touch."[2] There are many approaches to the use of imagination when praying with scripture, but they all have in common the invitation to imagine the scene as though it is happening around us and as though we are active participants. Gerard W. Hughes provides some helpful guidance for praying imaginatively.[3] He recommends that we take our time when imagining the scene. There should be nothing hurried about it; we should feel free to take a look around and "let the scene build up."[4] He recommends that we notice what we see and hear, talk to the characters, listen to them, and notice how we feel as we do so. The idea is to let our imaginations lead but remember that the focus of our attention should be on Jesus. This form of prayer aims to enable a person to experience God speaking through the text, and when Jesus is present in the story, it is possible for God to speak in ways that go well beyond words.

A type of imaginative prayer that is usually undertaken in a group setting is guided meditation. In a guided meditation, a leader uses questions or prompts to guide participants through their prayer. Participants are invited to enter into the scene, to use their senses, to be attentive to their emotions, and to experience being in Jesus' presence. While this process can be undertaken individually, often the prompting of the leader in a group setting can support participants to set aside any distractions and be more present to the prayer. The leader might take the approach of retelling the narrative, pausing often to allow time for the imagination, or they might pose a series of questions to help guide the meditation. Some questions that might be used in a guided meditation on Jn 2:13-19 include: As you enter the temple compound, what do you see? What do you hear? What do you smell? Taste? Touch? How do your senses speak to you? Where do you find yourself? Are you a character in the story? If so, who? Are you in the midst of the action, or do you watch from the sidelines? How do you feel as you see the events unfolding around you? Where is Jesus? What do you notice about him? What does he do and say? Does Jesus speak to you? How does

---

[1]Fleming, *What Is Ignatian Spirituality?* 25.
[2]Fleming, *What Is Ignatian Spirituality?* 26.
[3]Gerard W. Hughes, *God of Surprises*, Rev. and updated ed. (Darton, Longman and Todd, 2008), 52–3.
[4]Hughes, *God of Surprises*, 52.

it feel to be addressed by him? If you could ask Jesus one question or say one thing in this moment, what might it be? In our reflection below, we have used a number of these questions to contemplate the text. We have placed ourselves in the midst of the action and tried to capture a sense of what it might have been like to be there.

Guided Meditation on John 2:13-19

My friend and I have come to the outer court of the temple. Passover is near, and temple tax is due. We must pay in silver, so we need to exchange our Roman coins.[5] The scene is chaotic. Doves, mostly in cages, are cooing and flapping their wings. Some have escaped and are flying around. Oxen and sheep shuffle and bleat. They chew on piles of hay and long grasses. Do they have any idea of the slaughter that awaits them, I wonder. The sweet smell of grasses mixes with the stench of the livestock. There is chatter, laughter, people calling out, old friends exchanging greetings, shaking hands, embracing one another. I hear music a little way off, with clapping and dancing feet. Excitement and anticipation fill the air. The sellers stand by their tables, calling to one another and to people in the crowd: "Oxen here!" "Buy your doves!"

A woman—a beggar—hunches over in the corner, exhorting me with an outstretched hand, but she is unable to meet my gaze. I wonder who this woman is when she is away from the crowds. Does she laugh with her friends as I do? Does she hold her children close and tell them stories of far-away places? Does she hope? Does she dance? I wonder what she thinks of this spectacle. To many here, she is invisible. What would she say if she knew that what she said would be heard? A young boy comes to join her. He sits down beside her and reaches an arm around her shoulder, and a smile crosses her face. He talks excitedly and incessantly. I cannot hear his words above the noise, but his mother is soon engrossed in his story.

Then I see *him*—Jesus of Nazareth. He is usually gentle but authoritative when he teaches, but something is different today. He moves quickly into the space and his eyes dart around the forecourt, taking in the scene. As he turns on his heel, his face grows increasingly red with anger. Without a word, he removes the cords tethered around the necks of livestock nearby. He twists the cords together into a whip, and with a crack of the whip and a hand to their rumps, he releases the beasts. They run around the space and then out the gate as people leap out of their way. All eyes are on him now. There he stands, arms outstretched, breathing deeply, eyes aflare, with the whip held

[5]We realize that this task was likely reserved for adult men in first-century Jerusalem, but as this is an imaginative contemplation, we see no reason why we can't imagine ourselves as females and also in the midst of the action.

ready. *What has made him so angry?* People nearby stare at him in alarm and rush to the side as he begins to wield the whip, driving out the rest of the cattle. He is yet to say a word. He strides over to the moneychangers, upturning their tables and sending their coins flying. Only then does he speak. He addresses the dove-sellers directly, but his tone leaves no doubt that he is speaking to all: "Take these things out of here! Stop making my Father's house a market-place!"

I find myself unable to move. I am transfixed by him. His face is red, his eyes wild, his voice sharp. He is almost unrecognizable. Anger seems to have arisen in him like a match which sets gas aflame, spewing forth from his body. His anger is so palpable I can almost taste it. It is all-consuming. I want to speak to him, but what would I say? I remember the Psalm (69:9-12):

> zeal for your house consumes me,
> and the insults of those who insult you fall on me.
> When I weep and fast,
> I must endure scorn;
> when I put on sackcloth,
> people make sport of me.
> Those who sit at the gate mock me,
> and I am the song of the drunkards.

The psalmist is indeed a prophet. As I stare at Jesus, I can almost hear his thoughts ... *How dare you! How dare you forget your call to serve! You worship my Father and yet you use your worship for your own gain. You love this house for what it can give you. You take from it. You rid it of its warmth. You forget the love that that sits at its heart. Your love is ugly and twisted ... It is your twisted love that consumes me.* With a sharp breath and arms outstretched in cruciform, he screams: "Get out!!!"

All I can utter is "It is *you* Lord, here, today, in all of your humanity and vulnerability. In your anger, you call us to be more."

Engaging in Critical Dialogue with Biblical Tradition

This narrative is amongst the most well known of Jesus' ministry, and there is almost unanimous agreement among biblical scholars that the event is historical.[6] The story appears in all four gospels, but with a

[6]For a survey of literature on the question of historicity, see Klyne R. Snodgrass, "The Temple Incident," in *Key Events in the Life of the Historical Jesus: A Collaborative Exploration of Context and Coherence*, ed. Darrell L. Bock and Robert L. Webb (Mohr Siebeck, 2009), 429–80.

different placement and much more detail in John. Here, we find it at the beginning of Jesus' ministry (early in the Book of Signs, 1:19-12:50) as a foreshadow of the resurrection. In the synoptics, it is placed at the end of his ministry and linked with his trial and passion.[7] Only in John's account do we read of Jesus driving out the cattle and sheep, wielding a whip of cords, pouring out the coins of the money-changers, and speaking to the dove-sellers, and only here do we read that the disciples are present and that they remember the words of scripture: "Zeal for your house will consume me" (v. 17).[8] There is no doubt that the scene is vivid, emotive, and full of action, but the reasons for Jesus' anger are not given explicitly in the gospel accounts.

Earlier in this book when we explored the death of Lazarus, we spoke of the theological development that took place between the First and the Fourth Gospels, and we noted that John reaches back to the creation of the world to show that God speaks God's Word (or Wisdom) in flesh in the God-human Jesus: "In the beginning was the Word, and the Word was with God, and the Word was God. ... And the Word became flesh and lived among us" (1:1, 14). This deep theological insight is the hermeneutical lens we (the readers) are invited to use as we engage with the whole Johannine text. Mary Coloe expresses this clearly when she writes, "because the world was created through the Word and became the *locus* for the Word, material reality is open to and can mediate a transcendent reality."[9] The hermeneutics of the Prologue, therefore, invites, even "*demands* a 'symbolic' reading of the text."[10] While the event itself is understood to have taken place in history, in the Johannine account, Jesus' emotions, actions, and words, the disciples, "the Jews," and even the temple itself function as symbols.[11]

The focus of our attention here is the curious juxtaposition of the lively marketplace in the outer court of the temple in the lead-up to Passover and Jesus' visceral anger as he enters and takes in the scene. It was not unusual,

---

[7]Recall that in Chapter 5, we noted that John's Gospel can be divided into four main sections: the Prologue (1:1-18); the Book of Signs (1:19-12:50); the Book of Glory (the Easter events) (13:1-20:29) and a conclusion (20:30-31), with an epilogue (chapter 21) most likely to have been added later. Moloney, *Sacra Pagina: the Gospel of John*, 43–4.

[8]Moloney notes that v. 17 reimagines Psalm 69:9 in the future tense—the Johannine text reads "*will* consume me," rather than "*has* consumed me." Moloney, *Sacra Pagina: The Gospel of John*, 98. More on that later.

[9]Mary L. Coloe, *God Dwells with Us: Temple Symbolism in the Fourth Gospel* (Liturgical Press, 2001), 80.

[10]Coloe, *God Dwells with Us*, 79.

[11]Recall from Chapter 5 that in John, "the Jews" is a narrative device that is used to refer to a specific group of people who oppose Jesus or who are in conflict with Jesus and his followers. "Jewish people as such are not represented by the term 'the Jews,' and the Fourth Gospel must not be read as if they were." Moloney, *Sacra Pagina: The Gospel of John*, 30–3. For a detailed description of how "the Jews" is used in John's gospel as a narrative device, see R. Alan Culpepper, *Anatomy of the Fourth Gospel: A Study in Literary Design* (Fortress, 1983), 125–31.

after all, for the sellers and money changers to be there—ritual sacrifice and the payment of the temple tax were part of the yearly cycle of worship—but Jesus' actions and words present a curious challenge to the reader to consider the cause of his anger (or what his anger might symbolize), the particular message/s the author is trying to convey, and what the text might be telling us about who and how God is.

Enshrined in the book of Deuteronomy is the prescription for the Jewish community to travel to Jerusalem three times a year and offer a "gift" to God:

> Three times a year all your males shall appear before the Lord your God at the place that he will choose: at the festival of unleavened bread, at the festival of weeks, and at the festival of tabernacles. They shall not appear before the Lord empty-handed; all shall give as they are able, according to the blessing of the Lord your God that he has given you.
>
> (Deut. 16:16-17)

The Festival of Unleavened Bread refers to the seven days immediately following Passover (*Pesah*), which remembers Israel's liberation from Egypt when the Hebrews who had been enslaved by Pharaoh were instructed by Moses to slaughter a lamb, paint the blood of the lamb on their doorframes so that the angel of death "passes over" their house that night, and bake unleavened bread for the long journey they were to take out of Egypt the next morning (Exod. 12). During the Second Temple period (from the end of the Babylonian exile, c. 515 BCE, to the temple's destruction during the Roman-Jewish war in 70 CE), Jewish families would commemorate Passover by slaughtering a lamb in the temple and taking it home to be roasted (in accordance with Deut. 16:5-8).[12] Then they would eat unleavened bread for seven days. Other animals were sacrificed and burnt on the altar daily for seven days, in line with the ritual enshrined in the Hebrew texts (Num. 28:16-25).[13]

The Festival of Weeks (*Shabu'ot*) is the feast of the harvest. It is celebrated seven weeks (or fifty days) after Passover in thanksgiving to God for the

---

[12]Most scholars date the opening of the building around 515 BCE, noting that it began with the arrival of the Babylonian exiles to Israel in 539. Some scholars refer to the time between 63 BCE and 70 CE as the Third Temple period, due to the extensive renovations carried out by Herod. For a summary and images, see Paul J. Achtemeier, *Harper's Bible Dictionary*, 1st ed. (Harper & Row, 1985), 1021–32.

[13]From the writings of Josephus, we know that there were two altars in the temple: a bronze altar, which was used for animal sacrifices, and a gold altar, which was used for the burning of incense in front of the Ark of the Covenant. Josephus *Ant.* VIII. 104–5, cited in Maria-Zoe Petropoulou, "Jewish Animal Sacrifice in the Period 100 bc–ad 200," in *Animal Sacrifice in Ancient Greek Religion, Judaism, and Christianity, 100 BC to AD 200* (Oxford University Press, 2008), 138.

abundant harvest of wheat and includes the offering of bread (this time baked with yeast) as well as animals for burning:

> You shall bring from your settlements two loaves of bread as an elevation-offering, each made of two-tenths of an ephah; they shall be of choice flour, baked with leaven, as first fruits to the Lord. You shall present with the bread seven lambs a year old without blemish, one young bull, and two rams; they shall be a burnt-offering to the Lord, along with their grain-offering and their drink-offerings, an offering by fire of pleasing odour to the Lord. You shall also offer one male goat for a sin-offering, and two male lambs a year old as a sacrifice of well-being. The priest shall raise them with the bread of the first fruits as an elevation-offering before the Lord, together with the two lambs; they shall be holy to the Lord for the priest.
>
> (Lev. 23:17-20)

The Festival of Tabernacles (or *Sukkot*) is also an agricultural feast, which marks the harvesting of fruit and the end of the full harvest season. Like Shabu'ot, it is a festival of thanksgiving for the abundance of God. It is also called the "Festival of Booths" because it was expected that males reside in a shelter outside the temple to commemorate the Israelites' travel through the desert after liberation from Egypt. The proximity of the "tents" to the temple, especially for travelers, enabled them to attend daily temple offerings of burnt animals, grain, and wine (Num. 29:12-39).

In her study of Jewish sacrifice in the late Second Temple period, Maria-Zoe Petropoulou notes the continued importance of public offerings in the temple, despite the fact that many members of the Jewish community were by then living away from Jerusalem (in other parts of Judea, Syria, Babylonia, Rome, and the Roman provinces of Crete, Cyrenaica, and Egypt).[14] She explains that animal sacrifices were made throughout the year, even under difficult circumstances: "for instance, when Pompey captured the temple: the priests continued to make the daily offerings as if nothing had happened, and they were slaughtered during their ministry."[15]

The temple was divided into several courts: moving inward from just inside the outer walls, we would first find the court of Jews and Gentiles, then the court for male and female Israelites only, then the court reserved for male Israelites, and finally the court for priests. Only the High Priest was allowed to enter the Holy of Holies—the sanctuary—which stood at the center of the temple complex.[16] Such was the centrality of sacrifice in the temple that, of course, it became "a magnet for merchants" who

---

[14]Petropoulou, "Jewish Animal Sacrifice," 128.
[15]Petropoulou, "Jewish Animal Sacrifice," 142.
[16]Petropoulou, "Jewish Animal Sacrifice," 139.

sold sacrificial animals and other religious and worship-related goods.[17] The marketplace for merchants would have been found just inside the outer walls, where Jews and Gentiles, male and female, were welcome, and its presence would not have been seen as offensive. Instead, it was particularly helpful for pilgrims who had travelled long distances and were unable to bring their own livestock with them for sacrifice. The sellers enabled pilgrims to participate in Israel's practices of worship.[18]

The annual "temple tax" was due around the time of Passover. Enshrined in Exod. 30:11-16, it was seen as an offering of atonement to God and was used for the temple's upkeep and to subsidize the temple's sacrifices.[19] It consisted of a half-shekel and was to be paid in silver coins from the mint of Tyre (hence they were known as Tyrian shekels). These shekels were not part of the Roman currency, and the people would have had to exchange Roman currency for acceptable coins. This places the moneychangers also in the outer court of the temple and, as Coloe notes, their presence was permitted by the rabbis.[20]

With this in mind, we return to the question that arose in our contemplation of this text: *What was the cause of Jesus' anger?* We have seen that the presence of the sellers and money changers was warranted, so what is it about the scene that has Jesus so angry?

Cecilia Wassen notes that a common argument made for Jesus' actions is that he is protesting against the "commercialism" of the temple trade, but it is not as simple as that (as we have seen) because the very nature of temple sacrifice required the supply of livestock.[21] Other possibilities relate to allegations of corruption on the part of the temple priests and the abuse of temple funds, as well as corrupt partnerships between temple leaders and the Roman government. Analyzing these allegations in light of extra-biblical sources from the first century—especially the Qumran texts, known as the Dead Sea Scrolls, and the texts of Josephus—Wassen finds that while the particulars of these allegations do not have extra-biblical support, it is likely that Jesus is "protest[ing] over corruption in general" and is therefore calling for reform.[22] Jesus' actions certainly seem to confirm this because they are not directed at individuals within the temple court: across the accounts

---

[17]Petropoulou, "Jewish Animal Sacrifice," 142.

[18]"Their presence made possible the cultic participation of every Israelite, and it was not only not a blemish on the cult but part of its perfection." Jacob Neusner, cited in Coloe, *John 1–10*, 69.

[19]Nehemiah 10:32-33.

[20]Coloe, *John 1–10*, 68.

[21]Cecilia Wassen, "The Use of the Dead Sea Scrolls for Interpreting Jesus's Action in the Temple," *Dead Sea Discoveries* 23, no. 3 (2016): 285–6.

[22]Wassen contends that while Jesus had no direct contact with members of the Qumran movement, their texts "provide evidence for the historical context of Jesus's deeds and words ... [and] provide a window into the Jewish world." Wassen, "The Use of the Dead Sea Scrolls," 280, 287.

given in each of the four gospels, his actions include overturning tables and chairs, and driving out moneychangers and sellers as well as members of the public. Drawing on the work of Craig Evans, Wassen takes this a step further to contend that although temple corruption might not have been taking place during Jesus' time in particular (and there is no compelling evidence of such corruption in the Qumran texts), there is certainly a *perception* at the time that the temple "is polluted and its priesthood corrupt."[23]

One compelling argument that Wassen makes in this regard relates to apocalyptic expectations that were widespread early in the first century. In the Qumran texts, Jewish Pseudepigrapha, Jewish prophetic literature and texts written around the time of the Maccabean revolt (*c.* 167 BCE)—which had been "reinterpreted by later generations as pertaining to their own time"—the temple is central to speculations about end times, when it "would become perfect as a true dwelling place for God."[24] She finds two central motifs in the literature: the perception of temple pollution and corruption coupled with the desire for "an eschatological renewed or rebuilt temple."[25]

Wassen's analysis of the Damascus Document (from the Qumran texts) reveals repeated references to the defilement of the temple at the end times, through the "sexual misdeeds of the people," the "corruption of the priesthood in general" (which includes the sinful acquisition and misuse of wealth), and the "defilement of the sanctuary."[26] For Wassen, the charges that relate to corruption are "reminiscent of the critique of the prophets against the wealthy."[27] In the Pseudepigrapha (the Jewish apocalyptic texts), there are also numerous references to this. Wassen writes:

> Jub. 23:21 claims that the priests will "pollute the holy of holies with their pollution and with corruption of their contamination." Similar accusations concerning greed, pride, and sexual depravity of the priests

[23]Wassen, "The Use of the Dead Sea Scrolls," 292. Wassen cites Craig A. Evans, "Jesus' Action in the Temple: Cleansing or Portent of Destruction?" in *Jesus in Context: Temple, Purity, and Restoration*, ed. Bruce Chilton and Craig A. Evans (Brill, 1997), 395–439.

[24]Wassen, "The Use of the Dead Sea Scrolls," 303. The catalyst for the Maccabean revolt was Antiochus IV's desecration of the temple and his issuing of a decree forbidding Jewish worship. When the temple was recaptured in 164 BCE by the group who came to be known as the Maccabees (because they were led by Judas Maccabeus and his family), it underwent a ritual cleansing, which is now remembered in the feast of Hanukkah.

[25]Wassen, "The Use of the Dead Sea Scrolls," 294.

[26]James H. Charlesworth, ed., *Damascus Document, War Scroll and Related Documents, vol. 2 of The Dead Sea Scrolls: Hebrew, Aramaic, and Greek Texts with English Translations* (Mohr Siebeck/Westminster John Knox, 1995), cited in Wassen, "The Use of the Dead Sea Scrolls," 294, 296.

[27]Wassen cites, for example, Mal 3:5; Jer 7:5-6; Amos 2:6-7, 4:1; Wassen, "The Use of the Dead Sea Scrolls," 295 n258.

> that defile the temple are found in the Testament of Levi (T. Levi 14-17). ... [F]uture priests are charged with corruption in the Testament of Moses (T. Mos. 5:4-5). Enoch 89:73 in the Animal Apocalypse claims that the priests will offer polluted food after the rebuilding of the temple ("tower"). The book of Daniel also predicts a future defilement of the temple in connection to its destruction, in very specific terms: 9:26-27:71.[28]

On this reading, "the expectations [*sic*] of an impure temple goes hand in hand with the strong hope for a new or renewed temple ... a new, glorified temple of divine origin."[29] It is against the backdrop of this literature, Wassen argues, that Jesus' actions in the temple must be understood: "Jesus, like the Qumran sectarians, assumed that the temple would become defiled and profaned at end times, which he believed was his own time."[30] She explains,

> The anticipation of the defilement of the temple offers an interpretative key for understanding Jesus's violent reaction in the temple. Simply put, Jesus believed the temple was defiled because it was supposed to become defiled at the end time. This explains the rage that he expressed. His last visit to Jerusalem began with an extraordinary entry whereby he acted as a royal character riding into Jerusalem and being hailed by his supporters as a Davidic king (Mark 11:9-10; Zech 9:9), which was followed by his enacted prophecy about destruction in the temple. These actions strongly suggest that Jesus was convinced that God's reign would begin instantaneously, which also implies that the temple had already begun to be defiled, and that destruction was looming overhead ....
>
> ... Anticipating the defilement and destruction of the temple as part of the end time scenario, Jesus enacted its demise symbolically by attacking people and things. It is inconceivable that Jesus would have acted in this way without being angry about something, without protesting against current practice. ... [H]e undoubtedly protested against the current defiled state of temple practice, although we cannot know if there was a specific aspect at which he aimed his anger.[31]

---

[28]Wassen, "The Use of the Dead Sea Scrolls," 298.

[29]Wassen, "The Use of the Dead Sea Scrolls," 299. Wassen cites Ezekial 295:211; 298–9.

[30]Wassen, "The Use of the Dead Sea Scrolls," 300.

[31]Wassen, "The Use of the Dead Sea Scrolls," 302, 303.With regard to this last point, Alicia D Myers argues that this is "what happens when the sacred is profaned." For Myers, "John uses this scene to amplify and confirm Jesus's identity as God's glory made flesh ... Jesus's arrival in the temple, therefore, is nothing less than a clash resulting from the holiness of God's glory encountering the profane in what should be a sacred place. The intensity of Jesus's reaction not only further reveals his identity but also reinforces the depth of the problem he faces in the world: Not even God's people can recognize the glory in the chosen sacred space." Alicia D. Myers, "Revelation Through Violence? Jesus in the Temple in John 2:13–22," *Review & Expositor* 120, no. 1–2 (2023): 47.

Admittedly, Wassen is drawing from the Markan account of this event, but we know from the gospels that central to Jesus' ministry is his teaching on the imminence of the reign of God and the enacting of that reign through his words and deeds. For this reason, Wassen's argument is particularly compelling. However, her questions center on the historical details surrounding the text and pertain to a literal reading of the events, even while asking questions of the particular apocalyptic understandings of the people of the first century. While there is much we can learn from this analysis, our contention throughout the present book has been to demonstrate that the meanings of biblical texts go far beyond literalist readings, especially if we take into account the recognition that the gospels were written post-Easter—and for very different audiences with very different circumstances from those of the community of people who followed Jesus early in the first century. To this end, we now turn to two Australian scholars who have presented more symbolic readings of this text.

Moloney argues that Jesus' actions and words in the temple, as described by John, are both a direct attack on the abuse of the temple (*hieron*) and a statement about Jesus' particular relationship with God. In his exegesis of the text, Moloney focuses on the three Greek words used for temple: *heiron* (which refers to the whole temple complex, made of stone), *oikos* (house), and *naos* (the innermost part, or sanctuary, of the temple). When Jesus upturns the tables and drives out the moneychangers and sellers, the temple (*heiron*) has "degenerated" into a marketplace (*oikos emporiou*). But for Jesus, "it is not merely a building where people gather (*to heiron*) ... it is 'the house of my Father' (*ton oikon tou patros mou*)."[32] When Jesus first speaks (at v. 16), the Greek word used for temple shifts from *heiron* to *oikos* (house)—not in the sense of *oikos emporiou* (house of trade), a term the evangelist had used only moments earlier, but in the sense of a dwelling place: the *oikos* of God. Moreover, Moloney notes, by calling the temple "the house of *my* Father," Jesus personalizes it; "[t]heir temple belongs to him in a special way." Moloney argues that Jesus' actions and words in the Johannine account enact his reclaiming of the temple while also saying something particular about who he is: "the *heiron* of 'the Jews' is in fact the *oikos* of the Father of Jesus."[33] As the scene shifts to the question from "the Jews" ("What sign can you show us for doing this?" v. 18), the text becomes prophetic: "Destroy this temple and in three days I will raise it up" (v. 19). The word Jesus uses here for temple is *ton naon*. In the resurrection, the temple will no longer be a temple of stone (*to heiron*): the dwelling place of God (the sanctuary, *naos*) is Jesus.

Coloe's exegesis takes a similar line: "Whatever this prophetic demonstration meant for the historical Jesus, the Johannine account is a

[32]Moloney, *Sacra Pagina: The Gospel of John*, 97.
[33]Moloney, *Sacra Pagina: The Gospel of John*, 98.

highly condensed theological presentation that Jesus/Sophia, not the temple system, is now the means of encountering God."[34] By the time John's gospel comes to be written, the temple in Jerusalem has been destroyed (*c.* 70 CE) and Jewish Christians (a large group within John's community) have been expelled from the synagogue.[35] Their center of worship has shifted. The Johannine community must make sense of the meaning of sacrifice without the temple and without all of the sacrificial imagery that it contains. For so long, the community's sense of identity has been associated with the temple, but this is now under threat.[36] Coloe argues that instead of calling the text under discussion by its common title, "The Cleansing of the Temple," a more apt title might be "The Displacement or Abrogation of the Temple."[37] John's text is a recontextualization of the temple in light of the resurrection: "the temple worship system is no longer needed. The Jerusalem temple, as the great symbol of God's presence in Israel's midst, is now embodied in Jesus."[38] Elsewhere, Coloe takes this a step further to argue that transferring the meaning of the temple symbol to the body of Christ would not have been enough for the Johannine community, because Jesus, too (at least in terms of his physical body), is now absent.[39] In the Johannine community, the sacrificial life that has been associated with the temple is now being transferred into daily life and living. Following this line of argument, Coloe explains that with the return of the phrase "my Father's house" on the lips of Jesus in Jn 14:2 ("In my Father's house there are many dwelling places"), the symbol of the temple moves "from the body of Jesus to the community of believers."[40]

One final element of the text invites further discussion in our dialogue with the biblical tradition: the words of the Psalm (slightly adapted), in the memory of the disciples, "Zeal for your house will consume me" (Jn 2:17). Psalm 69 (LXX 68), the text to which this verse refers, is a lament about "the righteous suffering king" and his plea for the deliverance from persecution.[41] The Psalm begins by relating the personal suffering and shame

[34]Coloe, *John 1–10*, 66. By using the Greek name, *Sophia*, in connection with Jesus, Coloe reaches back to the book of Wisdom, where God is referred to in the feminine.

[35]For a detailed study of the Johannine community, see Raymond E. Brown, *The Community of the Beloved Disciple* (Paulist, 1979), 25–58, 166–7; Pheme Perkins, "The Gospel According to John," in *The New Jerome Biblical Commentary*, ed. Roland E. Murphy, Joseph A. Fitzmyer, and Raymond E. Brown (Geoffrey Chapman, 1995), 945–6.

[36]Mary L. Coloe, "Temple Imagery in John," *Interpretation* 63, no. 4 (2009): 368.

[37]Coloe, "Temple Imagery in John," 371.

[38]Coloe, *John 1–10*, 69.

[39]Coloe, *God Dwells with Us*, 6–7.

[40]"In my Father's house there are many dwelling-places. If it were not so, would I have told you that I go to prepare a place for you?" (Jn 14:2).

[41]Matthew J. Klem, "Flipping Tables and Building Temples: An Intertextual Reading of Psalm 68:10 LXX in John 2:17," *Horizons in Biblical Theology* 43, no. 1 (2021): 75.

that the king experiences as a result of his sin (vv. 1-3).[42] His enemies add to his suffering, turning his love for God (expressed through ritual piety, vv. 10-11) against him. He laments that he has been consumed by this love ("It is zeal for your house that has consumed me," v. 9) and he cries out to God to save him (vv. 13-15). In doing so, he asks God to let his enemies' "table be a trap for them" (v. 22) and "let your burning anger overtake them" (v. 24). When John places Ps. 69:9 in the thoughts of the disciples at the temple, he retranslates it from the Greek aorist tense ("It is zeal ... *that has* consumed me," indicating a past or continuous action) to the future tense ("Zeal for your house *will* consume me"). Matthew Klem explains that in the context of the temple incident, Jesus' zeal can be understood in two ways.[43] One way of understanding the verse is to say that Jesus' zeal (as love for the temple) overwhelms him in the moment, and that is what leads him to act out in anger. Snodgrass takes this line, arguing that although there is "a temple-replacement theme in the Fourth Gospel, ... the temple is still the place where Jesus teaches regularly, and the explanation from the evangelist for the temple incident is that zeal *for* the temple caused Jesus to act."[44] Another approach takes in the prophetic nature of the narrative and sees it as pointing to Jesus' death. Coloe and Moloney take this approach. For them, the use of the Psalm in the context of Jesus' actions echoes the Passion and indicates that Jesus' present action in the temple, which will "set him in conflict with the authorities, will ultimately lead to him being consumed in death."[45] For Coloe, this is a more adequate reading of the original psalm: "the psalmist is not speaking of a zeal that totally dominates him, but one that brings him close to death."[46] When we come to our dialogue with the contemporary context, below, we will offer a third way of understanding the zeal to which the evangelist refers, which potentially draws each of these approaches together.

Engaging in Dialogue with Post-Biblical Tradition

Our imaginative contemplation brought us to focus on the nature of Jesus' anger and the effect it has on him, as well as on us, the viewers. Even in light of the analysis above, the scale of Jesus' anger in the Johannine text is curious. So, let us sit with this for a while longer as we consider how anger

---

[42]Moloney generalizes the character of the psalmist, positing that the story refers to "the person dedicated to Temple prayer." Moloney, *Sacra Pagina: The Gospel of John*, 98.
[43]Klem, "Flipping Tables and Building Temples," 79.
[44]Snodgrass, "The Temple Incident," 433.
[45]Coloe, *John 1–10*, 70; Moloney, *Sacra Pagina: The Gospel of John*, 98.
[46]Coloe, *John 1–10*, 70.

is understood within the broader context of philosophical and theological traditions and the ways it is contrasted with other emotions.

In the gospel narratives, we see Jesus being moved with compassion, being overcome by grief, feeling indignant, troubled, broken-hearted, being filled with joy, anguish, love, and distress.[47] Yet, in only one other story in the gospels do we find Jesus' emotional state explicitly labelled as angry (at least in the English translation).[48] In the gospel of Mark, the emotion is triggered when Jesus is challenged on the Sabbath. Entering the synagogue, he encounters a man with a withered hand and his anger is mixed with grief when he finds that those present would have him put the law of the sabbath before the needs of a person who is suffering: "He looked around at them with anger; he was grieved at their hardness of heart" (Mk 3:5). Implied in this account is that Jesus' anger is justified because it is a response to an injustice (more on that soon).

Despite Jesus being overcome by anger in the temple and in the synagogue, anger seems to be understood within the Christian scriptures as an emotion that should be avoided, or at least kept in check. Jesus himself explicitly prohibits anger in Matthew's account of the Sermon on the Mount: "I say to you that if you are angry with a brother or sister, you will be liable to judgement" (Mt. 5:22). In Paul's letter to the Galatians, he lists anger as a "work of the flesh" (treating it as an action) and warns that "those who do such things will not inherit the kingdom of God" (Gal. 5:21; 19-21).[49] In his subsequent letter to the Ephesians, Paul makes room for anger (as an emotion), but it comes with a warning: "Be angry but do not sin; do not let the sun go down on your anger" (Eph. 4:26). In the epistle of James, we find similar sentiments: "let everyone be quick to listen, slow to speak, slow to anger; for your anger does not produce God's righteousness" (Jas 1:19-20).

---

[47]For an extensive survey of these emotions in the person and actions of Jesus, as narrated in the gospels, see Voorwinde, *Jesus' Emotions*.

[48]The Greek word used for the intense emotions expressed by Jesus at John 11:33 when he hears of Lazarus' death is *embrimaomai* (anger), but most English translations use a version of the phrase ("he was greatly disturbed in spirit and deeply moved"). See Voorwinde, *Jesus' Emotions*, 173–6. There are also references to Jesus feeling indignant, which is often connected with anger. For example, in Luke, when Jesus heals a "crippled" woman (Lk 13:10-17) he indignantly calls the bystanders "hypocrites" (v. 15), and in Mark, Jesus was "indignant" and spoke sternly to the disciples: "Let the little children come to me; do not stop them; for it is to such as these that the kingdom of God belongs" (Mk 10:14).

[49]"Live by the Spirit, I say, and do not gratify the desires of the flesh. For what the flesh desires is opposed to the Spirit, and what the Spirit desires is opposed to the flesh; for these are opposed to each other, to prevent you from doing what you want. But if you are led by the Spirit, you are not subject to the law. Now the works of the flesh are obvious: fornication, impurity, licentiousness, idolatry, sorcery, enmities, strife, jealousy, anger, quarrels, dissensions, factions, envy, drunkenness, carousing, and things like these. I am warning you, as I warned you before: those who do such things will not inherit the kingdom of God" (Gal 5:16-21).

As the Christian tradition develops, so too does its teaching on anger. We will see shortly that Augustine and Thomas Aquinas, two of the most influential theologians within the tradition, take up the question of whether or not anger can be justified. In their deliberations the influence of their dialogue with philosophy is clear. James Averill provides a helpful overview of the philosophical discussion on anger prior to Augustine.[50] He explains that in the thought of Plato and Aristotle (fourth century BCE), anger is considered to be a natural response to a painful or unjust situation and a potential ally of reason. However, the Stoics (second century BCE to as late as the second century CE) "regard emotions as diseases of the mind" and recommend that people "strive to be rid of them" because they are commensurate with "false judgements concerning matters of good and evil."[51] Seneca, a Roman stoic who lived in Jesus' time (4 BCE–65 CE), refers to anger as "'the most hideous and frenzied of all emotions' … [It] entirely consumes its possessor and renders dull his [*sic*] capacity for reasoning and sensible action … [It is] akin to madness."[52] Some 250 years later, Lactantius, a Christian convert and reported spokesperson for Emperor Constantine, distinguishes between just and unjust anger. He argues that unjust anger is anger that cannot be found in God; that is, anger that seeks "to avenge injury or return pain for pain."[53] This kind of anger is akin to something like fury or rage. In contrast, he contends that *just* anger is "useful and necessary" for the development of a civilized society: "[I]t is necessary that things which are bad should displease one who is good and just, and he [*sic*] to whom evil is displeasing is moved when he sees [reproval] done."[54] Moreover, he argues that to watch calmly as another person commits an offense is unjust in itself: "He who is not moved at all, either approves the faults, which is more shameful and unjust, or he avoids the bother of correcting them, bother which a calm spirit and quiet mind shuns and rejects unless anger has goaded and aroused it."[55]

In the early fifth century, and influenced by these debates, Augustine undertakes an exegesis of the Sermon on the Mount with a section focused on Matthew 5:22, Jesus' prohibition of anger. The translation he uses is the pre-Vulgate ("Old Latin") translation, which includes a qualifier: "Whoever is

[50] James R. Averill, *Anger and Aggression: An Essay on Emotion* (Springer, 1982), see chapter 4, 73–101. See also Michael Potegal and Raymond W. Novaco, "A Brief History of Anger," in *International Handbook of Anger: Constituent and Concomitant Biological, Psychological, and Social Processes*, ed. Michael Potegal, Gerhard Stemmler, and Charles Spielberger (Springer, 2010), 9–21.

[51] Averill, *Anger and Aggression*, 83.

[52] Seneca, *De Ira*, 107, cited in Averill, *Anger and Aggression*, 83.

[53] Averill, *Anger and Aggression*, 87.

[54] Lactantius, *De Ira Dei*, 102, cited in Averill, *Anger and Aggression*, 87.

[55] Lactantius, *De Ira Dei*, 102, cited in Averill, *Anger and Aggression*, 87.

angry with his brother [*sic*] *without cause*, shall be in danger of judgement."[56] According to William Mattison, Augustine uses this clause to qualify the kind of anger that is permissible under Jesus' teaching and he differentiates between anger that has just cause—which therefore prompts action to right the wrong—and "anger alone, ... anger prompting unintelligible utterance, [and] anger leading to verbal assault."[57] Curiously, despite the fact that some 30 years later when Augustine is writing his *Retractiones* he becomes aware that the original Greek does not include the additional clause, he does not change his teaching. He argues that the clause is implied in the Greek text because it refers to anger *at sin*, rather than at a person:

> one is not angry *with one's brother* when one is angry *at the sin* of one's brother ... [T]herefore the one who is angry at the sin of the brother, and not at the brother himself, does not sin and thus has anger with cause. It is only anger *with one's brother* that is condemned by Jesus in this passage.[58]

This early qualification was to become known in the Christian moral tradition as the person/sin distinction. Aware of the Stoics' debate about the rationality of anger, Augustine turns to the reasons *why* a person might be angry when considering anger's justification. His ultimate contribution to the discussion includes three tenets: the delineation of "the morality of anger based on its target; anger at a person is sinful; [and] anger at sin is virtuous."[59]

By the time Thomas Aquinas' thought is developing in the thirteenth century, the person/sin distinction has become commonplace. Centuries earlier, Gregory the Great had distinguished between "zealous anger," which is anger aimed at sin—a judgment of sin—and which is therefore justified and even virtuous, and "vicious anger," which is anger aimed at a person and therefore considered to be sinful.[60] This distinction finds its way into the writings of Thomas' contemporaries, such as William of Auxerre and Bonaventure. However, Thomas ultimately rejects the person/sin distinction, arguing that anger is justified "when it is 'reasonable in object,' that is, when it is directed at the right person (in response to a genuine offense), for

---

[56]See Augustine, *Exposition of the Sermon on the Mount: Drawn from the Writings of St. Augustine*, ed. Richard Chenevix Trench (J. W. Parker, 1844), 33–4; also William C. Mattison, "Jesus' Prohibition of Anger (MT 5:22): The Person/Sin Distinction from Augustine to Aquinas," *Theological Studies* 68, no. 4 (2007): 841–2.

[57]Mattison, "Jesus' Prohibition of Anger," 842.

[58]Mattison, "Jesus' Prohibition of Anger," 843. Mattison here paraphrases Augustine's *Retractionum Libri II*, CCSL 57 (Brepols, 1984) 57.

[59]Mattison, "Jesus' Prohibition of Anger," 846.

[60]Mattison, "Jesus' Prohibition of Anger," 849, 852.

the right goal, and toward proper *vindicatio*."[61] By the end of this period, Mattison explains, "reasonable anger" has become clearly defined:

> [It is] (1) prompted by an occasion of genuine injustice, (2) directed at the perpetrator of injustice, and (3) directed at fair *vindicatio* with the further goal of restoring justice, including reconciliation with, rather than banishment of, the offender. Such anger is compatible with charity, since the "harm" it seeks for *vindicatio* is actually constitutive of the reestablishment of right relationship.[62]

Much later, in the early seventeenth century, Descartes defines anger, along with indignation, as a species of hatred, which he in turn defines as "an emotion caused by ... the desire to be separated from the objects which present themselves as hurtful."[63] However, Thomas has previously rejected this equation, arguing that while hatred seeks harm "simply for itself," anger, properly justified, seeks the good (*vindicatio*).[64]

This foray into the philosophical and theological world of anger is helpful for our purposes to the extent that it provides a theoretical framework for understanding Jesus' experience and expression of anger. Whatever it is that causes his anger as he arrives at the temple, and despite the potential "irrationality" of his actions given that they draw the attention of the Roman authorities, Jesus is moved by an experience of injustice. His anger becomes manifest in his whole body: his voice, his gestures, his words and his actions all reflect a wholly human experience of anger. There is nothing unequivocal about it.

Engaging in Dialogue with the Current Context

Anger is a social emotion.[65] Today, anger is often linked with conversations about violence and aggression, especially against vulnerable people. This is reflected, for example, in public advertisements designed to decrease instances

---

[61]*ST* 2–2, q. 158, a. 2–4, cited in Mattison, "Jesus' Prohibition of Anger," 859. Elsewhere, Mattison qualifies his use of the Latin term *vindicatio*: "Common translations such as 'vengeance', 'revenge,' or 'vindication' have negative connotations. That was not the case in Latin, where the term has a neutral sense of 'righting an injustice' (which could be done virtuously or sinfully). In fact, Thomas treats *vindicatio* as a virtue in his treatise on justice. See ST 2–2, q. 108." Mattison, "Jesus' Prohibition of Anger," 855, n847.

[62]Mattison, "Jesus' Prohibition of Anger," 863.

[63]Descartes, *The Passions of the Soul* (1649/1968), LXXIX, cited in Averill, *Anger and Aggression*, 93.

[64]Mattison, "Jesus' Prohibition of Anger," 857.

[65]See Ann M. Kring, "Gender and Anger," in *Gender and Emotion: Social Psychological Perspectives*, ed. Agneta H. Fischer, Studies in Emotion and Social Interaction (Cambridge University Press, 2000), 211–31, 212.

of domestic violence which, in Australia, have been increasingly reported.[66] While both men and women get angry, studies suggest that the *expression* of anger by women is stereotypically considered (even by women themselves) to be less appropriate than the expression of anger by men.[67] For women, the expression of anger typically becomes part of an "unwanted identity," which brings about shame.[68] Our text about Jesus' expression of anger could open onto a discussion of this anger-bringing shame, reinforcing a theme that is taken up in a number of other places in this book. Instead, however, we take up part of Maloney's argument, that Jesus' actions are a direct response to the abuse of the temple (which he understood to be the house of God), coupled with Wassen's discussion of actual or perceived corruption taking place within the temple court, to consider another circumstance when anger at "temple" hypocrisy is right and just.

In our imaginative contemplation, we were drawn to the slightly modified words of the psalmist in the memories of the disciples: "Zeal for your house will consume me" (2:17). Some of the scholars we explored proffer that the disciples might have been thinking of Jesus' love (zeal) for the temple, which was consuming him in the face of defilement, while others see the insertion of the Psalm as prophetic, pointing to Jesus being ultimately consumed in death as a result of his actions. We wonder whether a third way of thinking about the insertion of Ps. 69:9 is possible. In the text, zeal is a noun, but it is not attached to a possessive pronoun (for example, "*my* zeal for your house ..."). Perhaps, then, the words could be understood as "*your* zeal for your house ...," with Jesus challenging the peoples' love for a temple of structure and stone over God's creative work in the world. We saw in our dialogue with Maloney that the story of Jesus' anger in the temple is a statement about Jesus' particular relationship with God. Here, God's house has degenerated into a marketplace, and the temple and all of the sacrificial ritual that it contains are used by the marketeers and the temple officials alike for their own gain. Corruption—real or perceived (if we take Wassen's analysis seriously)—is part of the story attached to the temple. Its function as a place of worship and as the place in which God dwells has been undermined and subverted. *How dare you forget your call to serve! You worship my Father and yet you use your worship for your own gain. You love this house for what it can give you. You take from it. You rid it of its warmth. You forget the love that sits at its heart.*

When it came time for the homily at Mass on the Sunday after the final report of Australia's Royal Commission into Institutional Responses to Child Sexual Abuse was handed down in 2017, a parish priest stepped down

[66] Christopher Dowling, "Police Training in Responding to Family, Domestic and Sexual Violence," *Trends and Issues in Crime and Criminal Justice*, no. 689 (2024): 1–25.

[67] Kring, "Gender and anger," 222.

[68] Ioana Latu, Susanne Kaiser, and Marianne Schmid, *Gender and Emotion: An Interdisciplinary Perspective* (Peter Lang, 2013), 158–9.

from the sanctuary and sat in the pews with the congregation in silence.[69] No words could have expressed the hurt and devastation that he and many members of the community were feeling. By then, the scale of the abuse was known to most, but the hurt and devastation were deepened by the Royal Commission's finding that the Australian Catholic Church in particular was culpable in the cover-up of abuse and the protection of abusers. The Royal Commission heard from over 16,000 people who had experienced sexual abuse as children within institutions in Australia, and there are countless others who did not feel able to share their trauma. 58.6 percent of the survivors who came forward reported having been abused by members of a religious organization. Of that 58.6 percent, 61.8 percent said that the abuse occurred within Catholic institutions.[70] This percentage reflects almost 2,500 survivors of abuse perpetrated by "priests, religious brothers and sisters, ministers, church elders, teachers in religious schools, workers in residential institutions, volunteers, youth group leaders and others."[71] As we mentioned, this number does not include those people who were unable or not ready to tell their story, nor does it include those who died prior to the Royal Commission who had no one to speak for them or people who were abused as adults (women in the novitiate and in religious orders, for example, or adults with disabilities in care facilities run by the Catholic Church).

In the executive summary of the report, we read these chilling words:

> Many children have been sexually abused in religious institutions in Australia. Based on the information before us, the greatest number of alleged perpetrators and abused children were in Catholic institutions. In many religious institutions, the power afforded to people in religious ministry and the misplaced trust of parents combined with aspects of the institutional culture, practices and attitudes to create risks for children. Alleged perpetrators often continued to have access to children even when religious leaders knew they posed a danger. We heard that alleged perpetrators were often transferred to other locations but they were rarely reported to police.
>
> The failure to understand that the sexual abuse of a child was a crime with profound impacts for the victim, and not a mere moral failure

---

[69]The report was presented to the Governor-General on December 15, 2017. The Royal Commission was established by then Prime Minister Julia Gillard on November 12, 2012.

[70]Compared to other Christian organizations: Anglican, 14.7 percent; Salvation Army, 7.3 percent; Protestant, 4.2 percent; Presbyterian and Reformed, 2.9 percent; Uniting Church, 2.4 percent; Baptist, 1.0 percent; Pentecostal, 0.9 percent. Commonwealth of Australia, *Final Report: Preface and Executive Summary*, Royal Commission in Institutional Responses to Child Sexual Abuse (Australian Capital Territory: Commonwealth of Australia, 2017), 11–2, https://www.childabuseroyalcommission.gov.au/sites/default/files/final_report_-_preface_and_executive_summary.pdf.

[71]Commonwealth of Australia, *Final Report*, 43.

> capable of correction by contrition and penance (a view expressed in the past by a number of religious leaders) is almost incomprehensible. It can only be explained by acknowledging that the culture of some religious institutions prioritised alleged perpetrators and institutional reputations over the safety of children.[72]

The Commission reports that "catastrophic failures of leadership of Catholic Church authorities over many decades" have caused irreparable harm to children and their families. It finds that in most cases "the abuse could have been avoided had Catholic Church authorities acted in the interests of children rather than in their own interests."[73] Contributing factors named by the commission include areas of theology, governance, and culture, specifically: organizational structure and governance, leadership, clericalism, canon law, theologies of priesthood (including the requirement for celibacy), the theologies and practices surrounding the sacrament of reconciliation, and the screening and formation of priests, deacons, and lay people working in ministry.[74] The Commission notes that "the same theological, governance and cultural factors that contributed to the occurrence of the abuse also contributed to inadequate responses of Catholic institutions to that abuse."[75] Writing on the crisis as it came to light in the United States, James F. Keenan adds that "many priests and their bishops simply were more concerned about the image of the Church than they were with these vulnerable children or their parents and family members who, in their vulnerability, came to us."[76]

Pope Francis has spoken often on the issue of clericalism. In an address to Bishops in 2018, he says,

> Clericalism arises from an elitist and exclusivist vision of vocation, that interprets the ministry received as a *power* to be exercised rather than as a free and generous service to be given. This leads us to believe that we belong to a group that has all the answers and no longer needs to listen or learn anything, or that pretends to listen. Clericalism is a perversion and is the root of many evils in the Church: we must humbly ask forgiveness for this and above all create the conditions so that it is not repeated.[77]

---

[72]Commonwealth of Australia, *Final Report*, 6.
[73]Commonwealth of Australia, *Final Report*, 61.
[74]Commonwealth of Australia, *Final Report*, 67–73.
[75]Commonwealth of Australia, *Final Report*, 67.
[76]James F. Keenan, "Vulnerability and Hierarchicalism," *Melita Theologica* 68, no. 2 (2018): 131.
[77]Pope Francis, "Address by His Holiness Pope Francis at the Opening of the Synod of Bishops on Young People, the Faith and Vocational Discernment" (October 3, 2018), https://www.vatican.va/content/francesco/en/speeches/2018/october/documents/papa-francesco_20181003_apertura-sinodo.html.

Clericalism is not simply confined to those in ordained positions within the Church, though. It is facilitated and perpetuated by many lay members of the Church, who are part of an often internalized and unspoken culture that upholds a division between the clergy and the laity, even in communities where the laity take leadership roles.[78] As Massimo Faggioli and Alana Harris point out, "the abuse crisis in the Catholic Church is not just a series of individuals committing or covering up crimes: it is the history of a complex institution within a social and spiritual ecosystem that facilitated and enabled abuse and that is now seeking to deal with a deplorable past."[79] It is clear that all members of the Church community have a role to play in ensuring that the ecosystem that enabled sexual abuse to occur and remain hidden is dismantled.

Many Catholics around the world are rightfully angry—and their anger is justified—but this anger has not always led to action. As Jennifer Beste reports, only a slim minority of Catholics have responded by supporting survivors, advocating for children's safety and well-being, and working for genuine Church reform.[80] Clergy sexual abuse strikes at the very heart of the Church's mission, which we might define as witnessing to and mediating the presence of Christ who, through the Holy Spirit, is present in an ongoing way in the world. As we noted earlier in our discussion of Coloe's exegesis, the Church is not a place of bricks and mortar; it lives in the lives and experiences of Christians who witness to the reality of God's grace in the world. The Church, properly conceived, is not a hierarchy of persons sustained by leadership and power but a movement of love and service that supports the creation of conditions for the acceptance of revelation.[81] The

---

[78]Gideon Goosen has analyzed the experience of clericalism in parish communities in Australia and offers helpful insights and ideas for undermining such a culture. See *Clericalism: Stories from the Pews. A Workbook for Parishes* (Coventry, 2020).

[79]Massimo Faggioli and Alana Harris, "Pursuing the Long Shadow over the 'Domestic Church': Toward a Global History of Abuse in Catholic Settings," *The Catholic Historical Review* 110, no. 2 (2024): 347.

[80]Beste notes that since the Boston sexual abuse crisis erupted in 2002, "common reactions among US Catholics have included (1) feelings of anger, disgust, frustration, and betrayal, (2) disaffiliation from Catholicism, (3) avoidance of the topic, (4) denial that clergy sexual abuse occurred, (5) minimization of the abuse, (6) disbelief and blame toward clergy sexual abuse victims, (7) defensiveness, and (8) complacency (believing that sufficient measures are already in place to respond to clergy sexual abuse and that the church can 'move on' from the crisis). Currently, many survivors continue to feel alone, unsupported, and/or retraumatized by the institutional church and even by those in their own parishes." Jennifer Beste, "Envisioning a Just Response to the Catholic Clergy Sexual Abuse Crisis," *Theological studies* 82, no. 1 (2021): 30, 30–1.

[81]Beste offers a particularly sharp analysis of the way in which the mission of the Church (understood as witnessing to Christ's revelatory mission) is undermined by clergy sexual abuse: "Catholic theology affirms that God offers Godself to all persons, inviting them to be in communion with the divine and all of creation. God's self-offer (uncreated grace) enables our freedom to accept that offer. This 'yes' to God is expressed in and mediated by our loving

house of God (the people of God) has been defiled and humiliated by the abhorrent abuse of the most vulnerable people in our midst by precisely those whose role it is to witness to God's unending love. And those who covered it up—who moved abusers from one place to another, used Church funds to ensure silence, and continued to enable abusers to enact their abuse—have shown a love for Church (as a hierarchical system of power) over love for God and God's people. Jesus would cry: *how dare you!*

The mission of the Church—witnessing to and mediating Christ's presence—is incumbent upon all members of the Church by virtue of their baptism. To this end, we cannot but employ some of Jesus' "zealous" anger: anger that *turns tables*; anger that is aimed at sin and the perpetrators of sin while recognizing our own complacency and need for conversion; anger that subverts clericalism and hierarchicalism; anger that is charged with the desire to restore justice and reconcile relationships; and, most importantly in the case of clergy sexual abuse, anger that is informed by a willingness to walk in empathy with the victims and their families.

How Is the Text Speaking to Me (or Us) Today?

In our engagement with the narrative of Jesus turning the tables in the temple, we chose to bring the text into dialogue with the findings of Australia's Royal Commission into Institutional Responses to Child Sexual Abuse. There are, of course, many other issues that could be brought into the discussion, issues for which the tables must be turned. Some of these issues have come into our dialogue elsewhere in this book. In naming this particular issue together with Jesus' anger in the temple, we implore ourselves as much as we implore our readers to raise our voices when we, the Church, place ourselves over God and fail to live up to the call to witness to God's love in our midst. In November 2023 Pope Francis issued an apostolic letter, *motu proprio* (meaning, "of his own accord"), laying out new conditions and frontiers

---

relationships with others. But, as noted above, research consistently finds that persons' capacities for healthy forms of relationality and agency can be severely impeded by abusive interpersonal relations ... [T]aking trauma studies of child sexual abuse seriously entails confronting the possibility that severe interpersonal harm diminishes and may possibly destroy persons' capacity to receive and respond to divine grace. In short, God's healing grace, revealed in Christ, is mediated to the victims of abuse through the church, its ministers, and creation more broadly, but persons' ability to receive and respond to such grace is subverted by the very clergy who are supposed to be instrumental for these graces ... [T]he extent of harm they [clergy perpetrators] inflict on victims very well may destroy their capacity to fulfill God's purpose for their lives: to receive and experience God's love and grace and be freed to love God, others, and themselves. The number of suicides committed by clergy sexual abuse victims attests to this reality." Beste, "Envisioning a Just Response," 40.

for the exercise of theology. In the letter, he calls for a "courageous cultural revolution" that commits itself to "reading and interpreting the Gospel in the conditions in which [human beings] live daily," and to a mission and theology that is "outgoing," enacted and elaborated "on its knees" in prayer, attentive to the voices of the people.[82] This book is part of our contribution to this cause. And so, we challenge you to listen to the voices of the people. Where is your anger needed? What tables should you turn?

[82]Pope Francis, "Ad theologiam promovendam," 3, 4, 7.

Has he been behind them all the way, or does he just appear—as if from nowhere? They have been engrossed in their talking and grieving, perhaps so engrossed that they have failed to notice for a while that he is there. Perhaps he comes upon them suddenly. Has he been trying to catch up with them, or has he reached them because their walk has been slowed by the weight of their burdens? Do they resent the intrusion? Do they fear he has been spying on them and will report them to the authorities as companions of Jesus? The law of hospitality insists. They make room for him to walk with them. He asks them what they have been talking about with such earnestness—evidently, he has observed them for some time.

Let us be clear: the disciples see only another man beside them on the road. They are not looking at *Jesus* because they are not expecting to see him. The disciples tell their story, but it is hard not to hear an unfortunate tone of condescension, or at least a hint of disrespect, in the man's response: "you fools!" The man continues, perhaps with more affection: "You're so slow of heart to believe!" In this he accomplishes an interruption—*You've got it all wrong!* The disciples have been wrapped up in their own version of events. If they can just allow themselves to hear what he's saying, they'll find they have been jumping hastily to the wrong conclusions.

The remainder of the journey to Emmaus is spent going over texts that they have known since childhood and reinterpreting them in light of recent events. The man "interrupts" their reading of the narrative traditions—more than that, he brings the texts to life in a way they have never experienced before. So, the light dims, and at last they get to the Emmaus turn-off on the highway. Something makes the disciples want him to stay with them. Perhaps they just have good manners and cannot leave a stranger without a meal and a bed for the night. Or, perhaps they feel they have found some consolation in their grief and don't want that feeling to end. They urge the man to stay, and he accepts.

Now we get to the part that is often considered to be the climax of the story. The three companions sit down to eat together. Their guest says the blessing, breaks the bread, and—suddenly—they recognize Jesus. Yet, no sooner does Jesus appear than he disappears. Recognition and disappearance are part of a piece. It is not as though Jesus' image is run through a database, and he is finally recognized because there is a digital match on the measurements of the distance between his eyes, the precise arc of each eyebrow, and the angles of his nose and chin. He is not recognized by the application of an algorithm, or by the provision of an adequate concept, but because of the prepredicative experience of love. This is the kind of recognition made where one's heart veritably *leaps*. It is not unlike the recognition of Jesus by Mary Magdalene in John 20, where he speaks her name (v.16) and she knows it is him, not because of how he appears, but by the tone of his voice. Heart speaks to heart, which is one of the reasons why we could interpret this properly eschatological moment as an event of revelation taking place in the affect. What the disciples are given in their experience of Jesus after his death is overlaid on their experience of Jesus during his life with them. The love that Jesus has previously expressed to them and that he stirs in them—their affective experience of him—renders him overwhelmingly "present" to them. It is only later that this is more fully articulated by the early church community—insufficiently and always inadequately, no doubt—with reference to God. And what could such a reference from Jesus to God possibly mean, except as a recognition in the affect?

The story has not finished, though. Two crucial details remain. First, the disciples reflect on what has happened to them that day. In verse 32, we overhear them saying to one another: "Were not our hearts burning [within us] while he was talking to us on the road, while he was opening the scriptures to us?" In their reflection, they come to realize that the joyous recognition they have now is linked to the mood that has accompanied his presence with them on the road, and that very probably lies behind their motivation to urge him to stay. Once again, it is quite possible that it is also linked to their experience with Jesus when he was living with them. If we were to give to their burning hearts an Ignatian inflection, we might add that this experience is directly contrary to the mood that affected them prior to meeting Jesus on their journey. This new mood has come, as it were, from no-where (or from elsewhere), since it cannot possibly follow from the disciples' feelings of utter desolation, and most certainly does not come from any preconceived expectation that Jesus will rise from the dead.

The second and related detail is that the disciples arise immediately to return to Jerusalem, even though it is night and they have already travelled a long distance on foot. The slow and undoubtedly heavy rhythm of walking to Emmaus is replaced by a rapid turnaround and an adrenaline-fueled run back to Jerusalem. Whatever has happened to them in the event in which they recognize Jesus has transformed them entirely. The event whereby the disciples recognize Jesus is no thing: it delivers no object or thing or even concept to be grasped, but only the extraordinary joy of recognition. It transforms their lives: they go from being fearful and grief-stricken to being bold and hope-filled. When they get back to Jerusalem, the other disciples are still up. Cleopas and his companion breathlessly proclaim to the others their experience of the resurrected Jesus, and joy has suddenly dispelled all fear.

Engaging in Critical Dialogue with Biblical Tradition

What kind of text is Luke 24? It contains three stories relating to Jesus' resurrection. The first is an account of the empty tomb, versions of which are common to all the synoptics and, more briefly, in John. In Luke, this account ends with the apostles' rejection of the women's testimony that the tomb is empty (24:11). The second story is that of the road to Emmaus. There is no parallel to this story, but a possible link can be made with the longer ending of Mark, at verses 12-13 ("After this he appeared in another form to two of them, as they were walking into the country. And they went back and told the rest, but they did not believe them"). The third story is the appearance of Jesus to the disciples, paralleled only in John 20:19-23. At the end of chapter 24, the Lucan writer brings the Gospel to an end with reference to Jesus' ascension, which also appears in the second Lucan text, Acts, in chapter 1:6-11, and in the longer ending of Mk (16:19).

A question that is often addressed to the Emmaus account concerns its historicity. Yet, we must clarify the type of historicity for which we are seeking. Are we asking about the historicity of the episode? Are we asking about the historicity of the text? Or, are we asking about the historicity of the text in its Lucan formulation? Responding to the first question, and in light of the outcomes of critical-historical analysis of the Emmaus narrative in the 1960s, Hans Dieter Betz writes that the text "reflects theologically and programmatically upon the problem of how Christian faith is made possible and what elements constitute its nature."[1] While identifying the importance of the text and recognizing that its interpretation "will bring to light the very concerns which the text wanted to express in its original historical setting," Betz argues that it is not "an account of a historical event" but a "cult legend."[2] In 1989, Eben H. Scheffler gives a thorough account of the factors that could influence a decision about an interpretation of the text as a retelling of historical events.[3] Scheffler concludes that while "Luke's account may therefore contain a 'historical core', his version cannot be regarded as a truly historical account." At the same time, Scheffler insists that the Emmaus story "explain[s] the origin of the resurrection faith. It is therefore probable that two disciples had an experience in which they observed that Christ was alive."[4] In other words, Scheffler cannot provide historical proof of the details of the story but does allow for the legitimate possibility of the

---

[1]Hans Dieter Betz, "The Origin and Nature of Christian Faith According to the Emmaus Legend: (Luke 24:13–32)," *Interpretation* 23, no. 1 (1969): 3.

[2]Betz, "According to the Emmaus Legend," 32, 33.

[3]Eben H. Scheffler, "Emmaus—A Historical Perspective," *Neotestamentica* 23, no. 2 (1989): 251–68. Historical problems Scheffler identifies in the Emmaus account include our inability to locate the village of Emmaus; the place and time-sequence of Jesus' appearances; a conflict between the claim for a first appearance to the Emmaus disciples and a claim for Peter as the first to see Jesus post-resurrection (1 Cor 15:5); a lack of clarity about who counts as a disciple (the two are not part of the eleven remaining in Jerusalem); the unusualness of the two leaving Jerusalem immediately after hearing of the empty tomb; clearly narrated parts of the text (the two disciples answer Jesus in chorus); the contradiction between 24:12 and 24:24 about who goes to the grave; and the way that the narrative is similar to other Lucan accounts and appears heavily redacted (pp. 254–9). The arguments for historicity are slim by comparison (259–60).

[4]Scheffler, "Emmaus—A Historical Perspective," 260.

resurrection appearances. We should not simply conclude, then, that Luke invented the episode for narrative effect.[5]

Responding to the second question, Betz maintains that the story contains a number of elements that are fundamentally pre-Lucan—"a description of the appearance of Jesus skilfully combined with a dialogue between the two disciples and Jesus"—but has been modified by the Lucan author in its incorporation into the Gospel.[6] Joseph Fitzmyer argues that the following pre-Lucan elements are evident: the reference in Mk 16:12-13 to Jesus' appearance to two disciples walking in the country; the mention of Emmaus (even though this village has never been decisively identified); the mention of Cleopas (Fitzmyer suggests that if the story has been simply the production of Luke's imagination, the other disciple would have been named as well, for consistency); the form of words in verse 34 (which incorporates non-Lucan vocabulary); verses 22-24, which seem to interrupt Luke's story; and the specific use of the verbs in verse 30, which echo a more traditional formulation "'take', 'utter a blessing', 'broke', and 'offered'."[7] Scheffler also concludes that Luke relies on an earlier tradition.[8] We must be cautious, however: Frank Moloney notes that admitting the likelihood of pre-Lucan content does not go so far as to support the existence of "Proto-Luke," an intermediary source proposed to explain the variations between Luke and Matthew, who both rely on Mark as well as the hypothesized source of Jesus' "sayings" (Q).[9] In sum, scholars have not uncovered an earlier version of the Emmaus story, but it seems likely that such a version was part of the early tradition.

In view of the third question, most scholars agree that Luke has heavily redacted the earlier material for his own purposes in order to help make sense of his own historical context, often approximated to be 75-85 CE. As Scheffler propounds: "The text as we have it is part of history itself and it is communicated as a *complete Lucan text* (even if it is regarded as a fictitious narrative or legend) within a historical situation."[10] That historical situation is likely to have been characterized by communal anxieties about the reality of the resurrection and the delay of Christ's promised return, as

---

[5]François Bovon, *Luke 3: A Commentary on the Gospel of Luke 19:28-24:53*, trans. James E. Couch, ed. Helmut Koester (Fortress, 2002).

[6]Betz, "According to the Emmaus Legend," 34.

[7]Joseph A. Fitzmyer, "Jesus Appears on the Road to Emmaus (24:13–35)," in *The Gospel According To Luke (X–XXIV)* (The Anchor Yale Bible, 1985).

[8]"I am of the opinion that Luke in all probability has an Emmaus tradition at his disposal." Scheffler, "Emmaus—A Historical Perspective," 260; Bovon et al., *Luke 3: A Commentary on the Gospel of Luke 19:28-24:53*, 369.

[9]See Francis J. Moloney, *The Resurrection of the Messiah: A Narrative Commentary on the Resurrection Accounts in the Four Gospels* (Paulist, 2013), 64 n.61.

[10]Scheffler, "Emmaus—A Historical Perspective," 261.

well as the suffering of the Christian community taking place.[11] This leads us to ask about Luke's purpose in writing. Luke Timothy Johnson argues that "Luke's original contribution to Christian literature was connecting the events of the early Church to those of Jesus' ministry, and to the whole story of God's people, indeed of humanity."[12] In particular, Luke has to deal with the movement of nascent Christianity away from Judaism and toward the Gentiles.[13]

The theology of the Emmaus story hinges on how it is possible for Jesus to continue being with the disciples when this is no longer apparent to them in the same way it was during his earthly life. This is shown in an ongoing play of presence and absence: Jesus is with the disciples in the discussion of the scriptures (on the road, Jesus is with the disciples even though they cannot recognize him, with a kind of presence-in-absence), and Jesus is with the disciples in the breaking of the bread (which is a moment of recognition rather than a vision, a sort of absence-in-presence).[14] As François Bovon et al. argue of the Emmaus text, the Christian community needs to know that "in life [Christ's] presence is real but invisible."[15] Frank Matera draws three significant theological points from the pericope.

> First, it is possible to be in the presence of the risen Christ, converse with him, and still not recognize him. Second, to believe in the resurrection, one must understand that Moses and the prophets had spoken about the Christ. Third, the risen Lord is present to the community of his disciples in the breaking of the bread. This presence, however, is elusive. For, while believers encounter him in Word and sacrament, they cannot control his presence.[16]

While Raymond Orlett observes in 1959 that "there can be little doubt that Lk intends to describe the meal at Emmaus as a Eucharistic celebration," Scheffler warns against "reading notions of the later practice of the eucharist into Luke's account."[17] Moloney, more broadly, maintains that "the memory of the many meals that Jesus has shared with them, and especially the meal he shared on the night before he died (22:14-38) opens their eyes

---

[11]Scheffler, "Emmaus—A Historical Perspective," 262. "We have no external evidence of Luke's situation" (261).

[12]Luke Timothy Johnson and Daniel J. Harrington, *Sacra Pagina: The Gospel of Luke*, vol. 3 (Liturgical Press, 1991), 15.

[13]Johnson and Harrington, *Sacra Pagina: The Gospel of Luke*, 20.

[14]See the discussion in E. Harold Breitenberg, "Luke 24:13–35," *Interpretation* 64, no. 1 (2010): 75–6.

[15]Bovon et al., *Luke 3: A Commentary on the Gospel of Luke 19:28-24:53*, 375.

[16]Frank J. Matera, *Resurrection: The Origin and Goal of the Christian Life* (Liturgical Press, 2015), 53.

[17]Raymond Orlett, "An Influence of the Early Liturgy upon the Emmaus Account," *The Catholic Biblical Quarterly* 21, no. 2 (1959): 219; Scheffler, "Emmaus—A Historical Perspective," 262.

and anticipate[s] the many meals that will be celebrated in the future."[18] Luke alone, Moloney notes, records the fulfilment of Jesus' promise to the disciples when he declares he shall neither eat the bread nor drink the wine until the kingdom of God is fulfilled (22:16, 18).[19] "What Jesus promised at the final meal with his disciples takes place *within the story*," in the two meals he shares with them in chapter 24. Further, Moloney postulates: "These meals form the bridge for the apostles out of the story of their association with Jesus into their mission."[20] The Lucan narrator shows the way forward for the Christians of his generation. The Emmaus story reveals something fundamental: Jesus is with them at all times but in an entirely new way. Moreover, as Johnson suggests, the story illustrates the growing need for and occurrence of theological reflection: "as people tell the story to each other, they also interpret the story." He continues: "Luke shows us narratively the process by which the first believers actually did learn to understand the significance of the events they had witnessed, and to resolve the cognitive dissonance between their experience and their convictions."[21]

Engaging in Dialogue with Post-Biblical Tradition

There are many places in the tradition where Christian thinkers have engaged with the Emmaus story.[22] In writing against Marcion, for example, Tertullian uses Luke's Gospel (which the heretic Marcion partially accepts) to "prove" that Christ is the son of the same Creator to whom the Old Testament attests. This is by means of the two witnesses (the two being important), whose slowness to believe means that Christ can demonstrate his identity anew. Tertullian writes: "But at no time even after His resurrection did He reveal Himself to them as any other than what, on their own showing, they had always thought Him to be."[23] Origen makes a similar argument in *Against Celsus*.[24] When other writers mention the Emmaus story in early patristic literature, it is frequently only fragmentary. However, common fragments drawn from the narrative relate to the powerful images of "hearts burning" and "the breaking of the bread," although they do not yet give consideration to its eucharistic significance.[25]

[18]Moloney, *The Resurrection of the Messiah*, 61.
[19]Moloney, *The Resurrection of the Messiah*, 57.
[20]Moloney, *The Resurrection of the Messiah*, 57.
[21]Johnson and Harrington, *The Gospel of Luke*, 435.
[22]In recounting this history, we are following Bovon et al., *Luke 3: A Commentary on the Gospel of Luke 19:28-24:53*, 376ff.
[23]Tertullian, *Adversus Marcion* 3, book IV, chapter 43.
[24]Origen, *Against Celsus* 4, book II, chapter 62.
[25]Bovon et al., *Luke 3: A Commentary on the Gospel of Luke 19:28-24:53*, 377.

This situation changes with Augustine. In preaching during the Easter Octave, Augustine devotes a sermon to the Emmaus story.[26] He emphasizes, first, that Jesus is the way, but that the Emmaus disciples had "wandered off the way."[27] With some insight, Augustine then describes how the trauma of Jesus' death has robbed the disciples of the capacity to recognize him, because they are simply not expecting to see him again.[28] "Christ, being alive, found the hearts of the disciples dead, appearing to their eyes, and not appearing. He was at one and the same time seen, and concealed." Augustine immediately applies the story to his own context, explaining that Jesus wants to be recognized in the breaking of bread: "if you listen to the word of God in fear and hope, you may take comfort in the breaking of bread. The Lord's absence is not an absence. Have faith, and the one you cannot see is with you." Yet, what is needed in order for Christians everywhere to recognize Jesus is the exercise of generous hospitality: "Constrain the stranger, if you want to recognize the Savior." Augustine argues that the faithful will recognize the Lord "when [they] eat him."[29] Finally, Augustine attempts to give an explanation for Christ's sudden disappearance in the narrative, that Christ withdrew from the disciples bodily in order to build up their faith.[30]

The theme of hospitality is also central to the homily of Gregory the Great on Lk. 24:13-35. Having experienced doubt about Jesus' resurrection, Gregory explains: "it had to be shown whether those who did not as yet love him as God were at least able to love him as a stranger." Christ manifests himself "before the eyes of their bodies in accord with what was going on inwardly before the eyes of their hearts"; Gregory perceives that the disciples were both "loving and doubting." The disciples urge the stranger to stay and eat with them; they "set the table, brought food, and recognized in the breaking of the bread the God they did not know as he explained the sacred scriptures." Words are not enough, Gregory insists. Instead, we must act. He then draws together a number of scriptural references on hospitality, emphasizing the welcome of the stranger in Mt. 25:35.[31]

To take another example of historical use of the Emmaus text, we look to Bonaventure's Commentary on Luke. Bonaventure focuses on "Christ's threefold accompaniment of the disciples": accompaniment on their journey, accompaniment in conversation, and accompaniment at

[26]Augustine, Sermon 235, *The Works of Saint Augustine: A Translation for the 21st Century III: Sermons*, ed. John E Rotelle, trans. Edmund Hill (New City Press, 1993), 40–3.
[27]Augustine, *Sermons,* 40.
[28]We could say this, too, of Mary in her experience with the gardener in John 20:15.
[29]Augustine, *Sermons,* 41.
[30]Augustine, *Sermons,* 42.
[31]Gregory the Great, *Forty Great Homilies*, trans. David Hurst (Cistercian Publications, 1990), homily 23.

table.[32] Like many others, Bonaventure mistakenly identifies Emmaus with the town of Nicopolis.[33] However, in his consideration of the conversation of the two disciples, he insightfully observes the significance of their discussion: "Now *they were talking* about this because it was especially on their minds, and it was on their minds because they love Christ. For Matthew 12:34 says; 'From the abundance of the heart the mouth speaks'."[34] If we momentarily jump forward to the twenty-first century, we find a similar emphasis on the significance of the activity of talking: Jean-Luc Marion remarks that the saturated phenomenon of revelation is frequently *felt* in the one who witnesses to it by their being unable to stop talking about it.[35] The disciples' talking expresses their deep love. Bonaventure underlines both the goodness of the disciples, who become "worthy to have Christ as a companion," as well as their doubt—which means that they cannot at first see him.[36] Their eyes are not opened by Christ's explanation of the scriptures, but only after they have shown love for Christ as a complete stranger, in offering him hospitality. Bonaventure emphasizes, as Augustine before him, and drawing from Bede and others, that it is not simply in words—in listening to the scriptures—but in action that the Christian becomes incorporated into Christ's body.[37] Another important part of Bonaventure's commentary is that he notes the urgency of the disciples' return to Jerusalem, linking it with the comment in 2 Kgs 7:9: "This is the day of good news. If we keep silence and do not tell it till the morning, we will be charged with a crime."[38] The whole commentary is, in fact, a weaving together of Hebrew and Christian scriptures so that it becomes an experience, for the reader, of the disciples' own experience of Jesus in the Emmaus story, with the reader similarly invited to act.

Engaging in Dialogue with the Current Context

In his 2021 reflections on the Gospel of Luke, Pope Francis sets the Emmaus story in the context of those who have left the Church, that is, of those who walk away from Jerusalem like the two disciples in the wake of their

---

[32]Bonaventure and Robert J. Karris, *St. Bonaventure's Commentary on the Gospel of Luke*, vol. 3: chapters 17–24, Works of St. Bonaventure, vol. 8, pt. 3 (Franciscan Institute, 2004), 2203.

[33]Bonaventure and Karris, *Bonaventure's Commentary on Luke*, 2205. On the historical difficulties of locating Emmaus, see Scheffler, "Emmaus—A Historical Perspective," 254–5.

[34]Bonaventure and Karris, *Bonaventure's Commentary on Luke*, 2206.

[35]Jean-Luc Marion, *In Excess: Studies of Saturated Phenomena*, trans. Robyn Horner and Vincent Berraud (Fordham University Press, 2002), 162; Jean-Luc Marion, *D'Ailleurs: La Révélation* (Grasset, 2020), 266.

[36]Bonaventure and Karris, *Bonaventure's Commentary on Luke*, 2207.

[37]Bonaventure and Karris, *Bonaventure's Commentary on Luke*, 2221–3.

[38]Bonaventure and Karris, *Bonaventure's Commentary on Luke*, 2226.

utter disillusionment and disappointment. Francis writes with compassion for those who "now think that the Church—their Jerusalem—can no longer offer them anything meaningful and important."[39] He reflects:

> So they set off on the road alone, with their disappointment. Perhaps the Church appeared too weak, perhaps too distant from their needs, perhaps too poor to respond to their concerns, perhaps too cold, perhaps too caught up with itself, perhaps a prisoner of its own rigid formulas; perhaps the world seems to have made the Church a relic of the past, unfit for new questions; perhaps the Church could speak to people in their infancy but not to those come of age.[40]

Is it true that this is what contemporary people feel about the Church?

We could think about this question using the enormous amount of sociological and philosophical research that has been undertaken over the last decades concerning the changes in participation in institutional religions in the Western world: generally characterized as "secularisation."[41] While secularization theory has evolved considerably over time, secularization can reasonably be described as a "process of differentiation of the various institutional spheres or subsystems of modern societies, understood as the paradigmatic and defining characteristic of processes of modernization."[42] Yet, secularization alone does not completely describe the modern context. Scientific and technological advances in transportation and communications, as well as the vast movement of people around the world and a structural shift to globalized economies, have had a large part to

---

[39]Pope Francis, *The Gospel of Luke: A Spiritual and Pastoral Reading*, English ed. (Orbis Books, 2021), 248.

[40]Pope Francis, *Luke: A Spiritual and Pastoral Reading*, 249.

[41]On secularization theory, see the special issue debating Jörg Stolz, "Secularization Theories in the Twenty-first Century: Ideas, Evidence, and Problems," *Social Compass* 27, no. 2 (2020): 282–308.

[42]José Casanova, "The Secular, Secularizations, Secularisms," in *Rethinking Secularism*, ed. Craig J. Calhoun, Mark Juergensmeyer, and Jonathan Van Antwerpen (Oxford University Press, 2011), 1050. In context, Casanova writes: "Secularization ... usually refers to actual or alleged empirical-historical patterns of transformation and differentiation of the institutional spheres of 'the religious' (ecclesiastical institutions and churches) and 'the secular' (state, economy, science, art, entertainment, health and welfare, etc.) from early modern to contemporary societies. Within the social sciences, and particularly within sociology, a general theory of secularization was developed that conceptualized these modern European historical transformations, which later became increasingly globalized as part and parcel of a general teleological and progressive human and societal development from the primitive 'sacred' to the modem 'secular'. The thesis of 'the decline' and 'the privatization' of religion in the modern world became central components of the theory of secularization. Both the decline and the privatization theses have undergone numerous critiques and revisions in the last 15 years. But the core of the theory ... remains relatively uncontested in the social sciences, particularly within European sociology."

play in the greatly increased pluralization of societies.[43] Pluralization means that once relatively homogenous social groupings have been exposed to and disrupted by difference—different points of view, different religious beliefs and traditions, different ways of behaving, and different life options. In addition to secularization and pluralization, we can name processes of individualization, detraditionalization, a loss of collective tradition memory, and the distribution and homogenization of religious symbols as significantly impacting the move away from belonging to institutional religions.[44] Charles Taylor argues that these and other changes (such as the "disenchantment" of the world) relate to an enormous shift in our ways of thinking—what Taylor calls a change in "the social imaginary." From Taylor's analysis, we learn that in the contemporary West, many people live without the innate sense of transcendence and engagement of the self with forces beyond it that characterized the lives of the people of earlier times. Taylor speaks of this in terms of living in "the immanent frame": a context where it is understood as normative that this world is "all there is."[45] In light of all this research, we learn that for many people, religion just no longer makes any personal or communal sense.[46]

There is another type of literature we need to consider, however, which is the study of why people actually choose to leave the Christian—and more specifically the Catholic—Church. Needless to say, this is often the most difficult question to study because it requires the capacity to identify and to interview or survey those persons who consider themselves no longer part of an identifiable community. In an American survey in 2021, *The Pillar* asked why Catholics leave and why they stay.[47] America is often considered

---

[43]See Peter L. Berger, *The Sacred Canopy: Elements of a Sociological Theory of Religion* (Doubleday, 1967); Peter L. Berger, *The Many Altars of Modernity: Toward a Paradigm for Religion in a Pluralist Age* (De Gruyter, 2014); Peter L. Berger, "The Desecularization of the World: A Global Overview," in *The Desecularization of the World: Resurgent Religion and World Politics*, ed. Peter L. Berger (Ethics and Public Policy Center/Eerdmans, 1999).

[44]On individualization and detraditionalization, see Martin Fuchs, Antje Linkenbach, Martin Mulsow, Bernd-Christian Otto, Rahul Bjørn Parson, and Jörg Rüpke, eds., *Religious Individualisation* (De Gruyter, 2019); Danièle Hervieu-Léger, "The Distribution of Religious Belief in Individualist Societies," *Année sociologique* 60, no. 1 (2010): 41–62; Lieven Boeve, "Consumer Culture and Christian Faith in a Post-Secular Europe: Individualisation, Critical Agency and Reflexivity," *ET Studies* 17, no. 1 (2006): 105–25; Lieven Boeve, "From Secularisation to Detraditionalisation to Pluralisation: A Challenging Shift for Contemporary Theology," *Roczniki Teologiczne* 51, no. 7 (2004): 5–19; Paul Heelas, Scott Lash, and Paul Morris, *Detraditionalization: Critical Reflections on Authority and Identity* (Blackwell, 1996). On loss of tradition memory and the distribution and homogenization of religious symbols, see Danièle Hervieu-Léger, *Religion as a Chain of Memory*, trans. Simon Lee (Polity, 2000).

[45]Taylor, *A Secular Age*, 543–4.

[46]Horner, *The Experience of God*, chapter 1.

[47]Brendan Hodge, "Special Report: Why Catholics Leave; Why Catholics Stay," *The Pillar*, November 10, 2021.

an exception in the secularization literature, so it is significant to note that even in America, the demographics of institutional believing are shifting.[48] Participants in the survey who identified themselves as having "stopped attending Mass for a year or more" most commonly gave responses indicating that this was due to geographical relocation or a change in personal circumstances, making attendance more difficult or less habitual (20 percent). However, the next highest response (19 percent) was "'I did not feel that attending Church mattered'." Other reasons included: "'My beliefs about God or religious practice changed'" (14 percent); "'I felt my church or religious leaders were not living up to their beliefs'" (11 percent); "'I felt like my church or religious leaders endorsed moral or political views that were wrong'" (9 percent); "'I did not feel welcomed in my church'" (6 percent); and "'I stopped believing in God'" (4 percent). Further, it seems that in the wake of COVID-19, fewer people have returned to church, although early research suggests that this is partly because of ongoing shifts in the mode of attendance.[49]

In a very different context, information released by the Catholic Bishops' Conference in Germany recorded that over half a million people disaffiliated from the Church in 2022. These numbers can be known precisely, since belonging to a church in Germany requires the payment of an additional state tax. Reported in the National Catholic Register, this diminishment is seen to exemplify a trend in place since 1990, which has gained increasing momentum: the 2022 figure, for example, is 44 percent higher than the figure in 2021. Some of those disaffiliating from the Church reject the so-called Synodal Way that was promoted by Pope Francis. However, the author of the article claims:

---

[48]See Vidal Díaz de Rada and Javier Gil-Gimeno, "Have the Inhabitants of France, Great Britain, Spain, and the US Been Secularized? An Analysis Comparing the Religious Data in These Countries," *Religions* 14, no. 8 (2023): 1005; David Voas, "Is the Secularization Research Programme Progressing? Debate on Jörg Stolz's Article on Secularization Theories in the 21st Century: Ideas, Evidence, and Problems," *Social Compass* 67, no. 2 (2020): 323–9; Simon Brauer, "The Surprising Predictable Decline of Religion in the United States," *Journal for the Scientific Study of Religion* 57, no. 4 (2018): 654–75; David Voas and Mark Chaves, "Is the United States a Counterexample to the Secularization Thesis?" *American Journal of Sociology* 121, no. 5 (2016): 1517–56. See also Stephen Bullivant, *Nonverts: The Making of Ex-Christian America* (Oxford University Press, 2022).

[49]Janet Adamy, "Churches Changed During the Pandemic and Many Aren't Going Back," *Wall Street Journal (Online)* (November 12, 2021); Wendy Wang, *How the Pandemic Has Affected Attendance at U.S. Religious Services*, Institute for Family Studies (January 7, 2022); Bev Botting, Ken Eames, and Bob Jackson, *Church Attendance in October 2022: Post-Covid-19 Trends, Patterns and Possibilities*, Diocese of Oxford (March 2023); Justin Nortly and Michael Rotolo, *How the Pandemic Has Affected Attendance at U.S. Religious Services*, Pew Research Center (March 28, 2023); National Church Life Survey, *COVID and Church: What Effect Did It Have?* NCLS Research (September 2022).

> Most of the people who disaffiliate don't want to keep paying for a religious entity that either they no longer trust or that represents a faith that they no longer believe or practice.
>
> A 2021 report by CNA Deutsch noted that 1 in 3 Catholics in Germany were considering leaving the Church. The reasons for leaving vary, with older people citing the Church's handling of the sex-abuse crisis, which broke there in 2010, and younger people pointing to the obligation of paying the church tax, according to one earlier study.
>
> But while the sex-abuse crisis may certainly be a contributing factor to disaffiliation, as are practical economic concerns, a deeper cause of disaffiliation is likely the rising tide of secularism in Germany ... A 2021 estimate found that 42% of Germans are irreligious, up from 30% in 2010. By comparison, the percentage of people in Germany who weren't Catholic or Protestant in 1950 was only 4%.[50]

While this report was written after COVID-19, the author observes that Mass attendance prior to COVID in Germany was already less than 5 percent amongst registered Catholics.

A third study dealing with the question of the reasons why people leave the Catholic Church was published by Stephen Bullivant in 2019.[51] Bullivant draws from three earlier studies from the United States, before introducing the results of his own, British study. He notes from an American study from 2012 that the reasons for respondents leaving the Church included the sexual abuse crisis; a lack of genuine community; and disagreement over doctrinal issues such as "'the church's refusal to ordain women, to allow priests to marry, to recognize same-sex marriage and to admit divorced and remarried persons to reception of the Eucharist ..., [as well as] contraception'."[52] In a 2014 American study, doctrinal issues are the most serious reasons for those disaffiliating:

> six [doctrines] were cited by over half of all respondents as a factor for their having left: birth control, fertility treatments, homosexuality, women as priests, marital status of priests, and divorce/remarriage. In addition, the other two suggested doctrines, abortion and "The Bible," were cited by a third and a quarter of all respondents.[53]

---

[50]Jonathan Liedl, "Why Half a Million Germans Left the Catholic Church in 2022—And What It Means," *National Catholic Register*, no. 28 June (2023).

[51]Stephen Bullivant, *Mass Exodus: Catholic Disaffiliation in Britain and America Since Vatican II* (Oxford University Press, 2019); see also Stephen Bullivant, Catherine Knowles, Hannah Vaughan-Spruce, and Bernadette Duncan, *Why Catholics Leave, What They Miss, and How They Might Return* (Paulist, 2019).

[52]Bullivant, *Mass Exodus*, 59.

[53]Bullivant, *Mass Exodus*, 68–9.

Bullivant highlights the very personal nature of the effects of many of these doctrinal teachings on individuals, which causes them to leave. He also observes that other active Catholics, perhaps not so personally implicated and so not in a position of feeling obliged to leave, are, nevertheless, "*also* troubled by the same sorts of moral teachings."[54] Moral disagreement is especially true of young people and their decision to leave organized religion, suggested in Wallis' 2014 research finding that young people in the United Kingdom often choose "no religion" because they might disagree with one element of an organized religion: "there seemed to be an assumption that in order to identify as a religious person, you had to accept every belief attaining to the faith in question."[55] Returning to the 2014 American study, sexual abuse and cover-up looms large for disaffiliation.[56]

In Bullivant's *Mass Exodus* study, he lists six main "practical and experiential" reasons for disaffiliation from the Catholic Church: "life circumstances; parochial concerns; spiritual and liturgical disillusionment; attractions of other churches; negative experiences with clergy and sexual abuse and the Church."[57] Practical experiences include changes in habits of attending: "Once I was no longer 'required' to attend Mass at the request of my parents—at age 18—I stopped going. I had stopped believing by age 14."[58] The loss of pressure to attend and concomitant presumption of belief is experienced as a great freedom:

> Religion had an air of quite excruciating embarrassment about it and was never discussed at home. When I objected to going to church in my teens, my views were not listened to nor respected. Looking back now, I think I was poorly catechized, despite regular catechism lessons. Belief was assumed. No one ever took me through arguments for the existence of God ... When I went to university, I started off by regular Mass attendance but then it dawned on me that I was now free to do as I wished and gradually tailed off.[59]

The Church is sometimes seen as disingenuous: "I don't see most Catholics as informed or living out the Gospel, attending Mass always seemed more a habit and not an inner work of the Spirit."[60]

---

[54]Bullivant, *Mass Exodus*, 69.

[55]Simeon Wallis, "Ticking 'No Religion': A Case Study Amongst 'Young Nones'," *Diskus* 16, no. 2 (2014): 70–87, cited in Nicola Madge and Peter J. Hemming, "Young British Religious 'Nones': Findings from the Youth on Religion Study," *Journal of Youth Studies* 20, no. 7 (2016): 872–88, 875.

[56]Bullivant, *Mass Exodus*, 69.

[57]Bullivant et al., *Why Catholics Leave*, 22–3.

[58]Bullivant et al., *Why Catholics Leave*, 24–5.

[59]Bullivant et al., *Why Catholics Leave*, 27.

[60]Bullivant et al., *Why Catholics Leave*, 29.

> My daughter made her Confirmation then not long after said that there were so many things she didn't agree with that she couldn't continue to go to Mass. We talked a lot about the Catholic Church, and I found that there were so many things I didn't agree with either that it would have been hypocritical to continue going to church ...[61]

In all the studies that have been mentioned, there is also a phenomenon recognized where people slowly realize that while they have continued to attend Church, they have already left it.

There are "intellectual, doctrinal, and moral reasons" for leaving the Church, although Bullivant observes that the categories are not mutually exclusive. "Half of our respondents," he writes, "either agreed or strongly agreed with the following statement: 'I stopped believing in Catholic teaching'." He lists three significant themes, in particular: "philosophical and historical doubts; doctrinal and moral problems; [and] Vatican II and Liberalization."[62] This last theme is interesting, because as Bullivant notes in *Mass Exodus*, a decline in Mass attendance is observable prior to the end of Vatican II, suggesting that so-called liberalization is not universally considered a reason to leave.[63] Some respondents react to a renewed traditionalism in the Church that is also seen to be a problem:

> What has changed? The fear of priests who have, in my local area, gone back to "childhood," it seems, and who mention such things as the more attendance at Mass equals a better chance to get into heaven, as if some loyalty card exists! I thought such nonsense had disappeared after Vatican II ... Also, this obsession with the past, with Latin, with absolutism, with the perfect liturgy, with a male-dominated Church, with priests telling married couples what is right and what is wrong. It's so wrong and dysfunctional. My children have long left, angry, yet continue to have deep faith and an understanding of the love of God. They cannot understand why those who lead in the Church are so joyless! We are going backwards![64]

Amongst the reasons why people leave are experiences of complete moral rejection by the Church.

> At 15 years of age, pregnant and ashamed, I went into the confessional to ask for absolution ... In a rage, Father [X] dragged me out of the confessional into the vestry and told me that I had broken every

[61]Bullivant et al., *Why Catholics Leave*, 29–30.
[62]Bullivant et al., *Why Catholics Leave*, 60.
[63]Bullivant, *Mass Exodus*, 59.
[64]Bullivant et al., *Why Catholics Leave*, 45.

commandment, broken my mother's heart, and was so sinful that he demanded that I leave the church immediately. Sadly, I never returned.[65]

Bullivant ultimately highlights two overall themes that seem to affect Church participation. The first of these is stated with reference to Taylor: "the eclipse of God from our culture."[66] People not only struggle to believe that God exists, he maintains, but they find little that fulfils their search for meaning in the Church. He quotes one respondent, who says "I would like to feel welcomed as an imperfect being ... A place where serious discussions can be held, and it's OK to explore things deeply; where you can talk about doubts and difficulties, embrace complexity, and go forward in a positive way."[67] The second high-level theme identified by Bullivant relates to "the mystery of evil and disunity in the Church."[68] What he understands by this, however, seems especially to concern evil experienced *within* the Church—in sexual and other abuse, and in a sickly self-referentiality. Like several others, Bullivant arrives here at the question of how the Church can be both holy and sinful—a question that Bullivant does not answer in this text—but a theme to which we shall return in a moment.[69] However, with regard to self-referentiality, he quotes a female who has disaffiliated: "The Catholic Church really needs to change and become less of a Catholic club before I could even consider returning."[70] The experience of many, crystallized in response after response to the sexual abuse crisis, is that clericalism, in particular, is the enemy of holiness.[71]

So, let us return to the diagnosis of Pope Francis, made in light of his reflection on the two disciples walking away from Jerusalem after the devastation of the crucifixion:

> Perhaps the Church appeared too weak, perhaps too distant from their needs, perhaps too poor to respond to their concerns, perhaps too cold, perhaps too caught up with itself, perhaps a prisoner of its own rigid formulas; perhaps the world seems to have made the Church a relic of the

---

[65]Bullivant et al., *Why Catholics Leave*, 53.
[66]Bullivant et al., *Why Catholics Leave*, 136.
[67]Bullivant et al., *Why Catholics Leave*, 137.
[68]Bullivant et al., *Why Catholics Leave*, 141.
[69]Bullivant et al., *Why Catholics Leave*, 143.
[70]Bullivant et al., *Why Catholics Leave*, 144.
[71]Gerald A. Arbuckle, *Abuse and Cover-Up: Refounding the Catholic Church in Trauma* (Orbis Books, 2019); Desmond Cahill and Peter Wilkinson, *Child Sexual Abuse in the Catholic Church: An Interpretive Review of the Literature and Public Inquiry Reports*, RMIT University (Melbourne, 2017), https://www.rmit.edu.au/ ... /church-abuse/child-sex-abuse-and-the-catholic-church.pdf; Marie Keenan, *Child Sexual Abuse and the Catholic Church: Gender, Power, and Organizational Culture* (Oxford University Press, 2011); Mary Gail Frawley-O'Dea and Virginia Goldner, *Predatory Priests, Silenced Victims the Sexual Abuse Crisis and the Catholic Church* (Analytic, 2007).

> past, unfit for new questions; perhaps the Church could speak to people in their infancy but not to those come of age.[72]

In much of the material we have examined, these are, indeed, reasons why people leave the Church. We can agree with Francis that the Church has failed, "perhaps … [appearing] too weak, … too distant, … too poor, … too cold, … too caught up with itself, perhaps a prisoner of its own rigid formulas." The world may have "made the Church a relic of the past, unfit for new questions," but perhaps the Church has also made of itself such a relic. It is true to say that the current, Western context has, for the most part, slammed the door on the question of (divine) transcendence. At the same time, it is also true that just as the early twentieth-century Church condemned "modernism," on the eve of the twenty-first century it also condemned "postmodernism"—each time with a fear that new ways of thinking were a departure from the kind of static solidity with which the Church had imagined itself.[73] It is true that as John XXIII opened the metaphorical windows at Vatican II, John Paul II and Benedict XVI sought rapidly to close them. It is true that as Francis sought to engage in dialogue with the contemporary world, there were people of the Church out to discredit his papacy or even accuse him of heresy.[74]

Nevertheless, we must observe that while Francis is prepared to be critical of the Church, he writes constantly from the perspective of an unwavering commitment to the Church. This leads to a difficult juxtaposition. Immediately after he writes of the Church's weaknesses, he goes on to say: "It is a fact that nowadays there are many people like the two disciples of Emmaus, not only those looking for answers in the new religious groups that are sprouting up but also those who already seem godless, both in theory and in practice."[75] This could sound as if those finding themselves within the horizon of pure immanence are somehow to blame for their situation. And while Francis laments of those who suffer "enormous confusion and an emptiness … regarding the purpose of life, personal disintegration, the loss of the experience of belonging to a 'home' and the absence of personal

---

[72]Pope Francis, *Luke: A Spiritual and Pastoral Reading*, 249.

[73]Pius X, *Pascendi dominici gregis: On the Doctrines of the Modernists* (Libreria Editrice Vaticana, 1907); Pope John Paul II, *Fides et ratio: On the Relationship Between Faith and Reason* (Libreria Editrice Vaticana, 1998); Pope John Paul II, *Veritatis Splendor: The Splendor of Truth—Regarding Certain Fundamental Questions of the Church's Moral Teaching* (Libreria Editrice Vaticana, 1993).

[74]Reuters, "George Pell Wrote Memo Calling Papacy of Pope Francis a 'Catastrophe'," *The Guardian* (Australia) (January 13, 2023); Andrew Brown, "The War Against Pope Francis," *The Guardian Weekly* (October 27, 2017); Edward Pentin, "Full Text and Explanatory Notes of Cardinals' Questions on 'Amoris laetitia'," *National Catholic Register* (USA) (November 14, 2016).

[75]Pope Francis, *Luke: A Spiritual and Pastoral Reading*, 249.

space and strong personal ties," he also insists that this is because there has been "no one to accompany them or to show them with his or her own life the true way." It can be deeply distressing to be told that the Church possesses the "true way," when the Church's way has so often been one of triumphalism, colonialism, racism, sexism, clericalism, and abuse. From Francis' perspective the Church is the true way, so that even in a context of great pluralization, and although the Church has shown itself to be sinful, he does not let go of his commitment to it.

Yet, it is possible for the Church to be committed relationally to the truth of God (that the God who reveals Godself *is* truth) while simultaneously needing to search for truth as a task integral to being human. John Paul II describes this possibility with insight when he speaks of the role of the Catholic university "to unite existentially by intellectual effort two orders of reality that too frequently tend to be placed in opposition as though they were antithetical: the search for truth, and the certainty of already knowing the fount of truth."[76] From the perspective of an orientation to relationship with God who is called "one" and "love" and "truth," there is no need to assume that Francis is presuming in his commentary to know "the truth" of how the journey ends before people have made the quest together. Moreover, when he speaks of there being "no one to accompany them or to show them with his or her own life the true way," perhaps we should be focusing on the question of the one who shows or does the truth (to borrow from Augustine), as distinct from someone who simply "espouses" the truth. If someone were to live the true way with their life, and to witness with that life to the truth of their relationship with God, that would be an offering to others and not an act of violence. The Church, Francis says, needs to be

> capable of walking at people's side, of doing more than simply listening to them; [it needs to be] a Church that accompanies them on their journey; a Church able to make sense of the "night" contained in the flight of so many of our brothers and sisters from Jerusalem; a Church that realizes that the reasons why people leave also contain reasons why they can eventually return.[77]

In the same way that the Church can bear a relationship with God as truth, while needing to search for truth as part of the human condition, we argue that it can at once be holy (of God, or perhaps "close to God") while still needing to become perfect. How can the Church be the body of Christ if it is not perfect? As we say in Chapter 3, the International Theological Commission opts in 1999 to support an understanding that the Church

[76]Pope John Paul II, *Ex corde ecclesiae* (Libreria Editrice Vaticana, 1990), section 3.
[77]Pope Francis, *Luke: A Spiritual and Pastoral Reading*, 250.

as a spiritual reality is perfect while people belonging to the Church can be sinful. This reflects a distinction between the holiness *of* the Church and holiness *in* the Church.[78] In preference to perpetuating this fracture, we prefer to explain the current experience of holiness-yet-sinfulness in terms of the journey and growth to which both humans more generally and Christians specifically are called. The Church as we know it is human and *in via.* It is the body of Christ, but at times it does not reflect what it means to be that body. It is now but not yet. It is not the realization of the reign of God but the people on the way to it.[79] So, while Matthew observes the commandment of Jesus to be perfect: "Be perfect, therefore, as your heavenly Father is perfect" (5:48), he does this in the context of a series of commandments where the Christian is called to fulfil the intention and not just the letter of the law. Becoming perfect is about letting go of what holds us back. While Paul writes in Romans, "Do not be conformed to this world, but be transformed by the renewing of your minds, so that you may discern what is the will of God—what is good and acceptable and perfect" (12:2), he also tells the Corinthians, "This is what we pray for, that you may become perfect" (2 Cor. 13:9) and the author of the book of Hebrews exhorts: "let us go on towards perfection" (6:1). Such is the process of deification about which we read in early church literature: "deification [is] not the perfection of the Christian Gnostic through ethical purification but the participation of the rational creature, through the operation of the Son and the Holy Spirit, in a dynamic divinity that derives ultimately from the Father."[80] Brian Flanagan writes of simultaneous holiness and sinfulness in the Church:

> [we] must be able to account not only for future holiness in the full reign of God, but also for the phenomena of holy women and men, and holy communities, in the history of the church. Similarly, an adequate ecclesiology must be able to take account of collective holiness and collective sinfulness as realities of the church on its pilgrimage toward the reign of God.[81]

Let us again return to Pope Francis and the story of the road to Emmaus. We noted earlier his suggestion that we need "a Church that realizes that the reasons why people leave also contain reasons why they can eventually return." Then, he writes: "but we need to know how to interpret, with

---

[78]International Theological Commission, *Memory and Reconciliation*, section 3.2.
[79]See Horner, *The Experience of God*, 90–1. Also Karl Rahner, "The Church of Sinners," in *Theological Investigations Volume VI: Concerning Vatican Council II* (Helicon, 1969), 141; Flanagan, "Can the Church Be Both Holy and Sinful?"; Brian P. Flanagan, *Stumbling in Holiness: Sin and Sanctity in the Church* (Liturgical Press, 2018).
[80]Norman Russell, *The Doctrine of Deification in the Greek Patristic Tradition* (Oxford University Press, 2004), 12.
[81]Flanagan, *Stumbling in Holiness*, 141.

courage, the larger picture. Jesus warmed the hearts of the disciples of Emmaus," and he asks, "are we still a Church capable of warming hearts?"[82] The overwhelming message of his Papacy is that Christians must be a people of welcome and dialogue.[83] This means that the Church must be a Church that welcomes difference.

> I believe there is no discussion about the call being addressed to everyone. Jesus is very clear about this: everyone. The invited guests did not want to come to the banquet. So he sent out to the streets to call in everyone, everyone, everyone. So that it remains clear, Jesus says "healthy and sick," "righteous and sinners," everyone, everyone, everyone. In other words, the door is open to everyone, everyone has their own space in the Church. How will each person live it out? We help people live so that they can occupy that place with maturity, and this applies to all kinds of people.
>
> ... It is clear that today the issue of homosexuality is very strong, and the sensitivity in this regard changes according to historical circumstances. But what I don't like at all, in general, is that we look at the so-called "sin of the flesh" with a magnifying glass, just as we have done for so long for the sixth commandment. If you exploited workers, if you lied or cheated, it didn't matter, and instead sins below the waist were relevant.
>
> So, everyone is invited. This is the point. And the most appropriate pastoral attitude for each person must be applied. We must not be superficial and naive, forcing people into things and behaviors for which they are not yet mature, or are not capable. It takes a lot of sensitivity and creativity to accompany people spiritually and pastorally. But everyone, everyone, everyone is called to live in the Church: never forget that.[84]

Perhaps this means that there will be some grey areas about where the Church begins and ends. Sometimes those who perceive themselves to be outside the Church will one day find themselves to have been within it all along. And perhaps some of those who think they have left the Church will find themselves to have gone, instead, "further up and further in"—to recall a phrase from C. S. Lewis in *The Last Battle*.[85] There is no doubt in Luke's Gospel that when Cleopas and his companion recognized that Jesus was risen and with them in a new way, they turned around and ran back to Jerusalem.

---

[82]Pope Francis, *Luke: A Spiritual and Pastoral Reading*, 250.

[83]Pope Francis, *On Fraternity and Social Friendship: Fratelli tutti* (Libreria Editrice Vaticana, 2020), especially chapter 6. See also Congregation for Catholic Education, *Educating to Intercultural Dialogue in Catholic Schools Living in Harmony for a Civilization of Love* (Libreria Editrice Vaticana, 2013).

[84]Antonio Spadaro, "'The Water Has Been Agitated': Francis in Conversation with Jesuits in Portugal," *La Civiltà Cattolica* (August 28, 2023).

[85]C. S. Lewis, *The Last Battle* (The Bodley Head, 1956).

How Is the Text Speaking to Me (or Us) Today?

In this chapter, we have examined the Emmaus story in light of the challenge to find Jesus when the presence of God's word is simply not evident to us. God draws close, even when we are oblivious in the frozen, dead night of despair. Moreover, in the expression of hospitality—openness to and lovingkindness of the other—we may recognize the God who has been with us all along. The struggles we name in this book, especially the struggle to continue belonging to the Church when we can no longer find Christ there, call us to smile in the face of strangers in order to welcome God in.

8

The Spirit of God Pours Out into the World: The Experience of Difference

In Chapter 7, we were challenged to consider where we find Christ in the world. Moving to our final chapter, we are challenged to find where God's Spirit speaks in that same world. There are times when the Church is tempted to separate itself from a world that is judged to be ungodly, and there is no doubt that it is possible to live amidst all the noise and forget that God is to be found there. Yet, Pope Francis encourages us to go beyond our boundaries and embrace others as those in whom God is to be found:

> *Those who do not love a brother or sister whom they have seen, cannot love God whom they have not seen"* (*1 Jn* 4:20).
>
> ... this call to love could be misunderstood. Saint Paul, recognizing the temptation of the earliest Christian communities to form closed and isolated groups, urged his disciples to abound in love "for one another and for all" (*1 Thess* 3:12). In the Johannine community, fellow Christians were to be welcomed, "even though they are strangers to you" (*3 Jn* 5). In this context, we can better understand the significance of the parable of the Good Samaritan: love does not care if a brother or sister in need comes from one place or another. For "love shatters the chains that keep us isolated and separate; in their place, it builds bridges. Love enables us to create one great family, where all of us can feel at home ... Love exudes compassion and dignity."[1]

There is no doubting that to be Christian is to turn toward others as fellow children of God.

---

[1]Pope Francis, *Fratelli tutti: On Fraternity and Social Friendship* (Libreria Editrice Vaticana, 2020), Encyclical Letter, ss. 61–2.

The Text: Acts 2:1-23

When the day of Pentecost had come, they were all together in one place. And suddenly from heaven there came a sound like the rush of a violent wind, and it filled the entire house where they were sitting. Divided tongues, as of fire, appeared among them, and a tongue rested on each of them. All of them were filled with the Holy Spirit and began to speak in other languages, as the Spirit gave them ability.

Now there were devout Jews from every nation under heaven living in Jerusalem. And at this sound the crowd gathered and was bewildered, because each one heard them speaking in the native language of each. Amazed and astonished, they asked,

> *Are not all these who are speaking Galileans? And how is it that we hear, each of us, in our own native language? Parthians, Medes, Elamites, and residents of Mesopotamia, Judea and Cappadocia, Pontus and Asia, Phrygia and Pamphylia, Egypt and the parts of Libya belonging to Cyrene, and visitors from Rome, both Jews and proselytes, Cretans and Arabs—in our own languages we hear them speaking about God's deeds of power.*

All were amazed and perplexed, saying to one another, "What does this mean?" But others sneered and said, "They are filled with new wine."

But Peter, standing with the eleven, raised his voice and addressed them: "Men of Judea and all who live in Jerusalem, let this be known to you, and listen to what I say. Indeed, these are not drunk, as you suppose, for it is only nine o'clock in the morning. No, this is what was spoken through the prophet Joel:

> *'In the last days it will be, God declares,*
> *that I will pour out my Spirit upon all flesh, and your sons and your daughters shall prophesy,*
> *and your young men shall see visions, and your old men shall dream dreams.*
> *Even upon my slaves, both men and women, in those days I will pour out my Spirit; and they shall prophesy.*
> *And I will show portents in the heaven above and signs on the earth below, blood, and fire, and smoky mist.*
> *The sun shall be turned to darkness and the moon to blood,*
> *before the coming of the Lord's great and glorious day.*
> *Then everyone who calls on the name of the Lord shall be saved.'*

"You that are Israelites, listen to what I have to say: Jesus of Nazareth, a man attested to you by God with deeds of power, wonders, and signs that God did through him among you, as you yourselves know—this man,

handed over to you according to the definite plan and foreknowledge of God, you crucified and killed by the hands of those outside the law."

A Sensory Meditation on Acts 2:1-23

Ignatian sensory meditation is usually undertaken by placing ourselves into the context of the narrative and taking note of what might be experienced at the level of the senses: sights, sounds, smells, tastes, touch, feelings, and even thoughts. Sometimes, the process might be completely open to what emerges in the experience. At other times, we might begin with a specific question and focus on the question as we enter the scene. With the example below, we take the latter approach.

In the narrative of Jesus' ascension, he says to his apostles, "You will receive power when the Holy Spirit has come upon you; and you will be my witnesses in Jerusalem, and in all Judea and Samaria, and to the ends of the earth" (Acts 1:8). *What does this witness look like*?

As we enter the room, we see that the apostles "are all together in one place" (2:1). Are they in the "room upstairs" in the house where they are staying, in the same room where they elected Matthias, who replaced Judas as the twelfth member of their group (1:13, 26)? Or are they somewhere else? Does it matter? It is a room. They are together. Jesus, who had been with them, is now "out of their sight" (1:9). As we look around, we see them seated at a large, empty table. They have been in prayer, but now they talk in whispers. They wait. They worry. They fear the unknown.

Suddenly, a sound rushes in and fills the house. It is so loud that it jolts us awake; our senses are set on fire. The text uses the metaphors of "violent wind" and "tongues like fire," which unsettle us as we watch. But the disciples around us, strangely, do not jump! They remain in their seats. The Spirit "rests" on their shoulders ("a tongue *rested* on each of them," 2:3). The scene is not one of violence, but of peace. We are at once held captive by the thought of the fury of fire (the burning bush that was not consumed, Exod. 3:2) and consoled by the beauty of peace ("remove the sandals from your feet, for the place on which you are standing is holy ground," Exod. 3:5). This is a symbolic text; the clue is in the detail. And as symbol, it speaks so loudly. The sound—the interruption of the Spirit—*ruptures* the peace and yet brings peace. The fear in the room is gone.

The scene shifts to the crowd outside. There are people everywhere. It is noisy, busy, chaotic. It is the feast of *Shabu'ot*, which happens fifty days after Passover, and the people are all in Jerusalem to celebrate the first harvest of grain. It is a feast of thanksgiving and abundance. We hear laughing and music. We see friends greeting each other, embracing, sharing stories, dancing. There are tables of food scattered throughout the square—breads of different kinds, fruit, even wine. The smell of warm bread mixed with the potency of fresh wine is enough to make our senses sing. The crowd is diverse. The long list of cities Luke gives us spans from the far East to the far West, and Jews and proselytes (Jewish converts) alike have come to celebrate: "devout Jews from every nation under heaven" (2:5). They hear the sudden sound, too. Was it coming from the house at the edge of the square? Or from somewhere above it? They gather and hush. They begin to ask questions to one another. "What does this mean?" (v. 12). Expressions of "amazement," "astonishment," and "bewilderment" fill the air.

We do not get to see the disciples' responses when they begin to speak the languages of their neighbors—we are too busy looking at the crowd, noticing the colors of their clothes, their faces, their voices, the smells. We can only imagine the disciples' surprise. Are they surprised? Jesus had said, "You will receive power when the Holy Spirit has come upon you; and you will be my witnesses in Jerusalem, and in all Judea and Samaria, and to the ends of the earth" (Acts 1:8). But did they really realize what this meant?

Again, *how will they witness? What does their witness look like?* They witnessed first-hand the person of Jesus and the love that exceeded his person, and they witnessed "the sound like a rush of violent wind" (2:2) which signaled the coming of Jesus' Spirit, but the sense of witness of which Jesus speaks goes beyond this. In Jesus' sense, to witness is an *action*. Of course, to speak (in words) is an action, but Jesus' witness to the love of the Father is not just through words; it is also (and predominantly) through deeds—actions that say much more than words. Jesus had stretched out his hand and touched the man with leprosy (Mt. 8:3); he had wept with Mary at hearing the news of Lazarus' death (Jn 11:35); he had sat and talked with the man who was possessed by demons (Lk. 8:35); and he had washed the feet of his disciples (Jn 13:5). Actions speak louder than words. *What is the action here?*

As the disciples begin to speak to members of the crowd, the questions escalate: "How is it that we hear, each of us, in our own native language?" (2:8). It is not that they suddenly understand the language of the disciples; the disciples speak in *their* languages, languages "of every nation under heaven" (2:5). The Spirit had rested on each of the disciples ... Is it the Holy Spirit who speaks now, inspiring the words of the disciples as they speak "about God's deeds of power" (2:11) in a multitude of languages? Perhaps. But maybe it is the *action* of the Spirit that is revealed more clearly. The Spirit "rests" on each of their shoulders, but the sound is heard by all. Peter seems to know what it means.

We might have imagined Peter standing on a rock in the center of the square as he begins to speak. But strangely, here he is at the level of the crowd. He merely "raise[s] his voice" (2:14) and addresses them. We all turn and keen our ears to listen. A child in his mother's arms wriggles and squirms and is finally set free on the ground to play in the dirt. An elderly man leans on his cane and is propped up in the strong arms of his son.

Peter summons the words of the prophet Joel: "In the last days it will be, God declares, that I will pour out my Spirit upon all flesh" (2:17). The action! But surely, it's not that simple. There is more to this than meets the eye.

Peter continues, "Your sons and your daughters shall prophesy ... your young men shall see visions ... your old men shall dream dreams ... even upon my slaves, both men and women, ... I will pour out my Spirit" (2:17-18). We look around—women, men, young and old, sons, daughters, children, the rich, the poor, slaves. The child who was playing on the ground has scampered off; his mother is trying to catch him. Someone has found a chair for the man with the cane. "Devout Jews from every nation under heaven" (2:5). Even to the least of these, Christ's Spirit is poured out. The Spirit is poured out richly and warmly to all. And they are all so different!

How must the experience have felt to the members of the crowd gathered? As Galileans, are the disciples people of authority? Is Peter? He certainly speaks with authority: "This is what was spoken through the prophet Joel" (2:16). We wonder if the members of the crowd consider themselves to be "outsiders" or "insiders." Some are "amazed," "astonished," "perplexed," "bewildered," and some even cast doubt on the whole scene—the disciples must be drunk, they say (2:13). Those who are "amazed and astonished" do not seem to be fearful (in the modern sense of the word), but instead struck with a sense of awe. Perhaps they signify an openness to the new.

If we stay for a moment with those who sneer, we might sense fear. Might these be the same voices who sneered at Jesus when he challenged them to see themselves and held a mirror to their hypocrisy? ("Let anyone among you who is without sin be the first to throw a stone at her," Jn 8:7). It may be that they are simply reacting (in fear) to the unknown (the strange-r), or it may be that they suffer quietly and do not trust the love to which Peter witnesses—the love of God so powerful that it defies even death (2:24). Peter's words are accusing: "Jesus of Nazareth ... handed over to you according to the definite plan and foreknowledge of God, you crucified and killed by the hands of those outside the law" (2:22-23). The Spirit is poured out to them, too.

When the Spirit rests on each of the disciples, they are "together in one place," unified. They experienced the peace of Christ's Spirit—a symbol too large for words. But here, amongst the crowd, they must embrace diversity in order that their message be heard. It is no accident that the crowd hears the message in their own native tongues. The Spirit wills it (2:4). Here, difference is brought to the fore, and difference is not elided but embraced. "I will pour out my Spirit upon all flesh" (2:17). A symbol too large for words. *How will the disciples witness? What does their witness look like?*

Engaging in Critical Dialogue with Biblical Tradition

Scholars traditionally understand the *Acts of the Apostles* to have been written by the same author as the Gospel of Luke: an anonymous physician, well-educated, possibly a companion of Paul, who hailed from Syrian Antioch and wrote for a Greek Christian audience—Jewish diaspora as well as gentile Christians—sometime in the late first century.[2] Christopher Stroup contends that Acts is an "urban" text: it addresses broad concerns facing "elites who lived in Greek cities under Roman rule" and is deeply informed by central features of Hellenistic urban life, which reflect a strong connection between the *polis*, religious activity, and the construction of ethnic and civic identities.[3] Stroup argues that a central purpose of Acts is to legitimate the place of Christians in the city "through a retelling of Christian origins and a positioning of Christians within the hierarchy of civic ethics."[4]

Richard Dillon points out that Luke "is not an actor in the story," he is "the historian digesting and contouring the past."[5] This becomes especially clear when we consider the nature of the text under discussion. This is a theological and ecclesial narrative, not a historical one.[6] Joseph A. Fitzmyer

---

[2]Luke's gospel is traditionally dated between 75 and 85 CE. However, Stroup notes that scholars in increasing numbers argue for dating the writing of Acts in the 90s or even later. Compelling evidence for the single authorship of Luke-Acts includes their dual address to Theophilus (Lk 1:1; Acts 1:1) and reference to the "first book" in Acts 1:1, as well as the theological relationships between the two books. On this last point, see Richard A. Edwards' response to Hans Conzelmann and Helmut Flender: Richard A. Edwards, "The Redaction of Luke," *The Journal of Religion* 49, no. 4 (1969): 392–405. While we acknowledge that some contemporary biblical scholars contest the notion that Luke and Acts are written by the same author, we will follow the lead of the majority and refer to the author as "Luke" in the present work. For more discussion on the authorship of Acts, see Robert J. Karris, "The Gospel According to Luke," in *The New Jerome Biblical Commentary*, ed. Raymond E. Brown, Joseph A. Fitzmyer, and Roland E. Murphy (Prentice Hall, 1991), 675–6; and Christopher Stroup, "Recontextualizing Acts: Religious, Ethnic, and Civic Identity," in *The Christians Who Became Jews, Acts of the Apostles and Ethnicity in the Roman City* (Yale University Press, 2020), 19–20.

[3]Stroup, "Recontextualizing Acts," 21, 22.

[4]Stroup, "Recontextualizing Acts," 20. Stroup here provides a helpful summary of the nature and purpose of Christian apologetics in Acts.

[5]Richard J. Dillon, "Acts of the Apostles," in *The New Jerome Biblical Commentary*, ed. Raymond E. Brown, Joseph A. Fitzmyer, and Roland E. Murphy (Prentice Hall, 1991), 723.

[6]Wedderburn argues that there are parallels with a number of different oral and written texts in the construction of Acts 2:1-13: traces of Ex 19:16, Ex 20:18, Isa 66:15-20, Jubilees 1, 7 and 14 (from the *Apocrypha*), and documents of the Rabbinic traditions. However, few of these connections are thought to be deliberate on Luke's part: "if we find evidence of, say, three discrete perspectives on events then it may be more likely that a predecessor of Luke's had already merged two of them and Luke has imposed the third, his own personal one, rather than that he alone has brought all three together for the first time." Alexander J. M. Wedderburn,

notes that the Lucan account of the theophany of the Spirit is the only one of its kind in the New Testament.[7] Soon after Jesus' appearance to Mary Magdalene in the garden outside the tomb, John recounts Jesus appearing to the disciples, breathing on them and saying, "Receive the Holy Spirit" (Jn 20:22), and Paul's letters refer to the gift of the Spirit to the followers of Christ (Gal. 3:2; Rom. 8:4-11; Eph. 1:13). However, neither makes any mention of a Pentecost event, as such, and there is no mention of the event in either Mark or Matthew. Nevertheless, the event at Pentecost is positioned by Luke as the catalyst for the transformation of the disciples, the event that enabled the spread of the gospel beyond the bounds of Israel.

In our critical dialogue with the text in biblical and post-biblical tradition, three elements are central: the setting and the characters; the nature of speech and the miracle of speaking in other tongues; and what we see as Luke's deliberate insertion of Joel's prophecy into Peter's speech at 2:17-21.

The setting for Luke's account is the Feast of Weeks, seven weeks after Passover.[8] At Passover, unleavened bread is eaten in memory of the first Passover in Egypt; seven weeks later, farmers celebrate the harvesting of grain and offer the wheat of leavened bread to God.[9] Josephus tells us that the festival includes a "solemn assembly" of Jews.[10] This provides a helpful setting for Luke's narrative, where "devout Jews from every nation under heaven" (v.5) have gathered. The list of those in the crowd at vv. 9-11 is curious: Fitzmyer notes that Luke omits nations that one would expect to see (such as Achaia, Macedonia, Cilicia, Syria, and Galatia, all places mentioned elsewhere in Acts), and uses older names of places which by the first century had been changed.[11] Certainly, the nations of the Jewish diaspora are listed—regions of Asia, Asia Minor, and northeast Africa—but the inclusion of Rome and the explicit insertion of Judea has puzzled scholars. Fitzmyer suggests, with others, that Luke derived the list from an unknown source and inserted Rome because he knew of Jews who were

"Traditions and Redaction in Acts 2.1-13," *Journal for the Study of the New Testament* 17, no. 55 (1995): 44; also 28, 54.

[7]Joseph A. Fitzmyer, "The Mission of Testimony in Jerusalem (2:1–8:4)," in *The Acts of the Apostles: A New Translation with Introduction and Commentary* (The Anchor Yale Bible, 1998), 232.

[8]Understood by Christians to be "the fulfilment of Easter," the feast of the Pentecost has been celebrated annually 50 days after Easter since at least as early as the third Century (there is mention of it in the writings of Origen and Tertullian, and explicit mention in Augustine's *Oration 31*, "On Pentecost"). See Edwards, "The Redaction of Luke," 403.

[9]Fitzmyer, "The Mission of Testimony in Jerusalem (2:1–8:4)," 232; Rick Strelan, *Strange Acts: Studies in the Cultural World of the Acts of the Apostles* (De Gruyter, Inc., 2004), 68.

[10]According to Fitzmyer, Josephus uses the Aramaic word, *ăṣartā*, which is related to the Hebrew word *ăṣeret*: "solemn assembly." Josephus, Ant. 3.10.6, n. 252, cited in Fitzmyer, "The Mission of Testimony in Jerusalem (2:1–8:4)," 233.

[11]Fitzmyer, "The Mission of Testimony in Jerusalem (2:1–8:4)," 240.

residing there.[12] Wedderburn contends that the explicit reference to Judea suggests Luke's use of a source "that was not composed from a Judean perspective."[13] Somewhat differently, John Stott argues that "Luke's list comprises five groupings, as he moves with his mind's eye approximately from East to West": (i) "peoples from the Caspian Sea westwards, many of whom will have been descended from the Jewish exiles ... in the eighth and sixth centuries BC"; (ii) the areas of Asia Minor or Turkey, with the insertion of Judea intended to capture the wider area of Palestine and Syria; (iii) North African regions; (iv) Rome, symbolizing visitors from across the Mediterranean; and (v) Crete and Arabia.[14] Needless to say, the crowd gathered in Jerusalem is international and multilingual. For us, the diversity of the crowd is a most striking feature of this narrative, and one that will occupy much of our discussion.

The story opens with the narrator telling us that "they were all together in one place" (2:1). Scholars differ as to whether Luke is referring to the 120 believers who had been present at 1:14-15, or to the twelve apostles, who had been in "the room upstairs" (1:13) and had just elected the last member of their group (1:26). Those who lean toward 120 tend to do so in order to affirm the universal nature of the gift: as one scholar suggests, "the gift of the Spirit was not confined to a special group of spiritual persons."[15] Curiously, and despite these observations, a focus on the *twelve* as the ones who experience the theophany and share it with the crowd has become a dominant way of thinking about this text. Fitzmyer argues that the Pentecost event is "the first opportunity that the Twelve had to confront the twelve tribes of Israel in an official capacity and bear testimony to the risen Christ, having received the power from on high to do so." He maintains that in Acts, "this confrontation and testimony are far more important than the reception of Spirit baptism."[16] According to this reading, the kernel of the theophany is believed to be the "upper room" (1:13).[17]

Fitzmyer and Dillon read Acts 2:4 ("all of them were filled with the Holy Spirit and began to speak in other languages, as the Spirit gave them ability")

[12]Fitzmyer, "The Mission of Testimony in Jerusalem (2:1–8:4)," 240, 242. Barrett suggests that Luke made use of Philo. Charles K. Barrett, *Acts of the Apostles: A Shorter Commentary* (Bloomsbury, 2002), 20.

[13]Wedderburn, "Traditions and Redaction in Acts 2.1-13," 45. He cites Rudolf Pesch, *Die Apostelgeschicte* (Benziger, 1994), 106

[14]John R. W. Stott, *The Message of Acts* (InterVarsity, 1990), A.2.1.a.

[15]Barrett, *Acts of the Apostles*, 17.

[16]Fitzmyer, "The Mission of Testimony in Jerusalem (2:1–8:4)," 238. See also John Chrysostom, "Homily IV," in *Homilies on the Acts of the Apostles. Part I: Homilies 1–28*, Gorgias Occasional Historical Commentaries (Gorgias, 2011), 54.

[17]See, for example, Julianne R. Cenac, "Leader Emergence and the Phenomenological Work of the Holy Spirit in Acts 2," *Journal of Biblical Perspectives in Leadership* 3, no. 1 (2010): 128.

in light of Paul's first letter to the Corinthians.[18] Both here (in Acts) and in Paul, the resting of the Spirit on the believer comes with the attribution of gifts, and it is the giving of these gifts that is understood to have enabled the Christian community to flourish. Paul writes,

> Now to each one the manifestation of the Spirit is given for the common good. To one there is given through the Spirit a message of wisdom, to another a message of knowledge by means of the same Spirit, to another faith by the same Spirit, to another gifts of healing by that one Spirit, to another miraculous powers, to another prophecy, to another distinguishing between spirits, to another speaking in different kinds of tongues, and to still another the interpretation of tongues. All these are the work of one and the same Spirit, and he distributes them to each one, just as he determines.
>
> (1 Cor. 12:7-11)

In a similar vein, Julianne Cenac argues that Acts 2 provides the means by which a theology of leadership might proceed: it narrates the transformation of the disciples "from followers to leaders," formalizes their leadership through the narration of their influence on Jerusalem, and attributes their transformation and influence to the work of the Holy Spirit.[19] Taking the lead of others to read the theophany as an experience centered on the "upper room," Cenac observes,

> The upper room ... is symbolic as a place of gathering, prayer, and a place set apart from the others for purging and the ritual of transformation to take place among the disciples. The power and omniscience of the Holy Spirit here combined with the formality and distinction of the disciples seems to almost foretell or establish the significance of the event.[20]

The others (outside), Cenac contends, are merely observers.

In the theophany at Pentecost, the gifts of the Holy Spirit are audible and discernible. The Spirit enables the disciples to speak in other languages and to have the message of Christ's resurrection heard and understood by Jewish peoples from the East to the West of the known world. Some chapters later, we see that this event is closely connected with Peter's journey to the Gentile nations, where the Spirit "fell upon all who heard the word" (Acts 10:44-45).

---

[18]Fitzmyer, "The Mission of Testimony in Jerusalem (2:1–8:4)," 236; Dillon, "Acts of the Apostles," 731.

[19]Cenac, "Leader emergence," 127.

[20]Cenac, "Leader emergence," 128.

The text sits within the three-fold structure of Acts 2: the theophany itself, which enables speech in a diversity of languages (2:1-13), Peter's speech to the crowd in answer to the question "What does this mean?" (2:14-40), and the beginnings of the mission, which focuses on evangelization, conversion, baptism, fellowship, communal breaking of the bread, prayer, and the selling of worldly possessions (2:41-47). Scholars tend to argue that Luke has a dual purpose in Acts 2: to show that Jesus has fulfilled his promise of sending the Spirit and instilling in the disciples supernatural powers (*cf.* 1:8), and to demonstrate the universal nature of the good news.[21] Indeed, Luke attributes to the Spirit the disciples' newfound ability to "speak in other languages" (2:4) and presents this miracle as the catalyst for the mission of the early Church—the creation of unity from diversity. Interestingly though, both Fitzmyer and Dillon note that the phrase Luke uses in verse 4 refers not to *glōssolalia* (speaking in tongues, such as in ecstatic speech—the "tongues of angels"), but to *xenologia* (speaking in *foreign* tongues—"other human tongues").[22] This reminds us that in the context of this narrative, a variety of different languages are the means by which the good news is heard.

When Peter raises his voice and addresses the crowd (v.14ff.) he uses the words of Joel (2:28-32a, NRSVACE; found at 3:1-5a in other translations), which effectively presents the event at Pentecost as the fulfillment of an Old Testament prophesy. The text in Joel reads:

> Then afterwards
> I will pour out my spirit on all flesh;
> your sons and daughters shall prophesy,
> your old men shall dream dreams,
> and your young men shall see visions.
> Even on the male and female slaves,
> In those days, I will pour out my spirit.
>
> I will show portents in the heavens and on the earth, blood and fire and columns of smoke. The sun shall be turned to darkness and the moon to blood, before the coming of the great and terrible day of the Lord. Then everyone who calls on the name of the Lord shall be saved.

The almost verbatim use of Joel in Acts 2:17-21 is striking. The change in the first line—from "Then afterwards," to "In the last days it will be, God declares"—has the effect of explicitly attributing the event to the hand

---

[21]See, for example, Barrett, *Acts of the Apostles*, 16.

[22]Fitzmyer, "The Mission of Testimony in Jerusalem (2:1–8:4)," 236, 239; Dillon, "Acts of the Apostles," 730. Virginia Burrus uses the term, "heteroglossia," which she derives from *heterai glossai* (literally, "other tongues"). See Virginia Burrus, "The Gospel of Luke and the Acts of the Apostles," in *A Postcolonial Commentary on the New Testament Writings*, ed. Fernando F. Segovia and Rasiah S. Sugirtharajah (T & T Clark, 2009), 147.

of God and presenting it as the inauguration of a new Messianic age: the age of the last days. Stott writes that Joel's prophesy in the mouth of Peter cannot be read as though the pouring out of the Spirit is merely a partial fulfillment of the prophesy. Instead, it reflects the inauguration of the age of the Spirit—the age "between the two comings of Christ" (cf v.20b), an age marked by the abundant ministry of the Spirit.[23] Moreover, there are no social conditions for the reception of the Spirit: neither sex, nor age, nor social status are barriers for receiving the grace of God. Fitzmyer further connects the mission of the apostles with the inauguration of the last days: "For the time has come when the Christian message is about to move out from Jerusalem 'to the end of the earth' (1:8)."[24]

Engaging in Dialogue with Post-Biblical Tradition

The question that we hear from the members of the crowd is a good starting point for discussing how the text has been understood within the context of Christian tradition: "What does this mean?" (v. 12). One way of reading the text follows the approach taken by St John Chrysostom in the fourth century, which is to begin in the house and read the text through the lens of discipleship. Chrysostom declares that it is through the grace of the Spirit that Jesus' followers—those in the house—receive the Holy Spirit (and are thus shown to be "worthy") and it is the Spirit that enables them to bring the good news to all through the miracle of speech in diverse languages.[25] He sees v.17, "I will pour out my Spirit upon all flesh," as a logical extension of the theophany experienced by those in the house.

Another way of reading the text is to begin with what happens *outside* the house, focusing first on why it might be—and what it might mean—that members of the crowd hear the news of the resurrection, each in their own language (2:8). Many scholars who take this approach argue that the narrative of Pentecost enacts God's reversal of the diversity and disunity that was effected at Babel; they see the Pentecost as an event that unifies diverse nations under the particular message of Christ.[26] In the story of the *Tower of Babel* (Gen. 11:1-9) the Shemites are commanded by God to spread throughout their lands, but they ignore God's command, settle together and build a city with "a tower that reaches to the heavens" (v. 4).

---

[23]Stott, *Message of Acts*, A.2.2.b.

[24]Fitzmyer, "The Mission of Testimony in Jerusalem (2:1–8:4)," 252.

[25]Chrysostom, "Homily IV," 54; Fitzmyer, "The Mission of Testimony," 238.

[26]"At Babel human languages were confused and the nations were scattered; in Jerusalem the language barrier was supernaturally overcome as a sign that the nations would now be gathered together in Christ." Stott, *Message of Acts*, A.2.

In doing so they attempt to make a name for themselves and to impose their name and their language on the rest of the world. Scholars who take this line often observe that the narrative of Babel is more than simply an event of human disobedience; it reflects the human desire to *master* the universe and to claim that human beings know more than God.[27] In the end, the Shemites' attempt to unify their people, to make a name for themselves, and place themselves at the level of the heavens results not in unity but in God's radical intervention. God halts the building of the tower, confuses the Shemites' language, and scatters the people "over the face of the whole earth" (Gen. 11:9). The Shemites' claim toward totalization, in the end, results in their dispersal.

We see the reunification reading exemplified in the writings of Ambrose of Milan (fourth century): "if pride caused the division of tongues at Babel, humility was the condition necessary for the coming of the Spirit at Pentecost."[28] In the sixth century, Pope Gregory the Great similarly observes:

> You have heard that the Holy Spirit appeared above the disciples in fiery tongues, and gave them the knowledge of all languages. What does this miracle signify, but that the Church, filled with the same Spirit, was going to speak with the voice of all nations? Those who tried to build a tower in opposition to God destroyed communication in a single language, but in these who humbly feared God all languages were united. In these, humility was rewarded with power, in them pride was rewarded with confusion.[29]

Much later, John Calvin comments on the way in which Pentecost restores the capacity (lost at Babel) "to speak the language of Canaan":

> For whence came the diversity of tongues, save only that the wicked and ungodly counsels of men [sic] might be brought to nought? [Gen 11.7]. But God doth furnish the apostles with the diversity of tongues now, that

[27]Clifford and Murphy argue that the events of Babel reflect "the refusal to accept one's place as a human in the universe under God." See Richard J. Clifford and Roland E. Murphy, "Genesis," in *The New Jerome Biblical Commentary*, ed. Raymond E. Brown, Joseph A. Fitzmyer, and Roland E. Murphy (Geoffrey Chapman, 1990), 18, n. 15. This is a strong theme in Genesis 1-11, particularly since the one tree (of two named trees) identified in 2:8 from which Adam and Eve eat is the tree of the knowledge of good and evil.

[28]Ambrose, Sermo 36.32., *Ambrose: Select Works and Letters*, in *Nicene and Post-Nicene Fathers*, series II, vol. 10, ed. Philip Schaff (Christian Classics Ethereal Library, 2016).

[29]Gregory the Great, *Forty Great Homilies*, trans. David Hurst (Cistercian Publications, 1990), homily 30.

> he may bring and call home, into a blessed unity, men which wander here and there. These cloven tongues made all men to speak the language of Canaan as Isaiah foretold [Is: 19.18].[30]

Calvin's reference to the language of Canaan reminds us of the earnest search, through Jewish and Christian history, to discover the "primeval language" spoken at Babel, and, ultimately, spoken by God.[31] Calvin's contemporary, Lancelot Andrewes (Bishop of Winchester in the late sixteenth century), gives another example of the correction of Babel at Pentecost:

> In which, we behold the mighty work of God; that the same means of tongues, which was the destroying of Babel, the very same is here made to work the building of Sion; that means that scattered them from the tower of confusion, the very same to reduce them to the fold of unity; that so the curse might be taken away, and a blessing come in place, the confused tongues being united into God's glory.[32]

More recently still, at the opening of the Second Vatican Council, Pope John XXIII highlights the Church's desire for unity and ecumenism, explicitly appealing to the unity of Pentecost: "Renew Your wonders in our time, as though for a new Pentecost, and grant that the holy Church, preserving unanimous and continuous prayer … may increase the reign of the Divine Savior, the reign of truth and justice, the reign of love and peace."[33] Commenting on this appeal to Pentecost and engaging the insights of *Lumen gentium* and *Gaudium et spes*, Thomas Guarino claims,

> Vatican II … said the worldwide mission of the church was "fully confirmed on the day of Pentecost". But the council also acknowledged that this global witness to Jesus Christ is deeply injured by ecclesial divisions. Only the restoration of unity among Christians—the unity

---

[30]John Calvin, *The Acts of the Apostles*, trans. John W. Fraser and William J. G. McDonald, 2 vols., ed. David W. Torrance and Thomas F. Torrance (Eerdmans, 1965), 2.

[31]Of course, there are two opportunities in the first section of Genesis for thinking about the origins of language/s: the Babel story in Genesis 11:1-9, and also Genesis 10:5. For discussion, see Yuliya Minets, *The Slow Fall of Babel: Languages and Identities in Late Antique Christianity* (Cambridge, 2022), 100.

[32]*The Sermons of Lancelot Andrewes, vol. 2, Paschal and Pentecostal*, ed. Marianne Dorman (Pentland, 1993), 221–2, cited in David Lyle Jeffrey, "Acts 2, Translating Pentecost," in *The Book of Acts: Catholic, Orthodox and Evangelical Readings*, ed. Charles Raith II (Catholic University of America Press, 2019), 63.

[33]John XXIII, "Opening Address of the Second Vatican Council" (December 25, 1961), https://vatican2voice.org/91docs/convoke.htm.

witnessed at Pentecost—would provide effective testimony for the world today.[34]

So, on this reading, the healing of Babel and the drawing together of languages at Pentecost may represent the possible overcoming even of contemporary divisions.[35]

Christy Cobb, who reads the text through a post-structural and post-colonial lens, highlights some of the problems with this reading. She posits that *like the Shemites*, Peter and the other disciples seek to "make a name for themselves": it is Peter who provides the explanation, Peter who clears up the confusion, and Peter who becomes "the sole speaker" amongst the crowd who had, prior to Peter's speech, been increasingly vocal.[36] According to Cobb, "Peter's tongue becomes a would-be universal tongue."[37] In the section following his speech, listeners are implored to "repent," to "be baptised," to "save [them]selves from this corrupt generation" and "devote[-] themselves to the apostles' teaching" (2:38, 40, 42) so that "day by day the Lord added to their number" (v. 47). For Cobb, the tongue that brings diversity is cut out of the narrative and difference becomes subsumed into the master narrative. She goes so far as to contend that Peter's speech becomes an instrument of "colonial violence."[38]

We might wonder, then, whether the reunification theme is the only or the best reading of Acts 2. If we consider philosopher Jacques Derrida's reading of Babel, we might ask: Does Acts 2 simply reunite by the miracle of translation what was scattered by confusion? This would presume—if we follow his argument in *Des Tours de Babel* about the nature of translation—that the apostles' speaking in all the languages of the world could re-present the singularity of a people able to hold themselves level with God. Yet, God

---

[34]Thomas G. Guarino, "Vatican II and Analogical Thinking: A response to David Lyle Jeffrey," in *The Book of Acts: Catholic, Orthodox and Evangelical Readings*, ed. Charles Raith II (Catholic University of America Press, 2019), 67.

[35]Chrysostom reasons that because Peter is standing next to the apostles, he speaks for all of them and reflects their "common voice." The courage with which he speaks then becomes reflected in the other eleven as they "encounter their adversaries with great boldness" in the mission that follows. Chrysostom, "Homily IV," 60.

[36]Christy Cobb, "Entangled Tongues: A Poststructuralist and Postcolonial Reading of Acts 2:1-13," *Journal for Interdisciplinary Biblical Studies* 4, no. 1 (2022): 9. Cobb cites David Jobling, "Postmodern Pentecost: A Reading of Acts 2," in *Postmodern Interpretations of the Bible*, ed. Andrew K. M. Adam (Chalice, 2001), 212.

[37]Cobb, "Entangled Tongues," 9.

[38]Cobb, "Entangled Tongues," 13. Cobb cites Jennings, who contends that it was in fact with the move into the Roman world later in Acts that Christianity took on colonial tendencies. See Willie James Jennings, *Acts, Belief: A Theological Commentary on the Bible* (Westminster John Knox, 2017), 31. See also, Virginia Burrus' incisive and thought-provoking discussion of Acts 8:25-40 and 16:11-40 in relation to the Lucan concept of mission and its tenuous and complex relationship with Roman imperialism: Burrus, "The Gospel of Luke and the Acts of the Apostles," 148–52.

is untranslatable. No human language is adequate to God's address. No translation ever re-presents its original: a translation is like a jug, which "is one with itself though opening itself to the outside, and this openness opens the unity, renders it possible, and forbids its totality. Its openness allows receiving and giving."[39] In translation, "the original becomes larger; it grows rather than reproduces itself."[40] In light of this, we might say that Pentecost does not reunite the world by restoring the capacity for all to speak the same language; instead, Pentecost frees the peoples of the world by giving dignity to the differences of their languages, by recognizing that the Spirit, inspiring translation, allows God's word to be heard *differently*.

The crowd's question, "how is it that we hear, each of us, in our own native language?" (v.8) reminds us that the text is not only a miracle of speech but also a miracle of *hearing*: as the Spirit is "poured out to all flesh" the crowd "hears the sound and gathers." The Spirit is not contained to the visual sense (tongues like fire) but extends to the aural sense and beyond.[41] The individual members of the crowd hear the good news spoken in their own languages. The disciples must embrace difference and diversity in order that their message be heard. And the members of the crowd respond in a myriad of ways: with awe, bewilderment, confusion, and even skepticism ("They are filled with new wine," v.13). The Spirit is, indeed, the first one who speaks here, and in a way that does not reduce differences but instead welcomes and embraces them.

We have noted the transformation of the disciples as they find a new confidence to speak and begin to speak in the native languages of the surrounding regions, but what seems to go unnoticed by many commentators is the transformation that also takes place in the individual members of the crowd.[42] Their wonder, awe, and confusion upon witnessing the theophany reflect an openness to the new; their worldview has been interrupted, and radically so. Moreover, while Peter and the other disciples cannot but speak about their experience in the house, the crowd speaks too (and at the same

[39]Jacques Derrida, "Des tours de Babel," in *Difference in Translation*, ed. Joseph F. Graham (Cornell University Press, 1985), 190.

[40]Derrida, "Des tours de Babel," 190.

[41]See Fitzmyer, "The Mission of Testimony in Jerusalem (2:1–8:4)," 236.

[42]Claude Romano argues that the event is only event when a change has taken place and when the change *appears*: "There is no event without change ... In order for there to be an event, a change has to appear, or rather, the event is the appearing of the change itself ... In order for a change to rate as an event, it has to appear to someone as change, that is, it has to modify something from the point of view of one's experience. In order for there to be an event, it does not suffice that something changes; it is necessary for this change to make a change *for* someone. The event is not the transformation itself, it is the appearing of that transformation in the world, or yet again: it is the taking place of that transformation, its occurrence." Claude Romano, *There Is: The Event and the Finitude of Appearing*, trans. Michael B. Smith (Fordham University Press, 2016), 217.

time as the disciples), with questions, gestures, and facial expressions, and their speaking is not homogeneous.[43]

In Chapter 7, we discussed some of the reasons why many Catholics no longer attend Sunday services or feel connected with a parish community. Perhaps they sense that there are those who are "in," who seem to know all the answers, and those who stand outside, who have more questions than answers. In Acts 2, the disciples witness to Jesus as they speak in the languages of their neighbors and place the event in the context of the Paschal mystery, but even they could never have fully grasped the mysterious revelation of God to the world in the Spirit of Christ: faith makes room for mystery. Those who stand outside are welcomed by the Spirit, too ("I will pour out my Spirit upon all flesh"), and in their responses to the event are no less loved by God. In this text, we see that there is room in God for those who have answers, those who ask questions, those who are brought to silence by a sense of awe, and even those who approach the whole thing with a healthy skepticism or even refusal. All of these responses have a place in the relational dialogue to which sentient (yes—all fleshly) beings are invited by God.[44] It is the Spirit who speaks here, in "sighs too deep for words" (Rom. 8:26).

Engaging in Dialogue with the Current Context

In 1975, during the apartheid era in South Africa, the Dutch Reformed Church (DRC) published a report that appealed to the Pentecost event as confirmation "that it is the will of God that each man [*sic*] should learn of the great deeds of God in his own language" and that in order for this to be achieved, each language group "must form its own separate, racial churches."[45] On this reading, the narrative of the Pentecost sanctioned apartheid. The DRC's stance on apartheid and their reading of the Pentecost has since been changed, of course, along with South African government policy, but the intergenerational trauma remains.[46]

---

[43]This argument is developed in detail in Teresa G. Brown, "Thinking God in Contemporary Theology: The Trinity and Christian Life Through the Lens of a Theology of Interruption" (Doctoral dissertation, Australian Catholic University, 2020), 243–4.

[44]"Through this revelation, therefore, the invisible God out of the abundance of God's love speaks to men and women as friends and lives among them, so that God may invite and take them into fellowship." Vatican II Council, *Dei verbum*, 2. Trans. modified.

[45]Dutch Reformed Church, "Human Relations and the South African Scene in Light of Scripture" (South Africa, 1975), 86, cited in Heidi J. Hornik and Mikeal C. Parsons, *The Acts of the Apostles Through the Centuries* (Wiley Blackwell, 2017).

[46]See, Zelda G. Knight, "In the Shadow of Apartheid: Intergenerational Transmission of Black Parental Trauma as it Emerges in the Analytical Space of Inter-Racial Subjectivities," *Research in Psychotherapy* 22, no. 1 (April 19, 2019): 128–37.

For those who might think this odd—a Christian church's support for racist policies—we need only look to our own backyard (here in Australia) to see that we have had our own version of apartheid, and that this, too, was supported by Christian churches. In 1788, British settlers overran what we know as Australia, despite the prior sovereignty of Aboriginal and Torres Strait Islander Peoples for over 60,000 years. In the 100 years that followed, the First Peoples of Australia were massacred, taken from their land, and treated in ways that deliberately dehumanized them and destabilized their cultures. During the period of 1890–1950, reserves, stations, and missions (missions mostly run by Christian churches, both Protestant and Catholic) were set up to segregate, house, and catechize the First Peoples, as part of an official government "protection" policy, which essentially aimed at segregation.[47] By 1915, amendments to the Aboriginal Protection Act allowed children to be forcibly removed from their parents in the missions and reserves and taken to boarding homes for training as workers (on farms and for domestic service) or to white (usually Christian) families in order to be "assimilated" into "white culture." When government policy began to move away from segregation, towards the deliberate eradication of Aboriginal and Torres Strait Islander Peoples' histories and cultures, it was thought that children were "more adaptable to white society than adults" and could more easily be assimilated.[48] The period of 1915–70 is known as the period of the "Stolen Generations," but the forced removal of children from Aboriginal and Torres Strait Islander communities continues to this day under paternalistic government policies.[49]

A not-so-well-known policy that existed between 1897 and 1967 was the "Aboriginal Exemption."[50] A clause in the Aboriginal Protection Acts of all Australian States allowed State governments control over the lives of First Peoples—over where they lived and worked, over who they interacted with and where they spent their money, even over their children and parental

---

[47]Walking Together Reconciliation Committee, "Protection and Segregation 1890s to the 1950s" (June 2020), http://www.workingwithindigenousaustralians.info/content/History_4_Protection.html.

[48]Australians Together, "The Stolen Generations: The Forcible Removal of First Nations Children from Their Families" (2023), https://australianstogether.org.au/discover-and-learn/our-history/stolen-generations.

[49]Michael McGowen reports: "In 2019/20, 952 Aboriginal children across NSW were removed from their families, a 2.6% increase on the year prior. In total, there were 6,688 Aboriginal children in what is known as 'out-of-home-care'—about 41% of the total number of kids in the system. This is despite Aboriginal children only making up 6% of Australia's under-18 population." Michael McGowan, "'People Think It's All in the Past': Push to Reform System Taking Aboriginal Kids from Families," *The Guardian* (March 14, 2022), https://www.theguardian.com/australia-news/2022/mar/14/people-think-its-all-in-the-past-push-to-reform-system-taking-aboriginal-kids-from-families?CMP=share_btn_link.

[50]Judi Wickes and Katherine Ellinghaus, "Women's Experiences of Aboriginal Exemption," *Agora* 56, no. 1 (2021): 9.

rights. Under State Aboriginal Exemption policies, a person could apply for and receive an exemption to this clause if they were judged to be "worthy" by government administrators.[51] The exemption enabled the recognition of basic human rights and a form of self-determination—access to education and health services, the ability to open a bank account, attend public venues, be served in stores, and access social security and pensions.[52] Aunty Judi Wickes, one of the contributors to an edited collection of stories from descendants of those who were granted an exemption, explains: "To many people the certificate of exemption was a way out, to get away from the government's control and have a voice for themselves. Even though they were under surveillance, they had more of a life than what they did when they lived under the Act. People had freedoms, people had choices that they didn't have before."[53] However, the exemption came at a high cost. Strict guidelines to keep it from being revoked (and to keep out of jail) included the requirement for people to renounce culture and heritage: to cut ties to their families and communities, to cease speaking in their native languages and participating in cultural celebrations, and be "always 'Clean, Clad and Courteous'."[54] In short, it meant "living as though they were assimilated."[55] Aunty Judi continues,

> One of the things of the certificate of exemption [was that] you were no longer classed as an Aboriginal person, you were a non-Aboriginal person. And one of the rules [was that] they weren't allowed to associate with other Aboriginal people. So we grew up really isolated in many ways from the community members … If we associated with other Aboriginal people, we could be automatically sent back to the mission. And so it really gave us a different viewpoint of growing up [from that of] other Aboriginal people who grew up on the communities or the missions.
>
> … People lived in fear. It stopped a lot of people interacting. And that's why today we have a lot of people looking for family. It's because of

[51]Aboriginal Exemption, "The History of Aboriginal Exemption," https://aboriginalexemption.com.au; also Australian Institute of Aboriginal and Torres Strait Islander Studies, "Exemption: the High Price of Freedom," https://aiatsis.gov.au/explore/exemption-high-price-freedom, accessed September 19, 2023.

[52]Sarah Collard, "'Stolen Twice': The Hidden Story of Exemption Certificates for Indigenous Peoples," *NITV News* (March 31, 2021), https://www.sbs.com.au/nitv/article/stolen-twice-the-hidden-story-of-exemption-certificates-for-indigenous-peoples/ebz7emgml.

[53]State Library Queensland, "Freedom: A Certificate of Exemption Story" (May 3, 2017), YouTube video, 7:49 min, at 2:17, https://youtu.be/syW1cC3F6hE?si=xGo0c-rqAX4K0hhM. For the collection, see Lucinda Aberdeen and Jennifer Jones, eds., *Black, White and Exempt: Aboriginal and Torres Strait Islander Lives Under Exemption* (Aboriginal Studies Press, 2021).

[54]Australian Institute of Aboriginal and Torres Strait Islander Studies, "Exemption: The High Price of Freedom."

[55]Wickes and Ellinghaus, "Women's Experiences of Aboriginal Exemption," 11.

this certificate of exemption. In essence, the government took away their identity of who they were. They were no longer Aboriginal people.[56]

Aunty Dorrie Moore, a Moyura Elder whose father was issued a certificate of exemption in 1957, shared her story with ABC Open's Object Stories Project.[57] Her niece, Maureen Davis, explains: "It was a licence that stripped us of our culture, our language, our family. Because once this licence was issued, you couldn't visit your family who remained on Wallaga Lake Mission. You couldn't speak the language, or practise the culture. Our elders did practise the culture, but it was all kept under lock and key with these licences. It impacted on many families."[58] Those who held an exemption certificate were also expected to carry it with them at all times, "to prove [their] status at any time and with any one"; they lived with constant external and internal shame.[59]

We cannot help but think about the striking resemblance of all of this to the antisemitic policies of the early twentieth century. In Germany, Jews had to produce papers to prove their status and eventually wear the Star of David to mark them as "other." By the time government policy on Australia's First Peoples shifted to integration and self-determination—following the 1967 referendum which recognized their citizenship (with the yes vote taking an overwhelming majority)—the damage had been done; the stage for intergenerational trauma had been set.

In 2023, Australians voted no in the referendum for an Indigenous Voice to Parliament enshrined in the Constitution, which would have enabled the First Peoples of Australia to have a say over government policies affecting them. In the lead-up to the vote, all types of media were full of misinformation, misrepresentation, and scare campaigns. Racism again reared its ugly head (did it ever really go away?).[60] The discussion was divisive, and the outcome led to more division, confusion, hurt, and shame.

Ben Abbatangelo, a Gunaikurnai and Wotjobaluk writer, shared a story that he believes illustrated the state of the campaign:

---

[56]State Library Queensland, "Freedom: A Certificate of Exemption Story," at 3:33, 37:02.

[57]Vanessa Milton, "Remembering the Days of the 'Dog Licence'," *ABC Local* (February 5, 2014), https://www.abc.net.au/rightwrongs/story/dog-licence/.

[58]Milton, "Remembering the Days of the 'Dog Licence'."

[59]Aboriginal Exemption, "The History of Aboriginal Exemption."

[60]The treatment of Stan Grant, Wirudjuri man and celebrated journalist, is a case in point. See Stan Grant, "For Years I've Been a Media Target for Racism and Paid a Heavy Price. For now, I Want No Part of It—I'm Stepping Away," *ABC Online* (May 19, 2023), https://www.abc.net.au/news/2023-05-19/stan-grant-media-target-racist-abuse-coronation-coverage-enough/102368652. See also Daniel James' discussion on the role that the Australian media plays in perpetuating racism and violence in the public sphere: Daniel James, "Stan Grant and the Anti-voice Trolls," *The Saturday Paper, Shwartz Media* (May 27, 2023), https://www.thesaturdaypaper.com.au/comment/topic/2023/05/27/stan-grant-and-the-anti-voice-trolls.

> [This story] was passed on to me a while back by Kado Muir, an esteemed Aboriginal artist, anthropologist and archaeologist.
>
> He told me his brother-in-law, when he was a young fella, used to be in a lot of spear fights. "Now, when a spear comes out of the woomera, there's two rotations that take effect," Muir told me. "The point and tail remain stable, but in the middle, there are two rotations in the shaft."
>
> Standing in front of it, the spear looks like a massive propeller. "When you're waiting down the end with your shield, the idea is to ignore all of the noise around it and focus on the little black dot, which is the tip of the spear," he said. "Because that little black dot is the difference between you walking or getting carried off. That little black dot is all that matters."
>
> I thought about this story as I looked at all the noise around the Voice to Parliament, all the nauseating discourse, the rigid binaries of "Yes" and "No," the total absence of space for curiosity, for exploring theories of change or examining doctrines of justice and fairness. Everything is the spinning shaft and no one is looking at the little black dot.
>
> There is a grotesque disconnect between what's being said and what's being done. The focus on the future is obscuring what's happening in the present—all of which is a violent continuation of the past.[61]

Now, let us return to the text at hand and the two phrases that have kept us occupied throughout this chapter: "How is it that we hear, each of us, in our own native language?" (Acts 2:8) and "I will pour out my Spirit upon all flesh" (2:17). Virginia Burrus considers the text from a post-colonial perspective. She argues that Luke is present and also "paradoxically, absent" as "author," not because he controls or disciplines speech by framing the event through the lens of Joel's prophecy, but because of his "mobilization of a heteroglossia that cannot finally be contained ... Speech in Luke-Acts remains textured by contingency, split or doubled by the awareness of other 'tongues', spaces and temporalities."[62] Burrus contends that we possibly hear in Acts 2 an "in-between" space "that may open the way to conceptualizing an *inter*national culture, based not on the exoticism of multiculturalism or the diversity of cultures, but on the inscription and articulation of culture's *hybridity*'."[63] Indeed, perhaps one way of thinking about the narrative of the Pentecost and the revelation that difference is welcomed and loved by God is to think about human culture itself as *hybrid*.

---

[61] Ben Abbatangelo, "Actions Speak Louder than the Voice," *The Saturday Paper* (June 10, 2023), https://www.thesaturdaypaper.com.au/comment/topic/2023/06/10/actions-speak-louder-than-the-voice.

[62] Burrus, "The Gospel of Luke and the Acts of the Apostles," 148. As we noted earlier, instead of using *xenologia*, in line with Fitzmyer and Dillon, Burrus uses the term *heteroglossia*, which she derives from *heterai glossai* (literally, "other tongues").

[63] Burrus, "The Gospel of Luke and the Acts of the Apostles," 148. She cites Homi K. Bhabha, *The Location of Culture* (Routledge, 1994), 38.

How Is the Text Speaking to Me (or Us) Today?

Let us return for a moment to Guarino's discussion of the connection between Vatican II and the Pentecost and recall his claim that "only the restoration of unity among Christians—the unity witnessed at Pentecost—would provide effective testimony for the world today."[64] We have tried to show in this chapter that the unity revealed at Pentecost is not a unity that elides differences, on the one hand, or brings division, on the other, but instead, a unity that embraces diversity simply because it is loved and affirmed by God. As you consider all that you have read in this chapter, think about what kind of unity you would like to see in your social, political, and religious communities today. How are you challenged to respond to the voices of difference in your own communities and nations? How might we ensure that a variety of voices are heard when decisions are being made? In colonized countries, how might we together discern a way forward that enables the voices silenced by colonization to speak? In light of all that you have read in this chapter, how does the Spirit call you to respond?

[64]Guarino, "Vatican II and Analogical Thinking," 67.

Conclusion

In choosing the title *Doing Theology in Plural Contexts* for this book, we wanted to underscore our conviction that engaging with scripture in theological ways (i.e., with reflection on the ways God might be speaking through the text) requires a particular type of intention. It calls us to go to the sources, to set aside pre-conceived ideas and assumptions, to build our understanding about the text so that we are primed for critical reflection, and to take seriously "the joys, hopes, griefs and anxieties" of people in the many contexts in which Christian faith is lived.[1] In each chapter, we have tried to show how a rigorous hermeneutical and critical engagement with scripture can help to create the conditions for authentic recontextualization. As we (the authors) move through the process of listening to a text in a number of different ways and then dialoguing with the biblical tradition and the post-biblical tradition, questions and insights emerge for us that lead us to think about a particular experience and a particular issue we find in our context. Our context is Australia. The issues and questions that emerge for us as we engage with the texts in this book reflect our awareness of the diverse religious and cultural communities in Australia and the colonial violence that marks our history. In Australia, as in many "Western" countries, mental health is on a steep decline, economic policy often takes precedence over the lives of human beings, public conversations about important issues often descend into hurtful assaults, and politicians weaponize these issues for political gain. Our reflections on the texts we have chosen for this book led us to consider the experiences of shame, abjection, hell, grief, anger, difference, and transformation, and to reflect on the way these experiences open onto issues of sexual abuse, gendered violence, discrimination on the basis of gender and sexuality, mental illness, colonization, clericalism, and disaffiliation from the Catholic Church. When we think about what it means to live Christian faith today—an authentic,

[1]Vatican II Council, *Gaudium et spes*, 1.

incarnational, and relational Christian faith—these issues and many others that affect Australian communities are front and center for us. Within your contexts, and through the lenses of different experiences and different times, the issues that emerge will be different.

We hope you have seen that recontextualization is not about replacing the text, or changing the text, or reading into the text merely what we want to hear or finding new meanings in the text that then become the new "fixed" meanings for today. Instead, recontextualization it is about engaging in a *repeated* process of meaning-making in order to listen to the way God continues to reveal Godself through the text in new contexts and in new times. It is about remembering that scripture mediates God's revelation—it is symbol in the richest sense of the word.[2] It holds multiple meanings, carries those meanings with it (we need only take the time to listen), and at the same time opens onto new meanings. When the symbol is placed into a new context, the symbol speaks anew. And when scripture, as *textual* symbol, is placed into a new context, God calls the reader to respond.[3]

At the beginning of this book, we noted: "it is a book that can be used by leaders and teachers in Catholic schools and systems (and those working in support of same) for the development of their theological knowledge, skills,

---

[2]In his extensive analysis of the documents of the Second Vatican Council, Ormond Rush notes in *Dei verbum* a clear differentiation between the *Word* of God—Christ, the divine Word—and the "written word of God." He writes, "*Both* 'tradition and scripture make up a single sacred deposit of the *word of God*, which is entrusted to the church' (DV 10). The phrase 'the word of God' here, as elsewhere in *Dei Verbum*—including those very first words of the document—is to be understood as a synonym for divine revelation itself: God's self-communication to human beings in Christ through the Spirit. God's personal address ('word') to humanity goes beyond 'words' and includes deeds, gestures, acts in history (DV 2). *Dei Verbum* does not refer to Scripture by itself as simply 'the word of God.' Scripture, rather, is spoken of as 'the word of God... in its written form' (DV 10) or 'the written word of God' (DV 24). *Scripture is not divine revelation itself, nor is the living tradition itself divine revelation, because neither is itself or together the living, personal, dialogic encounter between the triune God and human beings who respond in faith. They both, together, facilitate that encounter.*" Ormond Rush, *The Vision of Vatican II: Its Fundamental Principles* (Liturgical Press, 2019), 156. Emphasis added.

[3]When we use the term "response," here, we are thinking about it in two ways: 1) in terms of Rahner's contention that God invites the reader into relationship and (in grace) enables the possibility of a free response in faith; and 2) in terms of Reimund Bieringer's compelling argument for scripture to be read as "an invitation to participate in building a better world for full life for all." Bieringer considers biblical texts to be "a window into the mysterious reality of the future that God has in store for us." This "future orientation" of the text, he says, makes "ethical claims for the present that flow from the eschatological vision." Reimund Bieringer and Mary Elsbernd, "Introduction. The 'Normativity of the Future' Approach: Its Roots, Development, Current State and Challenges," in *Normativity of the Future: Reading Biblical and Other Authoritative Texts in an Eschatological Perspective* (Peeters, 2010), 22–4. In a somewhat similar vein, Sarra Lev proffers a fascinating discussion on the way a hermeneutical and critical reading of the Talmud, a Jewish text, summons readers "to become our best selves." See Sarra Lev, "Talmud That Works Your Heart: New Approaches to Reading," in *Learning to Read Talmud*, ed. Jane L. Kanarek and Marjorie Lehman (Academic Studies Press, 2016), 175–202.

and dispositions—knowledge, skills, and dispositions that will support their work to enhance the identity of Catholic schools today." Now that you have come to the end, we invite you to choose a text to undertake a process of recontextualization (you will find our process summarized for reference at the back of this book). In the belief that God continues to speak in human history, be open to what emerges and have the courage to ask how the text speaks to you today. As our colleague, Gina Bernasconi, observes in a challenging reflection on the present book: "there are no shortcuts—we have to do the work." We have to do the work.

SELECT BIBLIOGRAPHY

Aberdeen, Lucinda, and Jennifer Jones, eds. *Black, White and Exempt: Aboriginal and Torres Strait Islander Lives under Exemption*. Aboriginal Studies Press, 2021.

Alison, James. *The Joy of Being Wrong*. Crossroad, 1998.

American Psychiatric Association. *Diagnostic and Statistical Manual of Mental Disorders: DSM-5-TR*. 5th ed. American Psychiatric Association, 2022.

Anselm. *Basic Writings*. Edited and Translated by Thomas Williams. Hackett, 2007.

Aquinas, Thomas, Fabian Larcher, James A. Weisheipl, Daniel Keating, and Matthew Levering. *Commentary on the Gospel of John Chapters 6–12*. Catholic University of America Press, 2010.

Arbuckle, Gerald A. *Abuse and Cover-Up: Refounding the Catholic Church in Trauma*. Orbis Books, 2019.

Augustine. *Treatises on Marriage and Other Subjects: The Good Marriage, Adulterous Marriage, Holy Virginity, Faith and Works, The Creed, Faith and The Creed*. Translated by Charles T. Wilcox. Edited by Roy Joseph Deferrari. Catholic University of America Press, 1955.

Augustine. Sermon 235. *The Works of Saint Augustine: A Translation for the 21st Century III: Sermons*. Edited by John E. Rotelle. Translated by Edmund Hill, 40–3. New City Press, 1993.

Augustine. *The Confessions*. Edited and Translated by Thomas Williams. Hackett, 2019.

Averill, James R. *Anger and Aggression: An Essay on Emotion*. Springer, 1982.

Barrett, Charles K. *Acts of the Apostles: A Shorter Commentary*. Bloomsbury, 2002.

Basinger, David. *Miracles*. Cambridge University Press, 2018.

Berger, Peter L. *The Sacred Canopy: Elements of a Sociological Theory of Religion*. Doubleday, 1967.

Berger, Peter L., ed. *The Desecularization of the World: Resurgent Religion and World Politics*. Ethics and Public Policy Center/Eerdmans, 1999.

Berger, Peter L. *The Many Altars of Modernity: Toward a Paradigm for Religion in a Pluralist Age*. De Gruyter, 2014.

Bernard of Clairvaux. *Sermons on the Song of Songs*. Fig Classic Series, 2013.

Beste, Jennifer. "Envisioning a Just Response to the Catholic Clergy Sexual Abuse Crisis." *Theological Studies* 82, no. 1 (2021): 29–54.

Betz, Hans Dieter. "The Origin and Nature of Christian Faith according to the Emmaus Legend: (Luke 24:13–32)." *Interpretation* 23, no. 1 (1969): 32–46.

Bieringer, Reimund, and Mary Elsbernd, eds. *Normativity of the Future: Reading Biblical and Other Authoritative Texts in an Eschatological Perspective*. Peeters, 2010.

Black, David Alan, and Jacob N. Cerone, eds. *The Pericope of the Adulteress in Contemporary Research*. Library of New Testament Studies. Vol. 55. Bloomsbury, 2016.

Bockmuehl, Markus. "'The Form of God' (Phil. 2:6) Variations on a Theme of Jewish Mysticism." *Journal of Theological Studies* 48, no. 1 (1997): 1–23.

Boeve, Lieven. *Interrupting Tradition: An Essay on Christian Faith in a Postmodern Context.* Translated by Brian Doyle. Peeters, 2003.

Boeve, Lieven. *God Interrupts History: Theology in a Time of Upheaval.* Translated by Brian Doyle. Continuum, 2007.

Boeve, Lieven. *Lyotard and Theology: Beyond the Christian Master Narrative of Love.* T&T Clark, 2014.

Bonaventure, and Robert J. Karris. *St. Bonaventure's Commentary on the Gospel of Luke.* Franciscan Institute, 2004.

Boquet, Damien, and Piroska Nagy. "Medieval Sciences of Emotions during the Eleventh to Thirteenth Centuries: An Intellectual History." *Osiris (Bruges)* 31, no. 1 (2016): 21–45.

Borer, Michael Ian. "The New Atheism and the Secularization Thesis." In *Religion and the New Atheism: A Critical Appraisal*, edited by Amarnath Amarasingam, 125–37. Brill, 2014.

Bouwens, Jan. "Recontextualizing Catholic School Identity: Five Criteria." In *Teaching and Tradition: On Their Dynamic Interaction*, edited by Jos Moons, Rudi A. te Velde, and Archibald L.H.M. van Wieringen, 150–70. Brill, 2023.

Bovon, François, James E. Crouch, Donald S. Deer, Christine M. Thomas, and Helmut Koester. *Luke 3: A Commentary on the Gospel of Luke 19:28–24:53.* Hermeneia: A Critical and Historical Commentary on the Bible. Fortress, 2002.

Brachtendorf, Johannes. "'Et lacrymatus est Jesus': The Sorrow of Jesus in the Teaching of Augustine and Aquinas on the Affections." *Augustinian Studies* 48, no. 1–2 (2017): 225–45.

Breitenberg, E. Harold. "Luke 24:13–35." *Interpretation* 64, no. 1 (2010): 74–6.

Brown, Raymond E. *The Community of the Beloved Disciple.* Paulist, 1979.

Brown, Raymond E. *An Introduction to the New Testament.* Edited by Marion L. Soards. Abridged. Yale University Press, 2016.

Brown, Raymond E., Joseph A. Fitzmyer, and Roland E. Murphy, eds. *The New Jerome Biblical Commentary.* Prentice Hall, 1991.

Brown, Teresa G. "Thinking God in Contemporary Theology: The Trinity and Christian Life through the Lens of a Theology of Interruption." Doctoral dissertation, Australian Catholic University, 2020.

Bullivant, Stephen. *Mass Exodus: Catholic Disaffiliation in Britain and America since Vatican II.* Oxford University Press, 2019.

Bullivant, Stephen. *Nonverts: The Making of Ex-Christian America.* Oxford University Press, 2022.

Bullivant, Stephen, Catherine Knowles, Hannah Vaughan-Spruce, and Bernadette Durcan. *Why Catholics Leave, What They Miss, and How They Might Return.* Paulist, 2019.

Burrus, Virginia. "The Gospel of Luke and the Acts of the Apostles." In *A Postcolonial Commentary on the New Testament Writings*, edited by Fernando F. Segovia and Rasiah S. Sugirtharajah. The Bible and Postcolonialism 13, 133–55. T&T Clark, 2009.

Byrne, Brendan. *Lazarus: A Contemporary Reading of John 11:1–46.* St. Paul, 1991.

Cahill, Desmond, and Peter Wilkinson. *Child Sexual Abuse in the Catholic Church: An Interpretive Review of the Literature and Public Inquiry Reports.* RMIT

University (Melbourne: 2017). https://www.rmit.edu.au/ … /church-abuse/child-sex-abuse-and-the-catholic-church.pdf.

Calvert, David G. A. "An Examination of the Criteria for Distinguishing the Authentic Words of Jesus." *New Testament Studies* 18, no. 2 (1972): 209–19.

Calvin, John. *The Acts of the Apostles*. Translated by John W. Fraser and William J. G McDonald. Edited by David W. Torrance and Thomas F. Torrance. Eerdmans, 1965.

Casanova, José. "Rethinking Secularization: A Global Comparative Perspective." *The Hedgehog Review* 8, no. 1–2 (2006): 7–22.

Casanova, José. "The Secular, Secularizations, Secularisms." In *Rethinking Secularism*, edited by Craig J Calhoun, Mark Juergensmeyer, and Jonathan Van Antwerpen, 74–95. Oxford University Press, 2011.

Cenac, Julianne R. "Leader Emergence and the Phenomenological Work of the Holy Spirit in Acts 2." *Journal of Biblical Perspectives in Leadership* 3, no. 1 (2010): 123–35.

Chaves, Mark. "Secularization as Declining Religious Authority." *Social Forces* 72, no. 3 (1994): 749–74.

Chrysostom, John. "Homily IV." Translated by Charles Marriot. In *Homilies on the Acts of the Apostles. Part I: Homilies 1–28*, 53–66. Gorgias, 2011.

Clifford, Richard J., and Roland E. Murphy. "Genesis." In *The New Jerome Biblical Commentary*, edited by Raymond E. Brown, Joseph A. Fitzmyer, and Roland E. Murphy, 8–43. Geoffrey Chapman, 1990.

Cobb, Christy. "Entangled Tongues: A Poststructuralist and Postcolonial Reading of Acts 2:1–13." *Journal for Interdisciplinary Biblical Studies* 4, no. 1 (2022): 1–16.

Coloe, Mary L. *God Dwells with Us: Temple Symbolism in the Fourth Gospel*. Liturgical Press, 2001.

Coloe, Mary L. "Temple Imagery in John." *Interpretation* 63, no. 4 (2009): 368–81.

Coloe, Mary L. *John 1–10*. Wisdom Commentary Series. Liturgical Press, 2021.

Coloe, Mary L. *John 11–21*. Wisdom Commentary Series. Liturgical Press, 2021.

Congar, Yves. *Tradition and Traditions: An Historical and a Theological Essay*. Translated by Michael Naseby and Thomas Rainborough. Burns & Oates, 1966.

Congregation for Catholic Education. *Educating to Intercultural Dialogue in Catholic Schools Living in Harmony for a Civilization of Love*. Libreria Editrice Vaticana, 2013.

Coolman, Boyd Taylor. "Hugh of St. Victor on 'Jesus Wept': Compassion as Ideal Humanitas." *Theological Studies* 69, no. 3 (2008): 528–56.

Cope, O. Lamar. *Matthew: A Scribe Trained for the Kingdom of Heaven*. Catholic Biblical Association of America, 1976.

Cotter, Wendy. *The Christ of the Miracle Stories: Portrait through Encounter*. Brill, 2010.

Crouzel, Henri. "Divorce and Remarriage in the Early Church: Some Reflections on Historical Methodology." *Communio* 41 (Summer 2014): 471–503. "Divorce et remariage dans l'Église primitive." *Nouvelle Revue Théologique* 98, no. 10 (1976): 891–917.

Crowe, Frederick E. *Collection: Papers of Bernard Lonergan*. 2nd revised and augmented ed. Edited by Frederick E. Crowe. Vol. IV. University of Toronto Press, 1993.

Culpepper, R. Alan. *Anatomy of the Fourth Gospel: A Study in Literary Design*. Fortress, 1983.
David, Stephen T. "Is Kenosis Orthodox?" In *Exploring Kenotic Christology: The Self-Emptying of God*, edited by C. Stephen Evans, 112–38. Regent College, 2010.
Davies, Oliver. *A Theology of Compassion: Metaphysics of Difference and the Renewal of Tradition*. Eerdmans, 2003.
de Wet, Chris L. "John Chrysostom on the Healing of the Woman with a Flow of Blood: Exegesis, Tradition, and Anti-Judaism." *Journal of Early Christian History* 9, no. 2 (2019): 1–28.
Derrida, Jacques. "Des tours de Babel." In *Difference in Translation*, edited by Joseph F. Graham, 165–77. Cornell University Press, 1985.
Derrida, Jacques. *The Post Card: From Socrates to Freud and Beyond*. Translated by Alan Bass. University of Chicago Press, 1987.
Dinkler, Michal Beth. "Suffering, Misunderstanding, and Suffering Misunderstanding: The Markan Misunderstanding Motif as a Form of Jesus' Suffering." *Journal for the Study of the New Testament* 38, no. 3 (2016): 316–38.
Donahue, John R. *Sacra Pagina: The Gospel of Mark*. Liturgical Press, 2005.
Dulles, Avery. "Symbol, Myth, and the Biblical Revelation." *Theological Studies* 27, no. 1 (1966): 1–26.
Durken, Daniel, ed. *The New Collegeville Bible Commentary. New Testament*. Liturgical Press, 2009.
Eberstadt, Mary, and Naomi Schaefer Riley. *How the West Really Lost God: A New Theory of Secularization*. Templeton, 2014.
Edwards, Richard A. "The Redaction of Luke." *The Journal of Religion* 49, no. 4 (1969): 392–405.
Eliot, T. S. *Four Quartets*. Faber and Faber, 1944.
Endean, Philip. "The Ignatian Prayer of the Senses." *Heythrop Journal* 31, no. 4 (1990): 391–418.
Evans, Craig A. "Jesus' Action in the Temple: Cleansing or Portent of Destruction?" In *Jesus in Context: Temple, Purity, and Restoration*, edited by Bruce Chilton and Craig A. Evans, 395–439. Brill, 1997.
Eve, Eric. *The Healer from Nazareth: Jesus' Miracles in Historical Context*. SPCK, 2009.
Faggioli, Massimo, and Alana Harris. "Pursuing the Long Shadow over the 'Domestic Church': Toward a Global History of Abuse in Catholic Settings." *The Catholic Historical Review* 110, no. 2 (2024): 339–68.
Fallon, Michael. *The Gospel According to St Mark: An Introductory Commentary*. 2nd ed. Chevalier, 2009.
Falque, Emmanuel. *The Guide to Gethsemane*. Fordham University Press, 1999/2019.
Falque, Emmanuel. "Trinitarian Kenosis and the Limits of Phenomenology." *Revista portuguesa de filosofia* 76, no. 2–3 (2020): 883–902.
Fee, Gordon D. "The New Testament and Kenosis Christology." In *Exploring Kenotic Christology: The Self-Emptying of God*, edited by C. Stephen Evans, 25–44. Regent College, 2010.
Fisher, Kathleen M., and Urban C. von Wahlde. "The Miracles of Mark 4:35–5:43: Their Meaning and Function in the Gospel Framework." *Biblical Theology Bulletin* 11, no. 1 (1981): 13–16.

Fitzgerald, John T. *Passions and Moral Progress in Greco-Roman Thought.* Routledge Monographs in Classical Studies. Routledge, 2008.
Fitzmyer, Joseph A. "Jesus Appears on the Road to Emmaus (24:13–35)." In *The Gospel According to Luke (X–XXIV)*, 1553–72. The Anchor Yale Bible, 1985.
Fitzmyer, Joseph A. "The Mission of Testimony in Jerusalem (2:1–8:4)." In *The Acts of the Apostles: A New Translation with Introduction and Commentary*, edited by William Foxwell Albright and David Noel Freedman, 231–398. The Anchor Yale Bible, 1998.
Flanagan, Brian P. *Stumbling in Holiness: Sin and Sanctity in the Church.* Liturgical Press, 2018.
Flanagan, Brian P. "Can the Church Be Both Holy and Sinful?" *America* (October 22, 2018).
Fleming, David L. *What Is Ignatian Spirituality?* Loyola, 2011.
Fonrobert, Charlotte Elisheva. *Menstrual Purity: Rabbinic and Christian Reconstructions of Biblical Gender.* Stanford University Press, 2000.
Frawley-O'Dea, Mary Gail, and Virginia Goldner. *Predatory Priests, Silenced Victims: The Sexual Abuse Crisis and the Catholic Church.* Analytic, 2007.
Fuchs, Martin, Antje Linkenbach, Martin Mulsow, Otto Bernd-Christian, Rahul Bjørn Parson, and Jörg Rüpke, eds. *Religious Individualisation.* De Gruyter, 2019.
Gallagher, Timothy M. *Meditation and Contemplation: An Ignatian Guide to Prayer with Scripture.* Crossroad, 2008.
Gavrilyuk, Paul L. *The Suffering of the Impassible God: The Dialectics of Patristic Thought.* Oxford University Press, 2004.
Gench, Frances Taylor. "John 7:53–8:11." *Interpretation* 63, no. 4 (2009): 398–400.
Goetz, Ronald. "The Suffering God: The Rise of a New Orthodoxy." *Christian Century* (April 16, 1986).
Gondreau, Paul. *The Passions of Christ's Soul in the Theology of St. Thomas Aquinas.* University of Scranton Press, 2009.
Goosen, Gideon. *Clericalism: Stories from the Pews. A Workbook for Parishes.* Coventry, 2020.
Gregory the Great. *Forty Great Homilies.* Translated by David Hurst. Cistercian Publications, 1990.
Guarino, Thomas G. "Vatican II and Analogical Thinking: A Response to David Lyle Jeffrey." In *The Book of Acts: Catholic, Orthodox and Evangelical Readings*, edited by Charles Raith II, 67–78. Catholic University of America Press, 2019.
Hakola, Raimo. *Identity Matters: John, the Jews, and Jewishness.* Brill, 2005.
Harrington, Daniel J. *How Do Catholics Read the Bible?* Rowman & Littlefield, 2005.
Harrison, Anna. "'Jesus Wept': Mourning as Imitation of Christ in Bernard's Sermon Twenty-Six on the Song of Songs." *Cistercian Studies Quarterly* 48, no. 4 (2013): 433.
Harrison, Jim. "Modern Scholarship and the 'Nature' Miracles: A Defense of Their Historicity and Affirmation of Jesus' Deity." *Reformed Theological Review* 72, no. 2 (2013): 86–102.
Heelas, Paul. "Challenging Secularization Theory: The Growth of 'New Age' Spiritualities of Life." *Hedgehog Review* 8 (Spring/Summer 2006): 46–58.

Heelas, Paul, Scott Lash, and Paul Morris. *Detraditionalization: Critical Reflections on Authority and Identity*. Blackwell, 1996.

Hervieu-Léger, Danièle. *Religion as a Chain of Memory*. Translated by Simon Lee. Polity, 2000.

Hervieu-Léger, Danièle. "The Distribution of Religious Belief in Individualist Societies." *Année sociologique* 60, no. 1 (2010): 41–62.

Horner, Robyn. "Towards a Hermeneutic-Phenomenological Methodology for Theology." *International Journal of Practical Theology* 22, no. 2 (2018): 153–73.

Horner, Robyn. "A Phenomenology of Revelation: Contemporary Encounters with Saint Ignatius Loyola." In *The Challenge of God*, edited by Colby Dickinson, Hugh Miller, and Kathleen McNutt, 69–85. Bloomsbury, 2019.

Horner, Robyn. *The Experience of God: A Phenomenology of Revelation*. Cambridge University Press, 2022.

Horner, Robyn. "Enhancing Catholic School Identity: A Response to Peter McGregor." *Irish Theological Quarterly* 88, no. 2 (2023): 112–36.

Horner, Robyn, Didier Pollefeyt, Jan Bouwens, Teresa Brown, Christiaan Jacobs-Vandegeer, Maeve Heaney, and Michael Buchanan. "Openness to Faith as a Disposition for Teachers in Catholic Schools." *International Journal of Practical Theology* 24, no. 2 (2020): 231–51.

Hornik, Heidi J., and Mikeal C. Parsons. *The Acts of the Apostles through the Centuries*. Wiley Blackwell, 2017.

Hughes, Gerard W. *God of Surprises*. Rev. and updated ed. Darton, Longman and Todd, 2008.

Hume, David, Lewis A. Selby-Bigge, and Peter H. Nidditch. *David Hume: A Treatise of Human Nature*. 2nd ed. Oxford University Press, 1978.

Hunter, David G. "Augustine's Doubts on Divorce." *Augustinian Studies* 48, no. 1 (2017): 161–82.

International Theological Commission. *Memory and Reconciliation: The Church and the Faults of the Past*. Paulist, 1999.

International Theological Commission. *The Hope of Salvation for Infants Who Die without Being Baptised*. Catholic Truth Society, 2007.

Irenaeus. *Adversus Heresies*. Edited by Alexander Roberts, James Donaldson, and A. Cleveland Coxe. Translated by Alexander Roberts and William Rambaut. *Ante-Nicene Fathers*. 1. Christian Literature Publishing, 2007.

Jakelić, Slavica. "Secularization, European Identity, and 'The End of the West'." *Hedgehog Review* 8 (Spring/Summer 2006): 133–9.

Jeffrey, David Lyle. "Acts 2, Translating Pentecost." In *The Book of Acts: Catholic, Orthodox and Evangelical Readings*, edited by Charles Raith II, 48–66. Catholic University of America Press, 2019.

Jerome. *Commentaries on the Twelve Prophets. Volume 2*. Edited by Thomas P. Scheck. InterVarsity Press Academic, 2017.

Johnson, Luke Timothy, and Daniel J. Harrington. *Sacra Pagina: The Gospel of Luke*. Liturgical Press, 1991.

Keenan, James F. "Vulnerability and Hierarchicalism." *Melita Theologica* 68, no. 2 (2018): 129–42.

Keenan, Marie. *Child Sexual Abuse and the Catholic Church: Gender, Power, and Organizational Culture*. Oxford University Press, 2011.

Keener, Craig S. *Miracles: The Credibility of the New Testament Accounts*. Baker Academic, 2011.

Keith, Chris. "Recent and Previous Research on the Pericope Adulterae (John 7.53—8.11)." *Currents in Biblical Research* 6, no. 3 (2008): 377–404.
Kelley, Andrew J. "Miracles, Jesus, and Identity: A History of Research Regarding Jesus and Miracles with Special Attention to the Gospel of Mark." *Currents in Biblical Research* 13, no. 1 (2014): 82–106.
Kienstra, Natascha, Monique van Dijk-groeneboer, and Olav Boelens. "Religious-Thinking-Through Using Bibliodrama: An Empirical Study of Student Learning in Classroom Teaching." *Religious Education* 113, no. 2 (2018): 203–15.
Kieser, Doris M. "The Female Body in Catholic Theology: Menstruation, Reproduction, and Autonomy." *Horizons* 44, no. 1 (2017): 1–27.
Klem, Matthew J. "Flipping Tables and Building Temples: An Intertextual Reading of Psalm 68:10 LXX in John 2:17." *Horizons in Biblical Theology* 43, no. 1 (2021): 70–98.
Knust, Jennifer Wright. *To Cast the First Stone: The Transmission of a Gospel Story*. Edited by Tommy Wasserman. Princeton University Press, 2019.
Kring, Ann M. "Gender and Anger." In *Gender and Emotion: Social Psychological Perspectives*, edited by Agneta H. Fischer, 211–31. Cambridge University Press, 2000.
Kristeva, Julia. *Powers of Horror: An Essay on Abjection*. Translated by Leon S. Roudiez. Columbia University Press, 1982.
Lacoste, Jean-Yves. *In Search of Speech: Talking, Reading and Praying in an Age of Words*. Translated by Oliver O'Donovan. Bloomsbury, 2024.
Latu, Ioana, Susanne Kaiser, and Marianne Schmid. *Gender and Emotion: An Interdisciplinary Perspective*. Peter Lang, 2013.
Lawrence, Louise J. "'The Stilling of the Sea' and the Imagination of Place in a Cornish Fishing Village." *Expository Times* 120, no. 4 (2009): 172–7.
Lev, Sarra. "Talmud That Works Your Heart: New Approaches to Reading." In *Learning to Read Talmud*, edited by Jane L. Kanarek and Marjorie Lehman, 175–202. Academic Studies Press, 2016.
Levinas, Emmanuel. *On Escape: De l'évasion*. Translated by Bettina Bergo. Stanford University Press, 2003.
Levine, Amy-Jill. "Discharging Responsibility: Matthean Jesus, Biblical Law, and Hemorrhaging Woman." In *Feminist Companion to Matthew*, edited by Amy-Jill Levine and Marianne Blickenstaff, 70–87. Bloomsbury, 2001.
Levine, Amy-Jill. *The Misunderstood Jew: The Church and the Scandal of the Jewish Jesus*. HarperOne, 2007.
Lewis, C. S. *The Last Battle*. Bodley Head, 1956.
Lewis, C. S. *Poems*. Reissue ed. HarperOne, 2017.
Linehan, Marsha M. *Cognitive-Behavioral Treatment of Borderline Personality Disorder*. Diagnosis and Treatment of Mental Disorders. Guilford, 1993.
Linehan, Marsha M. *DBT Skills Training Manual*. 2nd ed. Guilford, 2015.
Linehan, Marsha M. *Building a Life Worth Living: A Memoir*. Penguin Random House, 2020.
Lonergan, Bernard. "The Transition from a Classicist World-View to Historical-Mindedness." In *A Second Collection: Papers by Bernard J. F. Lonergan, S. J.*, edited by William F. J. Ryan and Bernard J. Tyrrell, 1–9. Darton, Longman and Todd, 1974.
Luttick, Janine. "Purity, Anti-Judaism and Contemporary Biblical Interpretation." Master of Arts in Religion and Theology, Monash University, 2012.

Luttick, Janine. *Jairus' Daughter and the Female Body in Mark*. Society of Biblical Literature, 2023.

Madge, Nicola, and Peter J. Hemming. "Young British Religious 'Nones': Findings from the Youth on Religion Study." *Journal of Youth Studies* 20, no. 7 (2016): 1–17.

Marion, Jean-Luc. *In Excess: Studies of Saturated Phenomena*. Translated by Robyn Horner and Vincent Berraud. Fordham University Press, 2002.

Marion, Jean-Luc. *D'Ailleurs: La Révélation*. Grasset, 2020.

Matera, Frank J. *New Testament Christology*. Westminster John Knox, 1999.

Matera, Frank J. *Resurrection: The Origin and Goal of the Christian Life*. Liturgical Press, 2015.

Mattison, William C. "Jesus' Prohibition of Anger (MT 5:22): The Person/Sin Distinction from Augustine to Aquinas." *Theological Studies* 68, no. 4 (2007): 839–64.

Mayeski, Marie Anne. "'Like a Boat Is Marriage': Aelred on Marriage as a Christian Way of Life." *Theological Studies* 70, no. 1 (2009): 92–108.

McBrien, Richard P. *Catholicism*. Rev. and updated ed. CollinsDove, 1994.

Meier, John P. *A Marginal Jew: Rethinking the Historical Jesus*. Yale University Press, 1994.

Meier, John P. "5.7 The Historicity of Jesus' Miracles: The Global Question, 1994." In *Jesusforschung in vier Jahrhunderten*, edited by Zager Werner, 473–504. De Gruyter, 2014.

Milinovich, Timothy. "The Parable of the Storm: Instruction and Demonstration in Mark 4:1–41." *Biblical Theology Bulletin* 45, no. 2 (2015): 88–98.

Minets, Yuliya. *The Slow Fall of Babel: Languages and Identities in Late Antique Christianity*. Cambridge University Press, 2022.

Moloney, Francis J. *Signs and Shadows: Reading John 5–12*. Fortress, 1996.

Moloney, Francis J. *Sacra Pagina: The Gospel of John*. Edited by Daniel J. Harrington. Revised ed. Liturgical Press, 2005.

Moloney, Francis J. *The Gospel of Mark: A Commentary*. Baker Academic, 2012.

Moloney, Francis J. *The Resurrection of the Messiah: A Narrative Commentary on the Resurrection Accounts in the Four Gospels*. Paulist, 2013.

Moloney, Francis J. "A New Testament Hermeneutic for Divorce and Remarriage in the Catholic Tradition." *Australasian Catholic Record* 92, no. 3 (2015): 269–88.

Moore, Sebastian. *The Crucified Is No Stranger*. Darton, Longman and Todd, 1977.

Moore, Sebastian. *The Fire and the Rose Are One*. Darton, Longman and Todd, 1980.

Moore, Sebastian. *Let This Mind Be in You: The Quest for Identity through Oedipus to Christ*. Darton, Longman and Todd, 1985.

Moore, Sebastian. *Jesus the Liberator of Desire*. Crossroad, 1989.

Morgan, Eleanor. *Hormonal: A Conversation about Women's Bodies, Mental Health and Why We Need to Be Heard*. Hachette, 2019.

Myers, Alicia D. "Revelation through Violence? Jesus in the Temple in John 2:13–22." *Review & Expositor* 120, no. 1–2 (2023): 46–59.

Newman, John Henry. *An Essay on the Development of Christian Doctrine*. Cambridge University Press, 1845/2010.

Nussbaum, Martha C. *The Therapy of Desire: Theory and Practice in Hellenistic Ethics*. Revised ed. Princeton University Press, 2009.

O'Day, Gail R. "John 7.53–8.11: A Study in Misreading." *Journal of Biblical Literature* 111, no. 4 (1992): 631–40.

Orlett, Raymond. "An Influence of the Early Liturgy upon the Emmaus Account." *The Catholic Biblical Quarterly* 21, no. 2 (1959): 212–19.

Overgaard, Søren. "How to Do Things with Brackets: The *epochē* Explained." *Continental Philosophy Review* 48, no. 2 (2015): 179–95.

Pagola, José Antonio. *Jesus: An Historical Approximation*. 4th ed. Convivium, 2009.

Patrick, George-Thomas White, trans. and ed. *The Fragments of Heraclitus*. Digireads, 2013.

Pentin, Edward. "Full Text and Explanatory Notes of Cardinals' Questions on 'Amoris laetitia'." *National Catholic Register* (USA) (November 14, 2016). https://www.ncregister.com/blog/full-text-and-explanatory-notes-of-cardinals-questions-on-amoris-laetitia.

Petropoulou, Maria-Zoe. *Animal Sacrifice in Ancient Greek Religion, Judaism, and Christianity, 100 BC to AD 200*. Oxford University Press, 2008.

Phipps, William E. "The Menstrual Taboo in the Judeo-Christian Tradition." *Journal of Religion and Health* 19, no. 4 (1980): 298–303.

Pitzele, Peter. *Scripture Windows: Toward a Practice of Bibliodrama*. Alef Design Group, 1997.

Pollefeyt, Didier, and Jan Bouwens. *Identity in Dialogue: Assessing and Enhancing Catholic School Identity. Research Methodology and Research Results in Catholic Schools in Victoria, Australia*. Lit Verlag, 2014.

Pontifical Biblical Commission. *The Interpretation of the Bible in the Church*. Libreria Editrice Vaticana, 1993.

Pope Francis. "Address by His Holiness Pope Francis at the Opening of the Synod of Bishops on Young People, the Faith and Vocational Discernment" (October 3, 2018). https://www.vatican.va/content/francesco/en/speeches/2018/october/documents/papa-francesco_20181003_apertura-sinodo.html.

Pope Francis. *Fratelli tutti: On Fraternity and Social Friendship*. Libreria Editrice Vaticana, 2020.

Pope Francis. *The Gospel of Luke: A Spiritual and Pastoral Reading*. English ed. Orbis Books, 2021.

Pope Francis. "Spiritus Domini." Apostolic Letter issued Motu Proprio (January 10, 2021). https://www.vatican.va/content/francesco/en/motu_proprio/documents/papa-francesco-motu-proprio-20210110_spiritus-domini.html.

Pope Francis. "Ad theologiam promovendam." Apostolic letter issued Motu Proprio (November 1, 2023). https://www.vatican.va/content/francesco/it/motu_proprio/documents/20231101-motu-proprio-ad-theologiam-promovendam.html.

Pope John Paul II. *Ex corde ecclesiae*. Libreria Editrice Vaticana, 1990.

Pope John Paul II. *Veritatis Splendor: The Splendor of Truth—Regarding Certain Fundamental Questions of the Church's Moral Teaching*. Libreria Editrice Vaticana, 1993.

Pope John Paul II. *Fides et ratio: On the Relationship between Faith and Reason*. Libreria Editrice Vaticana, 1998.

Pope Paul VI, *Ministeria Quaedem*. Apostolic Letter issued Motu Proprio. Libreria Editrice Vaticana, 1972.

Pope Pius X. *Lamentabili sane: Syllabus Condemning the Errors of the Modernists*. Libreria Editrice Vaticana, 1907.

Pope Pius X. *Pascendi dominici gregis: On the Doctrines of the Modernists*. Libreria Editrice Vaticana, 1907.
Potegal, Michael, and Raymond W. Novaco. "A Brief History of Anger." In *International Handbook of Anger: Constituent and Concomitant Biological, Psychological, and Social Processes*, edited by Michael Potegal, Gerhard Stemmler, and Charles Spielberger, 9–24. Springer, 2010.
Punch, John David. "The Piously Offensive." In *The Pericope of the Adulteress in Contemporary Research*, edited by David Alan Black and Jacob N. Cerone, 7–32. T&T Clark, 2016.
Quack, Johannes, and Cora Schuh. *Religious Indifference New Perspectives from Studies on Secularization and Nonreligion*. Springer, 2017.
Rahner, Karl. *Theological Investigations*. XXIII vols. Darton, Longman and Todd, 1992.
Rambo, Shelly. "Trauma and Faith: Reading the Narrative of the Hemorrhaging Woman." *International Journal of Practical Theology* 13, no. 2 (2009): 233–57.
Reinhartz, Adele. "'Jews' and Jews in the Fourth Gospel." In *Anti-Judaism and the Fourth Gospel*, edited by Reimund Bieringer, Didier Pollefeyt, and Frederique Vandecasteele-Vanneuville, 341–56. Westminster John Knox, 2001.
Retief, Francois P., and Louise Cilliers. "The History and Pathology of Crucifixion." *South African Medical Journal* 93, no. 12 (2003): 938–41.
Ricoeur, Paul. *Hermeneutics and the Human Sciences: Essays on Language, Action and Interpretation*. Edited and Translated by John B. Thompson. Cambridge University Press, 1981.
Romano, Claude. *Event and World*. Translated by Shane Mackinlay. Fordham University Press, 2009.
Romano, Claude. *At the Heart of Reason*. Translated by Michael B. Smith. Northwestern University Press, 2015.
Romano, Claude. *There Is: The Event and the Finitude of Appearing*. Translated by Michael B. Smith. Fordham University Press, 2016.
Rush, Ormond. *The Vision of Vatican II: Its Fundamental Principles*. Liturgical Press, 2019.
Russell, Norman. *The Doctrine of Deification in the Greek Patristic Tradition*. Oxford University Press, 2004.
Ruys, Juanita Feros. "Carnal Compassion: Peter Abelard's Conflicted Approach to Empathy." In *The Intellectual Dynamism of the High Middle Ages*, edited by Clare Monagle, 24–44. Amsterdam University Press, 2021.
Sartre, Jean-Paul. *No Exit and Three Other Plays*. [1944] Vintage International Series, 2015.
Sartre, Jean-Paul, Michel Contat, and Michel Rybalk, eds. *Sartre on Theater*. Quartet Books/Random House, 1976.
Schaff, Philip, ed. *Nicene and Post-Nicene Fathers*. Christian Classics Ethereal Library, 1895–1899. https://www.ccel.org/.
Scheffler, Eben H. "Emmaus—A Historical Perspective." *Neotestamentica* 23, no. 2 (1989): 251–67.
Schenk, Richard. "And Jesus Wept." In *Reading John with St. Thomas Aquinas: Theological Exegesis and Speculative Theology*, edited by Michael Dauphinais and Matthew Levering, 212–37. Catholic University of America Press, 2005.
Schneiders, Sandra M. "Death in the Community of Eternal Life. History, Theology, and Spirituality in John 11." *Interpretation* 41, no. 1 (1987): 44–56.

Schönborn, Christoph, ed. *Catechism of the Catholic Church*. Libreria Editrice Vaticana, 1993, as updated.
Schrader, Elizabeth. "Was Martha of Bethany Added to the Fourth Gospel in the Second Century?" *The Harvard Theological Review* 110, no. 3 (2017): 360–92.
Selvidge, Marla J. "Mark 5:25–34 and Leviticus 15:19–20: A Reaction to Restrictive Purity Regulations." *Journal of Biblical Literature* 103, no. 4 (1984): 619–23.
Seneca, Lucius Annaeus. *Epistles. Volume I*. Harvard University Press, 1917.
Sheridan, Ruth. *Retelling Scripture: "The Jews" and the Scriptural Citations in John 1:19–12:15*. Brill, 2012.
Snodgrass, Klyne R. "The Temple Incident." In *Key Events in the Life of the Historical Jesus: A Collaborative Exploration of Context and Coherence*, edited by Darrell L. Bock and Robert L. Webb, 429–80. Mohr Siebeck, 2009.
Sorabji, Richard. *Emotion and Peace of Mind: From Stoic Agitation to Christian Temptation*. Oxford University Press, 2000.
Stewart, Alistair C. *The Didascalia Apostolorum: An English Version*. Brepols, 2009.
Stolz, Jörg. "Secularization Theories in the Twenty-First Century: Ideas, Evidence, and Problems." *Social Compass* 27, no. 2 (2020): 282–308.
Stott, John R. W. *The Message of Acts*. InterVarsity, 1990.
Strelan, Rick. *Strange Acts: Studies in the Cultural World of the Acts of the Apostles*. De Gruyter, 2004.
Stroup, Christopher. *The Christians Who Became Jews. Acts of the Apostles and Ethnicity in the Roman City*. Yale University Press, 2020.
Swidler, Leonard. *Jesus Was a Feminist: What the Gospels Reveal about His Revolutionary Perspective*. Sheed and Ward, 2007.
Taylor, Charles. *A Secular Age*. Harvard University Press, 2007.
Toensing, Holly J. "Divine Intervention or Divine Intrusion? Jesus and the Adulteress in John's Gospel." In *Feminist Companion to John*, edited by Amy-Jill Levine, 159–72. Bloomsbury, 2003.
Twelftree, Graham H. "The Miraculous in the New Testament: Current Research and Issues." *Currents in Biblical Research* 12, no. 3 (2014): 321–52.
United States Conference of Catholic Bishops. *The Bible, the Jews, and the Death of Jesus: A Collection of Catholic Documents*. United States Conference of Catholic Bishops, 2004.
van den Berg, Bas, and Fortuin van der Spek. "The Appropriation of Symbolic Language in Worldview Education through Bibliodrama." *Education Sciences* 9, no. 2 (2019): 88.
Vatican Council I. *Dogmatic Constitution on the Catholic Faith*. Libreria Editrice Vaticana, 1870.
Vatican Council II. *Lumen gentium: Dogmatic Constitution on the Church*. Libreria Editrice Vaticana, 1964.
Vatican Council II. *Dei verbum: Dogmatic Constitution on Divine Revelation*. Libreria Editrice Vaticana, 1965.
Vatican Council II. *Gaudium et spes: Pastoral Constitution on the Church in the Modern World*. Libreria Editrice Vaticana, 1965.
Vermès, Géza. *Jesus the Jew: A Historian's Reading of the Gospels*. Collins, 1973.

Voas, David. "Is the Secularization Research Programme Progressing? Debate on Jörg Stolz's Article on Secularization Theories in the 21st Century: Ideas, Evidence, and Problems." *Social Compass* 67, no. 2 (2020): 323–9.

Voas, David, and Mark Chaves. "Is the United States a Counterexample to the Secularization Thesis?" *American Journal of Sociology* 121, no. 5 (2016): 1517–56.

Voorwinde, Stephen. *Jesus' Emotions in the Fourth Gospel: Human or Divine?* T&T Clark, 2005.

Voorwinde, Stephen. *Jesus' Emotions in the Gospels*. Bloomsbury, 2011.

Wachsmann, Shelley. *The Sea of Galilee Boat: An Extraordinary 2000-Year-Old Discovery*. Plenum, 1995.

Wassen, Cecilia. "The Use of the Dead Sea Scrolls for Interpreting Jesus's Action in the Temple." *Dead Sea Discoveries* 23, no. 3 (2016): 280–303.

Wedderburn, Alexander J. M. "Traditions and Redaction in Acts 2.1–13." *Journal for the Study of the New Testament* 17, no. 55 (1995): 27–54.

Westphal, Merold. *Whose Community? Which Interpretation? Philosophical Hermeneutics for the Church*. Baker Academic, 2009.

Wheelwright, Philip. *Metaphor and Reality*. Indiana University Press, 1962.

Wheelwright, Philip. *The Burning Fountain: A Study in the Language of Symbolism*. 2nd ed. Indiana University Press, 1968. 1954.

Wickes, Judi, and Katherine Ellinghaus. "Women's Experiences of Aboriginal Exemption." *Agora* 56, no. 1 (2021): 9–12.

Wilson, Alistair I. "In the Same Boat? Jonah and Jesus as Wave-Beaten Heralds." *In die skriflig* 55, no. 1 (2021): 1–8.

Zylstra, Sarah Eekhoff. "Is 'Go and Sin No More' Biblical?: If the Earliest Manuscripts of the Gospel of John Don't Include the Story of the Woman Caught in Adultery, Why Is It in Our Bibles?" *Christianity Today* 52, no. 6 (2008): 46.

FOUR STEPS TO RECONTEXTUALIZATION: LISTEN, DIALOGUE, PERFORM, EVALUATE

Within the overall structure of four steps, the sub-steps will vary according to the text or local context.

STEP 1. LISTEN TO THE TEXT

Choose a Biblical Text for Recontextualization

Very often, it is good advice to choose one of the texts from the daily Mass or service. If you have the app *Universalis*, you will be able to select easily from the Lectionary or even from the Office of Readings of the Catholic Church. Many Christian denominations follow the same Lectionary cycle.

Sometimes you may have reason to choose a particular reading. It is easy to find a reading using keywords or a biblical reference using *BibleGateway*, which is searchable in your browser or as an app. Choose one of the New Revised Standard Versions of the Bible translations, as the NRSV is used by many biblical scholars and can be found in inclusive translation.

Read the Chosen Biblical Text Reflectively

The biblical text can speak in surprising ways if we allow it. Christians believe that God can speak to them by means of the text. This does not mean reading the text in a literal way but waiting to feel God's touch as the text is read or heard.

Do this alone or in a group. Begin when you are quiet, focused and sitting comfortably. If it is appropriate to you, place yourself before God in prayer and ask for God's help in reading or listening to the text. Read or listen to the text slowly, taking note of the words or phrases that strike you.

Reread or listen again to the passage and ponder those words or phrases especially (*lectio divina*). Make a written note of those items that have struck you about or in the text.

Deepen Your Experience of the Text by Placing Yourself in the Context of the Biblical Narrative

This can be undertaken alone or in a group, in appropriate ways, for example:

1. Listening to a phenomenological reading of the text (such as those contained in this book). A phenomenological reading of the narrative focuses on what in the text gives itself to the senses and the affect as well as to the intellect. It tries to bring to life what can be seen or heard or sensed as you allow the text to unfold in your mind.
2. Engaging in Bibliodrama.
3. Following a guided meditation on the text. In a guided meditation, the narrative is retold with an emphasis on the details as they are heightened for the imagination.
4. Finding or creating images of the narrative.
5. Engaging in a Colloquy, where you address Christ in the narrative.

STEP 2. ENTER INTO DIALOGUE

Engage in Critical Dialogue with the Biblical Tradition

In order to gain some understanding of how the text might have been understood in the context of its early telling or writing, it is important to read some of the critical commentary available. Unfortunately, much of this critical commentary is not online (conversely, much of what you might easily be able to find online is not very critical!). To be "critical" does not mean to be disapproving but to analyze "the merits and faults of a work of literature, music, or art" (OED).

As individuals, in small groups or in a larger group, read from a respected biblical commentary, such as the *New Jerome Commentary* (which has information on the entire Bible) or the *Sacra Pagina* series, which usually has an individual volume for each book. These resources will be available in various libraries. Find out: where, when, and why the text is likely to have been written or revised; the context of the story in the biblical book in which it is found; anything unusual about its history; and any words that might be ambiguous or difficult to translate from the language in which the text was written.

Engage in Dialogue with Post-Biblical Tradition

What has Christian (particularly Catholic) tradition said at different times about the subject of the text? This step is difficult to undertake without some tertiary-level theological knowledge. If necessary, find a colleague or contact with expertise to help you find some resources. The *Catechism* is *not* the most helpful resource, here, because *it does not give insight as to questions behind the doctrine.*

It is essential to read quality theological resources and to be open to a variety of perspectives about how the tradition has developed. These resources can be read by individuals and discussed for clarification of meaning in small groups, or with a larger group.

Engage in Dialogue with the Current Context

As an individual, or through open, respectful discussion with others, name some central issues for the contemporary context emerging from the work of steps one to five. What are the issues that arise? Do some research on those issues as they affect the contemporary community. Locate one or two resources that place those issues squarely in focus. These might be written resources, or they might be artistic resources.

STEP 3. PERFORM A RECONTEXTUALIZATION

Ask, "How Is the Text Speaking to Me (or Us) Today?"

Allow time to reflect quietly on the issues in light of the biblical text.

Consider or discuss what emerges from those moments of reflection and deepen the insights, testing their consonance with Christian faith as professed and exploring what such insights might mean for others. How does the text speak to the issues in the contemporary context? Does the text challenge the new context? How does the contemporary context speak to the text? Does the new context challenge the text? How does the recontextualized text challenge the Christian community? How does it challenge *us*, those engaged in the dialogue? How does it challenge *me*?

This exercise frequently opens questions that might have potential answers but cannot easily be resolved. Be prepared to keep the tension open and do not rush to make the text and new context harmonious. It is possible that the dialogue will not lead to easy responses or satisfactory resolutions. Be prepared to *dwell with* the issues arising. Resist platitudes or pious commentary. Remember, however, that *not* to respond is still to respond.

Have new understandings of the text arisen as a result of its being placed in a new context? What insights about the new context arise? As a result of this dialogue, what shifts have taken place in your understanding of the text and the contextual issue/s?

Document the Recontextualization

Document the recontextualization: in writing, in art, in music, in a personal reflection.

Begin when you are quiet, focused and sitting comfortably. If it is appropriate to you, place yourself before God in prayer and ask for God's help in reviewing the process of recontextualization. Go over the recontextualization process in your mind, as if you were watching it on film. Pause on any moments of insight or internal movement. What, if anything, has changed for you? Where, if at all, has God spoken?

What do you need to *do* in response to the recontextualization? Make a note of any important insights in a personal journal.

STEP 4. EVALUATE THE RECONTEXTUALIZATION

Assess the Effectiveness of the Recontextualization

Use the following questions to guide your evaluation:

1 Does it respect the text in its faith-context? OR does it twist or warp the text?

2 Does it respect the contemporary context in which the text has been placed? OR does it twist or warp the context?

3 Does it allow the text to speak powerfully in a new context? OR does it fall flat?

4 Does the recontextualization challenge or "interrupt" the faith context? How?

5 Does the recontextualization challenge or "interrupt" the contemporary context? How?

6 Is it a "strong" recontextualization (stays with you) or a "weak" recontextualization (becomes irrelevant quite quickly)?

The richest recontextualization leads to lasting transformation—of text, context, and reader. However, sometimes an attempt at recontextualization will "fail"; that is, it will not "hold together" or "gel." There is often as much to learn from this failure as from success. Ask why the text or the context seems resistant to recontextualization. Ask if there is something that has been misunderstood about the text or the context or understood in too facile a way.

NAME INDEX

Page numbers followed by n denote footnotes.

SUBJECT INDEX

Page numbers followed by n denote footnotes.

SCRIPTURE INDEX

Page numbers followed by n denote footnotes.